Author Mary Baxter takes us on a journey that reminds us of how much God really cares for us and watches over us. This book about angels is filled with her experiences in dreams and visions from God, but what she says is backed up by Scripture. You will rejoice in your spirit as you read about the miraculous and unusual ways God rescues and provides for His children. God is speaking to us through these words.

—*Jentezen Franklin*
Senior pastor, Free Chapel
Host, *Kingdom Connection* television program
Gainesville, Georgia

The work of angels, God's messengers, can be seen throughout Scripture. However, many believers today have a man-created vision of angels. Who they are and what they do are often misunderstood due to the work of the secular press and its influence over television, film, and popular literature. *A Divine Revelation of Angels* sets the record straight! A book that is both scripturally sound and easy for anyone to understand.

—*Rod Parsley*
Pastor and founder, World Harvest Church
Host, *Breakthrough* television program
Columbus, Ohio

Through the years, Mary Baxter has captured the imagination of the body of Christ and directed it heavenward. Her new book with Dr. T. L. Lowery, *A Divine Revelation of Angels*, takes us higher yet anchors our feet in solid doctrinal ground.

—*John A. Kilpatrick*
Former senior pastor, Brownsville Assembly of God
Pensacola, Florida

The Bible frequently mentions angels—God's heavenly messengers or servants. In *A Divine Revelation of Angels*, Mary Baxter combines biblical teaching with her own experiences, giving the reader thought-provoking and enlightening insights about the ministry of angels.

—*Dr. David Yonggi Cho*
Founder, Yoido Full Gospel Church
Seoul, Korea

A Divine Revelation of Angels describes the dreams, revelations, and visions of Mary Baxter, revealing angels at work today. It is most interesting and absorbing. I believe you will be inspired by this book.

—*Oral Roberts*
Founder, Oral Roberts University
Tulsa, Oklahoma

Mary Baxter's previous works have earned her thousands of fans all over the world. In *A Divine Revelation of Angels*, she tells of her own experiences with angels and makes a case for these heavenly beings at work in our lives. God cares enough about us to send us extra help in those special times when our strength alone is insufficient. You will be blessed by her work.

—*Dr. Bill George*
Editor in Chief, Church of God Publications
Cleveland, Tennessee

Mary K. Baxter's books have reached around this world and have impacted people in all walks of life. As people get the opportunity to meet her and witness the power of God on her life, they learn it truly is *A Divine Revelation* from God."

—*T. L. Gabbard, Sr.*
Pastor, Wynne, Arkansas

We have been blessed by Mary Baxter's ministry at our church.... Hundreds have been saved and filled with the Holy Spirit, and many have been healed and set free.

—*Winford Walters*
Pastor, Elyria, Ohio

Mary Baxter has been a great blessing to our church family. Through her preaching abilities, many people have gotten saved and delivered, and a great number of backsliders have rededicated their lives back to God.... I believe that her written testimonies will change the lives of countless unbelievers and strengthen the faith of many believers concerning heaven and hell.

—*Jason Alvarez*
Pastor, Orange, New Jersey

Mary Baxter has preached at our church many times, and lots of people were saved and healed.... Her ministry has touched many lives in the kingdom of God.

—*Gladys Boggs*
pastor's wife, Houston, Texas

Mary Baxter truly has an incredible testimony that needs to be shared with all. God surely is using Mary as a soul winner for Jesus Christ.

—*Eldred Thomas*
President, KLTJ–TV, Houston, Texas

I wish [Mary's] book[s] could be made available to everyone—to Christians as a warning to continue walking with Jesus, and to non-Christians to show them what is awaiting them if they do not commit their lives to Jesus Christ.

—*R. Russell Bixler*
Founder, Cornerstone TV, Wall, Pennsylvania

BEST-SELLING AUTHOR
MARY K. BAXTER

A DIVINE REVELATION OF ANGELS & DEMONS

WHITAKER
HOUSE

The Billy Graham excerpts in chapters 2 and 6 of *A Divine Revelation of Angels* are from his book *Angels: God's Secret Agents*, © 1995 by Billy Graham, and reprinted by permission of Thomas Nelson Publishers.

A Divine Revelation of Angels & Demons
Two Books in One

Mary K. Baxter
marykbaxter@yahoo.com
www.marykbaxterinc.com

Whitaker House compilation 2020

ISBN: 978-1-64123-406-1
Printed in the United States of America
A Note from the Publisher © 2020 by Whitaker House
A Divine Revelation of Angels © 2003 by Lowery Ministries International
A Divine Revelation of Deliverance © 2008 by Mary K. Baxter and
   George G. Bloomer

Whitaker House
1030 Hunt Valley Circle
New Kensington, PA 15068
www.whitakerhouse.com

2 3 4 5 6 7 8 9 10 11 ⅢⅡ 27 26 25 24 23 22 21 20

CONTENTS

A NOTE FROM THE PUBLISHER

In 1976, Jesus Christ appeared in human form to a woman in Belleville, Michigan. She was not anyone of importance in the eyes of the world. She was not a celebrity or scholar. She was not even an ordained minister with an impressive congregation and far-reaching influence. Nevertheless, for forty consecutive nights, Jesus appeared to her in dreams, visions, and revelations. The first thirty nights were spent on a horrifying tour of the realities of hell; the last ten nights on a glorious tour of the streets of heaven. The impact of these divine visitations would change the trajectory of Mary K. Baxter's life and send ripples of supernatural impact around the world.

The first two books she wrote about her experiences during that time were *A Divine Revelation of Hell* and *A Divine Revelation of Heaven*. Since its initial publication by Whitaker House in 1993, *A Divine Revelation of Hell* has sold nearly 1.4 million copies. Subsequent books inspired by divine visions have surpassed 2.7 million in sales, which does not include sales of eBooks and foreign language translations. Mary has since been ordained as a minister, received a doctorate in ministry, and taken the gospel message around the world. Signs, wonders, and miraculous testimonies of God's saving grace have followed her.

In 2019, Whitaker House published Mary K. Baxter's first two books in a single volume, entitled *A Divine Revelation of Heaven & Hell*. The response from readers was so positive that we are now making two additional books available in this format under the title *A Divine Revelation of Angels & Demons*.

In the first book of this volume, *A Divine Revelation of Angels*, Mary describes dreams, visions, and revelations of angels that God has given her over the years. God's holy angels are magnificent beings who are His messengers and warriors sent to assist, sustain, protect, and deliver us through the power of Christ. Mary explores the appearance and roles of angelic beings and how they operate, not only in the heavenly realms, but also in our lives here on earth. You will learn the difference between good angels and evil angels (demons) and their activities so you can distinguish angels of light from angels of darkness.

In the second book, *A Divine Revelation of Deliverance*, Mary explores the realm and work of Satan and his demons. As she exposes the schemes of Satan, she explains why many people have great difficulty overcoming sins and temptations, and why they experience recurring problems in their health, finances, and relationships. Through the Scriptures, visions of warfare, and personal encounters with evil spiritual forces, Mary K. Baxter has discovered powerful truths that will help you overcome your fear of the enemy, recognize and conquer satanic traps, experience victory over sins and failures, be free from unexplained attacks, and intercede for the deliverance of others. You will learn how to access the supernatural power of God and fight with the spiritual weapons He has provided.

We pray that you will be informed, encouraged, and strengthened by each of these books, becoming more spiritually discerning and recognizing that God has given believers protection and authority *"over all the power of the enemy"* (Luke 10:19).

—*Bob Whitaker Jr.*
President, Whitaker Corporation

A DIVINE REVELATION
OF ANGELS

CONTENTS

FOREWORD

Sir Francis Bacon said,

> Some books are to be tasted, others to be swallowed, and some few to be chewed and digested: that is, some books are to be read only in parts, others to be read, but not curiously, and some few to be read wholly, and with diligence and attention.

This is one of those books to be chewed and digested. It is to be studied and enjoyed. Its subject matter may at times be controversial, but the study of angels is of great importance in this day and age. The topic of angels is not a new one, yet it is current and relevant. There is much confusion about angels, and therefore much misinformation is being circulated about these heavenly beings. I believe it is vital that we know what the Bible, the great Word of God, has to say about this most important subject.

Mary Katherine Baxter is a choice servant of God. She is anointed and boldly fearless in her proclamation of the truth of God's Word. In these last days, the sovereign Lord has especially chosen her to receive marvelous and breathtaking revelations that give all of us amazing light on spiritual matters.

Her first book describing her divine revelations, *A Divine Revelation of Hell,* is an eyewitness account of what she saw taking place among the lost souls who refuse to believe and end up in hell.

A Divine Revelation of Heaven, her second book, describes the beauties and rewards that God permitted her to see so that she could "tell others about that wonderful place."

Her third book, *A Divine Revelation of the Spirit Realm,* is a treasure chest of resource and encouragement for those who are engaged in spiritual warfare.

This latest volume, *A Divine Revelation of Angels,* does two things. First, it presents the believer with a study of angels; it tells what the Bible has to say about them. Again, with all the misinformation and erroneous teaching about angels today, it is important that God's truth be known. I have collaborated with Mary Baxter in the writing of this book. We have searched the Scriptures diligently, and we present this material with the assurance that its teachings are backed up by the Bible. This book is solidly biblical.

Second, this book relates faithfully the visions and revelations that God has given to Mary Baxter concerning angels. What she writes and describes speaks to the heart about these spiritual, heavenly creatures.

This series of books has already blessed hundreds of thousands of people in many countries. The wide acceptance of these writings and the enthusiastic feedback from people whose lives have been changed by the reading of them is gratifying, indeed.

My prayer for you is that God will bless you and keep you. May He cause His face to shine on you, and may He bless you in everything you do. I pray that God will give you a fresh anointing and renewed vision as you read this book, so that you may be abundantly fruitful in building His kingdom and participating in the end-times harvest.

—*Dr. T. L. Lowery*

PREFACE

This book explores what the Bible says about angels. It is also a true account of the many experiences God has given to me concerning His heavenly messengers. I know that God has promised,

> *Because you have made the LORD, who is my refuge, even the Most High, your dwelling place, no evil shall befall you, nor shall any plague come near your dwelling; for He shall give His angels charge over you, to keep you in all your ways. In their hands they shall bear you up.* (Psalm 91:9–12)

I believe the angels were with me in the writing of this book. Also, many people helped to make this project possible. I want to acknowledge a few of them.

First, I want to thank my pastor, mentor, and spiritual advisor, the Reverend Dr. T. L. Lowery, for his invaluable assistance. Without him and his advice, prayer, and help, this book would not and could not have been written. I honor him and his beautiful wife, Mildred, for their support, encouragement, and valuable assistance in this ministry.

I gratefully recognize and credit those at Whitaker House in New Kensington, Pennsylvania, who have been so instrumental in making these messages from God available to the reading public.

Most of all, I am grateful to God who has called me to share these messages. I give all praise and honor and glory to God the Father, God the Son, and God the Holy Spirit.

PART I:
THE NATURE OF ANGELS

1

ARE ANGELS REAL?

People have been captivated by the idea of angels for centuries. Throughout history, most religions have held certain beliefs concerning spiritual beings, powers, and principalities. In ancient times, unenlightened pagans usually believed spiritual beings were the disembodied spirits of departed ancestors, spirits of things in nature, or fairy beings from another world.

Archaeologists have discovered representations of winged beings in early cave art, etched on walls and cliffs. The classical artists of the medieval period popularized the use of artistic symbols in their works, so that one could immediately recognize an angel in a painting. They usually showed angels as humanlike figures with wings, white robes, halos, and often harps or other types of musical instruments. The wings on the angels were meant to signify that they were celestial beings. Their white robes and halos symbolized purity and holiness. The musical instruments were included to indicate that angels sing praises to God. Depictions of angels in both medieval and Renaissance paintings contribute to many of our current ideas about what angelic beings look and act like.

"ANGEL MANIA"

Angels are a hugely popular subject in today's society. In my ministry travels over the past few years, I have observed a steadily rising interest in celestial beings among people of all walks of life. Everywhere I go, people ask me about angels. Even Christians from more traditional backgrounds that don't usually emphasize the supernatural realm show an increasing fascination with these heavenly creatures.

There are many signs of a widespread interest in angels not only in the church, but also throughout our society. Our museums are crammed full of paintings and sculptures of winged beings. Best-seller lists regularly feature titles about angels. Bookstores have whole sections of their displays devoted to celestial beings.

In addition, we regularly read and see reports in the media about angels. A current popular television show called *Touched by an Angel* suggests the existence of guardian angels. Not long ago, another highly rated program called *Highway to Heaven* featured an angel sent to earth to assist mortals.

The lyrics of many popular songs speak about angels. Representations of celestial beings also appear on birthday cards and wedding invitations. They abound as souvenirs, jewelry, and religious or semi-religious dust catchers. Artists and writers continue to depict angels in many forms.

Time magazine published a cover story entitled "Angels among Us." The writers of the article explained the phenomenon of the current craze for angels in this way:

> For those who choke too easily on God and his rules, theologians observe, angels are the handy compromise, all fluff and meringue, kind, nonjudgmental. And they are available to everyone, like aspirin.

It seems that many people today use the idea of angels to ease their consciences, escape the realities of life, and enter an imaginary world that seems pleasant and nondemanding.

What are angels? Do such creatures really exist? Or are they make-believe, like elves and fairies? Are they just beings that fertile minds have conjured up, imaginary figures that have become hopelessly suspended between reality and fantasy? If they do exist, how can we be sure? Can they be seen?

MY INTEREST IN ANGELS

My own interest in angels is more than a passing fad or craze. Many years ago, God began to give me dreams, visions, and revelations of the spiritual realm, including those that revealed the work of His angels. I am not referring to special people who are "angels" to us; I am talking about God's spirit messengers, His special agents who do His bidding and are sent to rescue His people. These visions and revelations usually came when I was in prayer and meditation on God's Word.

I have written about many of these experiences in my books *A Divine Revelation of Hell*, *A Divine Revelation of Heaven*, and *A Divine Revelation of the Spirit Realm.** In these accounts, I tell in great detail of the revelation knowledge God has given to me and what He has shown me over the years concerning His mysteries. In *A Divine Revelation of Angels*, I want to emphasize the visions and revelations of angels that God has given to me. I want to show what the work of angels in our lives means for us as we love and serve God.

In 1976, when I started telling the story of the revelations God had given to me, I was like a pioneer pushing into unfamiliar territory. When I went out to speak, there were times when I was mocked, persecuted, and ridiculed. But I kept telling my story

---

* Published by Whitaker House.

because I felt I had a mandate from God. Today, God is sending manifestations and revelations in abundance. God has mysteries to reveal to us at this hour, and we must believe Him.

THE PURPOSE OF GOD'S REVELATIONS

I am Christ's servant, and I'm excited about the fact that He is merciful and good to His servants. God has given me these visions and revelations so that, in turn, I can give them to the body of Christ and to those who are not yet believers. They are signs that God is working among us. The Bible says, *"Surely the Lord GOD does nothing, unless He reveals His secret to His servants the prophets"* (Amos 3:7). God has revealed these things to give us hope, to encourage us, and to show us that He is with us.

What I will relate to you lines up with the Word of God. I know from the Bible and from the revelations God has given me that angels—real angels—are not myths or legends. They are more than a marketing gimmick or a premise for a television program. They are true spiritual beings.

I write these things to lift up Jesus Christ, to exalt Him. The purpose of these revelations is to draw people close to God and to bring Him honor and glory. You need to know just how much Jesus loves and cares about you. There is so much He wants to talk to you about, so much He wants to open up your heart to. He desires your companionship. He desires to reveal Himself to you. You can talk to Him, and He will talk to you. He is an awesome, loving God!

I want you to know that I love the Lord Jesus with all my heart. He is so good to me. What I'm saying in this book is true. I want you to understand this so that you can sit with Christ in heavenly places. This is something He wants for all of us:

> *But God, who is rich in mercy, because of His great love with which He loved us, even when we were dead in trespasses, made us alive together with Christ (by grace you have been*

saved), and raised us up together, and made us sit together in
the heavenly places in Christ Jesus.   (Ephesians 2:4–6)

God has put it on my heart to write this book about angels. He is inspiring books to be written to let the world know what a good God He is and how He takes care of His people. I've seen angels in action many times, and I'm praying that the Holy Spirit will guide me as I relate some of these revelations to you. As I write down what God has given me to share, I pray that it will strengthen and enlighten you in the mysteries and revelations of God.

I also pray that this book will go all over the world to help many other people who need God—that these testimonies of angels in action will help thousands of people know the reality of God's love and concern for them. Through the truths presented here, I'm praying that God—either directly or through His angels—will undo heavy burdens, heal sicknesses and diseases in the name of Jesus, and help the oppressed go free. It is God's desire *"to loose the bonds of wickedness, to undo the heavy burdens, to let the oppressed go free, and...break every yoke"* (Isaiah 58:6).

I get excited all over again when I remember the marvelous revelations God has given me and what He has shown me about His holy angels. Truly God has mercy, and He has angels working for our benefit. In parts 1 and 2 of this book, I will explain what the Bible has to say about the nature and role of angels. In part 3, I will relate what the Lord has revealed to me by His Holy Spirit about these heavenly messengers. I will also share some visions I've seen of the angels of God in action. These visions emphasize the many ways that angels bring glory to God and carry out His commands to guide, protect, comfort, defend, and deliver His people.

In the next chapter, we will learn what is true and what is myth concerning God's heavenly messengers.

2

THE TRUTH ABOUT ANGELS

The study of angels is a serious and sacred pursuit. You have to be careful about some of the teachings you hear and read on the subject, especially what you find on the Internet. Much of so-called teaching on angels making the rounds these days—even in religious circles—is false, and it causes people to be deceived. In this day when we are experiencing a wave of "angel mania," it is important to know what God's Word says about angels. Uninformed conceptions of angels abound, as they have in the past, but I am writing these pages to declare the truth! The things I describe in this book are reality; none of them is fantasy.

GOOD AND EVIL ANGELS

Many people do not realize that there are *two* kinds of angels operating in the world today. This is why people can often become confused and deceived about the nature and role of celestial beings. Not all angels are kind and benevolent. There are good angels and there are evil angels.

Good angels continually seek to do God's will, and they work for our benefit. Evil angels seek to deceive us about their true intentions toward us. They are demons who want to harm us rather than help us. This is why it can be very dangerous to learn about angels from those who don't have a solid biblical understanding of their true nature and ways. I believe that one reason God wanted me to write this book was so people could know how to tell the difference between angels who want to help them and angels who desire to harm them. In this book, I mainly describe the things God has revealed to me concerning His good angels. We have to understand the truth about God's holy angels if we are going to be able to discern what is counterfeit.

ANGELS IN THE BIBLE

Angels have been written about prominently in the Scriptures, and the Bible teaches that they are real beings. The Bible is our best source for understanding the true nature of angels because it is God's own Word. *"Every word of God is flawless"* (Proverbs 30:5 NIV).

In the Scriptures, the words *angel* and *angels* appear about three hundred times (combined), and the work of angels is referred to almost two hundred fifty times. Angels are mentioned in thirty-four books of the Bible (a little over half the books). The Hebrew word for angel most commonly used in the Old Testament is *mal'ak*, and the Greek word for angel most frequently used in the New Testament is *aggelos*. Both of these words mean "a messenger." (See *Strong's* #G32; #H4397.)

Scripture makes reference to the origin of angels and various types of angels, and it reveals important facts about their character, habits, and actions—much of which are contrary to popular belief about angels today. I will talk more about the nature and ways of angels in the next chapter. However, we must first recognize the following truths about angels in order to understand who they are and how they work in our lives.

ANGELS WERE CREATED

First, what is the origin of angels? Did they always exist?

The Bible tells us that angels are a company of spiritual beings that were created by God Himself. For example, in the Old Testament, we read,

> *Praise [the Lord], all His angels; praise Him, all His hosts!...*
> *Let them praise the name of the LORD, for He commanded*
> *and they were created.*   (Psalm 148:2, 5)

In the New Testament, we find,

> *All things were made through Him, and without Him nothing*
> *was made that was made.*   (John 1:3)

> *By [Jesus] all things were created that are in heaven and*
> *that are on earth, visible and invisible, whether thrones or*
> *dominions or principalities or powers. All things were created*
> *through Him and for Him.*   (Colossians 1:16)

There is nothing anywhere that God did not create, including the angels.

The Bible doesn't tell us exactly when angels were created, but it indicates that they already existed and were present when God created the earth. God asked Job,

> *Where were you when I laid the earth's foundation? Tell me,*
> *if you understand. Who marked off its dimensions? Surely*
> *you know! Who stretched a measuring line across it? On what*
> *were its footings set, or who laid its cornerstone—while the*
> *morning stars sang together **and all the angels shouted for***
> ***joy?***   (Job 38:4–7 NIV, emphasis added)

ANGELS ARE NOT GODS

Second, many people today think that angels are divine, and they look to them for direction in life. I have seen some books advertised that purport to tell you how to contact "your" angel. Some who present themselves as experts on angels tell their followers to love their angels and call upon them for health, healing, prosperity, and guidance.

This teaching is contrary to God's Word. Angels are neither our gods nor our direct spiritual guides. They are not available for use at our convenience, like aspirin. They are not genies that we can summon to fulfill our wishes. We cannot call down an angel any time we want to, just by repeating certain phrases or reciting a magic formula or mantra. Angels are God's servants, not ours. They come and go at His bidding. They respond to His voice, not to our commands or requests:

> Bless the LORD, you His angels, who excel in strength, who do His word, heeding the voice of His word. Bless the LORD, all you His hosts, you ministers of His, who do His pleasure.
> (Psalm 103:20–21)

We are never to pray to angels or to call on angels for guidance or deliverance. We are to pray only to the Lord Himself. Praying to an angel may open you up to spiritual deception, especially if you are a new Christian or are not walking close to God. You won't be able to spiritually discern the true nature of an encounter with an angel. When you talk to a being that appears or claims to be an angel, you may be talking to a deceiving spirit masquerading as an angel of light. (See 2 Corinthians 11:14.)

However, when you talk to Jesus, you never go wrong. When you ask God to guide or deliver you, He may use an angel to help you. Yet make no mistake—it is God who is delivering you, even though He may do so *through* His angels.

It is God whom we are to trust, not angels. The Bible doesn't tell us to love angels; it tells us to love God. (See, for example, Matthew 22:37.) All the attention, emphasis, and glory should go to God, not to His servants! God Himself says, *"My glory I will not give to another"* (Isaiah 42:8).

As great as angels are, therefore, we are never to worship them. False teachers will draw you into the worship of angels, which will lead you away from God's truth and into deception. The Bible warns us about this:

> *Let no one cheat you of your reward, taking delight in false humility and worship of angels, intruding into those things which he has not seen, vainly puffed up by his fleshly mind, and not holding fast to [Christ].* (Colossians 2:18–19)

We should respect angels, admire their dedication to God, and appreciate their ministries to God and to us, but we are forbidden to worship them.

One thing I have noticed about real encounters with angels is that God's holy angels never bring attention to themselves. They usually just do their work quietly, often behind the scenes and unnoticed, and they leave when the work is done. Their lives and actions are always consistent with the character of Christ. They always glorify God, not themselves. Therefore, a true angel of God will not accept worship from a human being. Instead, he will always tell you to worship God. In Revelation 19, the apostle John wrote that when he encountered an angel, he was so awed that he *"fell at his feet to worship him"* (v. 10). However, the angel told John,

> *See that you do not do that! I am your fellow servant, and of your brethren who have the testimony of Jesus. Worship God! For the testimony of Jesus is the spirit of prophecy.* (v. 10)

Again, in Revelation 22, John wrote,

*Now I, John, saw and heard these things. And when I heard
and saw, I fell down to worship before the feet of the angel who
showed me these things. Then he said to me, "See that you do
not do that. For I am your fellow servant, and of your brethren
the prophets, and of those who keep the words of this book.
Worship God."*   (vv. 8–9)

Angels are fellow servants and co-worshippers of God with
human beings. In his vision of heaven, John saw all the angels giving
glory, honor, and praise to the One who sits on the throne. (See
Revelation 5:13; 7:11–12.) He described heavenly beings praising
God and exalting Him with the words, *"Holy, holy, holy, Lord God
Almighty, who was and is and is to come!"* (Revelation 4:8). He saw
the twenty-four elders fall down in worship and cast their crowns
before the throne. (See verses 9–10.) Then he heard their shouts
of praise: *"You are worthy, O Lord, to receive glory and honor and
power; for You created all things, and by Your will they exist and were
created"* (v. 11). When the prophet Isaiah described his vision of
heaven in chapter 6 of his book, he said that the cherubim angels
were crying out in a continual litany of worship, *"Holy, holy, holy
is the Lord of hosts; the whole earth is full of His glory"* (Isaiah 6:3).

The favorite activity of all the angels I have seen in my visions
of heaven seems to be the worship of God. Angels worship Him
constantly. Without ceasing, they sing God's praises. They bow
down before Him and worship Him. They obey Him, carrying out
His commands and doing His will.

Again, we are not to worship any other person or creature, no
matter who tries to persuade us to do so. God alone is worthy to
be worshipped and praised! However, we should know that He
provides us with divine help in the form of angels. God is with us.
He will never leave His children alone. Sending His angels to help
us is one of the ways He shows us that He is present with us.

JESUS CHRIST IS GREATER THAN THE ANGELS

Third, some people believe that Jesus Christ is on the same level as angels, or that He is lower than they are. They may have come to that conclusion after reading this Scripture passage:

> *But we see Jesus, who was made a little lower than the angels, for the suffering of death crowned with glory and honor, that He, by the grace of God, might taste death for everyone.*
>
> (Hebrews 2:9)

In this passage, the writer of Hebrews is quoting from Psalm 8:4–5, which talks about God's creating mankind with great worth and dignity:

> *What is man that You are mindful of him, and the son of man that You visit him? For You have made him a little lower than the angels, and You have crowned him with glory and honor.*

Jesus came to earth as a man, but He is both fully human and fully God. He voluntarily set aside the splendor—but not the reality—of His deity. The Scriptures say that He,

> *being in the form of God, did not consider it robbery to be equal with God, but made Himself of no reputation, taking the form of a bondservant, and coming in the likeness of men. And being found in appearance as a man, He humbled Himself and became obedient to the point of death, even the death of the cross.* (Philippians 2:6–8)

Christ became "*a little lower than the angels*" (became a flesh-and-blood man) for our sakes so that He could achieve our salvation. His glory was then restored to Him. The passage in Philippians continues,

> *Therefore God also has highly exalted Him and given Him the name which is above every name, that at the name of Jesus*

*every knee should bow, of those in heaven, and of those on
earth, and of those under the earth, and that every tongue
should confess that Jesus Christ is Lord, to the glory of God
the Father.*   (Philippians 2:9–11)

We also read in Ephesians,

*[God] raised [Jesus] from the dead and seated Him at His
right hand in the heavenly places, far above all principality
and power and might and dominion, and every name that is
named, not only in this age but also in that which is to come.
And He put all things under His feet, and gave Him to be
head over all things to the church, which is His body, the fullness of Him who fills all in all.*   (Ephesians 1:20–23)

First Peter 3:21–22 says, "*Jesus Christ...has gone into heaven and
is at the right hand of God, angels and authorities and powers having
been made subject to Him.*" Christ is forever higher and greater than
all angels! The Word of God says in Hebrews that Jesus is "*so much
better than the angels, as He has by inheritance obtained a more excel-
lent name than they*" (Hebrews 1:4). The passage continues,

*For to which of the angels did He ever say: "You are My
Son, today I have begotten You"? And again: "I will be to
Him a Father, and He shall be to Me a Son"? But when He
again brings the firstborn into the world, He says: "Let all
the angels of God worship Him." And of the angels He says:
"Who makes His angels spirits and His ministers a flame of
fire." But to the Son He says: "Your throne, O God, is forever
and ever; a scepter of righteousness is the scepter of Your kingdom."...But to which of the angels has He ever said: "Sit at My
right hand, till I make Your enemies Your footstool"?*
                                          (vv. 5–8, 13)

Do not let anyone tell you that Jesus is an angel, that He is on
the same level as angels, or that He is lower than the angels. Jesus

Christ is Lord over all the angels, and all the angels worship Him as God.

ANGELS ARE DISTINCT FROM HUMANS

Fourth, there is a popular idea that human beings become angels after they die. Yet the reality is that angels are completely distinct from people. A human is always a human—whether he or she is on earth or in heaven—and an angel is always an angel. People who belong to Christ immediately go to be with Him when they die. They will receive a glorious, resurrected body when Jesus returns for the church, but they do not become angels.

The apostle Peter said that angels *"are greater in power and might"* than humans (2 Peter 2:11). Angels were created before mankind, and throughout the Word of God, they are depicted as existing on a level somewhere between God and man.

Billy Graham, in his best-selling book *Angels,* said this about God's special agents:

> Angels belong to a uniquely different dimension of creation that we, limited to the natural order, can scarcely comprehend.... [God] has given angels higher knowledge, power and mobility than we.... They are God's messengers whose chief business is to carry out His orders in the world. He has given them an ambassadorial charge. He has designated and empowered them as holy deputies.

Angels are a higher form of creation than humans in this sense: Right now, they have higher spiritual knowledge, power, and mobility than we do. In addition, God's holy angels never sin against Him. As long as we are on earth and not yet totally free from *"this body of death"* (Romans 7:24), which is the way the apostle Paul described our tendency to sin, then we are not as morally good as God's holy angels. We still sin and go against the will of

God at times. Angels always work directly for God and with God, and they don't sin; therefore, they are "higher" than we are.

When we acknowledge that angels are higher than we are, we are not putting humanity down. King David recognized the dignity and glory of mankind:

> *You have crowned him with glory and honor. You have made him to have dominion over the works of Your hands; You have put all things under his feet.*   (Psalm 8:5–6)

This passage was so beautiful and important to the early Christians that the New Testament writer quoted it in his letter to the Hebrews (Hebrews 2:7–8), as I talked about in the previous section.

Notice that mankind is *"crowned...with glory and honor."* We were crowned with glory and honor because, first of all, we were created in the image of God. *"God created man in His own image; in the image of God He created him; male and female He created them"* (Genesis 1:27). The Bible doesn't say that angels were created in God's image—only that we were. That makes us precious to Him. Next, mankind was given dominion over all the works of God's hands on earth. God honored humanity by entrusting it with the stewardship and development of the entire world.

Also, we are so important to God that He sent His Son to earth to die for us! He didn't do that for the angels who fell and rebelled against Him. (I will talk more about that shortly.) Hebrews 2:16 says, *"For indeed He does not give aid to angels, but He does give aid to the seed of Abraham."* When mankind fell, God provided a way for us to be forgiven and restored to Him. We have been redeemed through the blood of Christ. This gives us a high and exalted position with God:

> *If God is for us, who can be against us? He who did not spare His own Son, but delivered Him up for us all, how shall He*

not with Him also freely give us all things?
(Romans 8:31–32)

Because Christ redeemed us, we have the righteousness of Jesus Himself! *"Christ Jesus...became for us wisdom from God; and righteousness and sanctification and redemption"* (1 Corinthians 1:30). Paul wrote of the time after Jesus comes back when Christians will exist in a glorified state:

> *I consider that the sufferings of this present time are not worthy to be compared with the glory which shall be revealed in us....*
> *Whom He predestined, these He also called; whom He called, these He also justified; and whom He justified, these He also glorified.*
(Romans 8:18, 30)

At that time, we will be higher than the angels, and we will even judge them. The Bible says, *"Do you not know that we [believers] shall judge angels?"* (1 Corinthians 6:3).

SOME OF GOD'S ANGELS REBELLED AGAINST HIM

Fifth, as I said earlier, many people think all angels are benevolent. However, we must realize that some of God's angels rebelled against Him, and that is the reason that they will one day be judged. They will be eternally punished at the end of the age.

If all angels were created holy, as God is holy, then what happened? The Bible indicates that, at some point, Satan—who is also referred to as Lucifer or the devil—rebelled against God and was expelled from heaven. Ezekiel 28 is apparently alluding to Satan before he fell when it talks about one who had been *"the anointed cherub who covers ["a guardian cherub"* NIV*]"* and who had been *"on the holy mountain of God"* (v. 14). Satan seems to have been one of a special group of angels known as cherubim, but his heart apparently became corrupted by pride:

You were the seal of perfection, full of wisdom and perfect in beauty. You were in Eden, the garden of God; every precious stone was your covering: the sardius, topaz, and diamond, beryl, onyx, and jasper, sapphire, turquoise, and emerald with gold. The workmanship of your timbrels and pipes was prepared for you on the day you were created. You were the anointed cherub who covers; I established you; you were on the holy mountain of God; you walked back and forth in the midst of fiery stones. You were perfect in your ways from the day you were created, till iniquity was found in you. By the abundance of your trading you became filled with violence within, and you sinned; therefore I cast you as a profane thing out of the mountain of God; and I destroyed you, O covering cherub, from the midst of the fiery stones. Your heart was lifted up because of your beauty; you corrupted your wisdom for the sake of your splendor; I cast you to the ground.... I brought fire from your midst; it devoured you, and I turned you to ashes upon the earth in the sight of all who saw you.

(Ezekiel 28:12–18)

Notice in this next passage from Isaiah that pride is again mentioned as being Satan's downfall:

How you are fallen from heaven, O Lucifer, son of the morning! How you are cut down to the ground, you who weakened the nations! For you have said in your heart: "I will ascend into heaven, I will exalt my throne above the stars of God; I will also sit on the mount of the congregation on the farthest sides of the north; I will ascend above the heights of the clouds, I will be like the Most High." Yet you shall be brought down to Sheol, to the lowest depths of the Pit. (Isaiah 14:12–15)

Other angels followed Satan in his rebellion, and they all fell from their sinless position in heaven. Based on the following passage from Revelation, many people believe that about a third of the angels of heaven rebelled:

> *And another sign appeared in heaven: behold, a great, fiery red dragon having seven heads and ten horns, and seven diadems on his heads. His tail drew a third of the stars of heaven and threw them to the earth.... And war broke out in heaven: [the archangel] Michael and his angels fought with the dragon; and the dragon and his angels fought, but they did not prevail, nor was a place found for them in heaven any longer. So the great dragon was cast out, that serpent of old, called the Devil and Satan, who deceives the whole world; he was cast to the earth, and his angels were cast out with him.*
>
> (Revelation 12:3–4, 7–9)

The Bible tells us that the fallen angels were cast into hell to await their judgment at the end of the age:

> *God did not spare the angels who sinned, but cast them down to hell and delivered them into chains of darkness, to be reserved for judgment.* (2 Peter 2:4)

> *And the angels who did not keep their proper domain, but left their own abode, [God] has reserved in everlasting chains under darkness for the judgment of the great day.* (Jude v. 6)

The Bible also reveals the solemn reality that, even though the angels who sinned were cast into hell, some, at least, continue to operate against God and His people:

> *For we do not wrestle against flesh and blood, but against principalities, against powers, against the rulers of the darkness of this age, against spiritual hosts of wickedness in the heavenly places.* (Ephesians 6:12)

Satan is the leader of the fallen angels, and Jesus said that the devil *"does not come except to steal, and to kill, and to destroy"* (John 10:10). Satan hates God, and he hates God's people with a passion.

All iniquity on earth stems from Lucifer's sin. In his desire to further hurt God and usurp His authority, Satan tempted God's beloved creation, mankind, so that humanity would also rebel against God and be a fallen, corrupt people. (See Genesis 3.) Humanity did fall, and Lucifer thought he had won a victory. However, the devil did not count on God's sending Jesus to redeem humanity. Now he works to keep lost souls in darkness by blinding them to the truth of the gospel, which is the message of salvation and freedom from sin through faith in Christ. When Satan rebelled, he exalted himself because he wanted to be worshipped as God. Today, he continues to try to exalt himself.

In fact, I believe that he and his fallen angels are behind much of the current angel craze in our culture. The Bible says that he *"transforms himself into an angel of light"* (2 Corinthians 11:14) in order to deceive people. His purpose is to cause us to worship him and his evil spirits rather than God. He knows that people were created as vessels of worship. Either we are worshipping the true and living God, or we are worshipping the devil and his demon forces. Those who do not know God are serving Satan—consciously or unconsciously.

Satan wants to draw all people to his counterfeit light. Your adversary is lying in wait to deceive you if he can. He wants to confuse you in regard to the truth. Once you are deceived, your mind and heart become open doors for him to attack. That is why it is extremely important in this age, when so many people are becoming interested in spiritual things, that we learn to recognize when the devil is at work and to discern the difference between good and evil angels.

HOW TO DISCERN THE SPIRITS

How are we to know if what presents itself as an angel is truly from God? The Bible tells us to try or test the spirits to see if they are authentic:

> Beloved, do not believe every spirit, but test the spirits, whether they are of God; because many false prophets have gone out into the world. By this you know the Spirit of God: Every spirit that confesses ["acknowledges" NIV] that Jesus Christ has come in the flesh is of God, and every spirit that does not confess ["acknowledge" NIV] that Jesus Christ has come in the flesh is not of God. And this is the spirit of the Antichrist, which you have heard was coming, and is now already in the world.   (1 John 4:1–3)

If we continually read and meditate on the Word of God, we can distinguish between the devil's deceiving angels and God's holy angels. You can tell whether or not an angel is from God by what he says about the Lord Jesus and the salvation He provided for humanity when He came to earth as a man and shed His precious, cleansing blood on the cross. If a spiritual being communicates any message that denies the deity, humanity, and salvation of the Lord Jesus, we can unmask him as the enemy. We can expose him through the power of the Holy Spirit. If his message promotes an unscriptural message or practice, if it draws attention to himself rather than Jesus, then that spirit being is a demon attempting to deceive people.

Therefore, if any being, or any person, claiming to be an angel begins to tell you something that is different from God's Word, or that goes against God's Word, you can know that an evil spirit from hell is behind it. Remember that Satan twisted the Scriptures out of context when he tried to tempt Jesus in the wilderness (see Luke 4:1–13), and he is still trying to manipulate the Scriptures to deceive people today. Make it a priority to study and learn the whole Word of God so you can tell when the Scriptures are being misquoted.

While fallen angels are working as hard as they can to do evil under the direction of the devil, righteous angels are diligently serving God and doing good under His direction. God's holy angels continually glorify Him. They acknowledge Jesus Christ and His coming into the world to redeem us from the enemy's bondage. They focus on Jesus and His deliverance. By their activities and actions, they continually emphasize God's work and will.

OUR ULTIMATE PROTECTION AGAINST DECEPTION AND EVIL

Your ultimate protection against the enemy's deception and evil is the Lord Jesus Christ Himself. The final destiny of Satan and his angels is to spend eternity in a burning lake of fire. Jesus said that there is an *"everlasting fire prepared for the devil and his angels"* (Matthew 25:41). It would be Satan's delight to take you and all your friends with him to hell. Let me beg you not to let this happen to you! Believe in the Lord Jesus Christ and accept Him as your Savior today. Then, as you study about angels, pray to God the Father, in Jesus' name, and ask for His direction and protection so that you will not be deceived by the enemy.

Remember that Jesus is *always* more powerful than the devil and his demons because they are only created beings, while Jesus is God. In addition, when we accept Christ's sacrifice on our behalf, we are safe in Him. Romans 8:38–39 says,

> For I am persuaded that neither death nor life, nor angels nor principalities nor powers, nor things present nor things to come, nor height nor depth, nor any other created thing, shall be able to separate us from the love of God which is in Christ Jesus our Lord.

When Jesus was about to be arrested and crucified, He said that He could easily call tens of thousands of angels to come to His aid: *"Do you think that I cannot now pray to My Father, and He will provide Me with more than twelve legions of angels?"* (Matthew 26:53). In Roman times, a legion could be made up of between three thousand and twelve thousand soldiers, including cavalry and support staff. Jesus could have destroyed His enemies then and there, but He allowed Himself to be crucified for our sakes. Through His death and resurrection, He restored our relationship with God. He paid a great price to provide us with forgiveness of sin and new life in Him.

Once, when I was diligently praying, I had a vision of the day Christ was crucified. It just broke my heart. I saw the Roman soldiers nailing His hands to the cross using huge nails. I saw His blood dripping and running down. I remember seeing the blood coming not just from His hands but from all over His body. He had been beaten so badly that I wanted to comfort my Lord and do something to help Him.

The men who were doing this terrible deed were cursing and blaspheming Him. All at once, the eyes of the Lord looked up. When He looked straight at the men, they fell backward. After a little while, they continued to prepare Jesus for crucifixion. Then I saw them lift up the Lord on the cross. It was so horrible and sad! I was crying and weeping as I saw this mighty vision.

Then I saw angels by the thousands. They seemed to be invisible to those who were at the crucifixion, but I could see them clearly. The angels placed every drop of blood that Jesus shed in vessels they held in their hands, and then they carried the blood of Jesus to heaven and laid it on the mercy seat. Just as atonement in the Old Testament was made by regularly applying the blood of animals to the mercy seat in the Holy of Holies (Leviticus 16:14–16), so Jesus' blood was applied to the mercy seat in heaven. Yet the Old Testament sacrifices were only a type of the sacrifice of Christ.

His blood alone was able to atone for the sins of the whole world once and for all.

The angels were crying as they carried those drops of blood up to the mercy seat. The precious treasure they carried represented a tremendous sacrifice for Jesus. As I watched in awe, I began to cry so hard that I could not see the vision anymore. I was overwhelmed by the awesome price Jesus paid for you and me. When He sacrificed His life, it hurt Him deeply. There was agonizing pain involved. Through this vision, I realized why He gave His life. He knew that He had to carry the weight of the whole world on His shoulders, but He was willing to do it in order to save us from a burning hell. Oh, what He has done for you and me!

I urge you to accept Jesus and His great sacrifice for you. If you do not know Jesus, read the Holy Bible and learn about Him. Understand who He really is. The Bible is the true Word of God, and it says you must be born anew into God's kingdom: *"Jesus answered and said to* [Nicodemus], *'Most assuredly, I say to you, unless one is born again, he cannot see the kingdom of God'"* (John 3:3).

Your sins can be washed away through the atonement Jesus accomplished by shedding His blood on the cross. Even if you think you are the worst person in the world, you can turn to Jesus for complete forgiveness. You can pray, "Jesus, I believe You're the Son of God and my Savior. I believe You died on the cross and rose again so that I can have new life in You. I ask You to wash away my sins through Your cleansing blood and make me clean. Fill me with Your Holy Spirit so that I can now live for You. I commit my life to loving and serving You. Amen."

If you prayed that prayer sincerely from your heart, God will be faithful to forgive you and cleanse you completely. He will give you the gift of the Holy Spirit, who will live within you and enable you to obey and serve Him. You will become a part of God's own family, and His angels will watch over you.

ANGELS IN ACTION

The activity of God's angels in the lives of His people was not just for Bible times. It continues today. Hebrews 1:14 says, *"Are not all angels ministering spirits sent to serve those who will inherit salvation?"* (NIV). Jesus affirmed the involvement of angels in people's lives when He said, *"Take heed that you do not despise one of these little ones, for I say to you that in heaven their angels always see the face of My Father who is in heaven"* (Matthew 18:10). Psalm 91:9–12 assures us,

> *Because you have made the LORD, who is my refuge, even the Most High, your dwelling place, no evil shall befall you, nor shall any plague come near your dwelling; for He shall give His angels charge over you, to keep you in all your ways. In their hands they shall bear you up, lest you dash your foot against a stone.*

God sends His holy angels to help and protect those who belong to Him—who love and serve Him. Angels have worked for each of you who are the children of God. It is possible that an angel will appear to some of you as you face a special need. All around us, the atmosphere is filled with marvelous, magnificent, heavenly angels, God's messengers and warriors. They are there to assist you, to help you, to lift you up!

I call these special messengers "angels in action." They come in the power of almighty God. They are intermediaries between God and man, and they work for people according to God's will. God sends His angels to strengthen me as I try to encourage people in the Lord through my ministry. I have seen so many beautiful things that God has done through His angels in various church services I have participated in. It is wonderful to see God undoing people's heavy burdens and to see lives changed.

In all my visions of Christ, angels constantly surround Him. I am grateful that God has called me to be His servant and has allowed me to see supernatural visions of angels in action. If you meet someone who doesn't believe in angels, just remember that the same situation existed in Jesus' day: *"Sadducees say that there is no resurrection; and no angel or spirit"* (Acts 23:8). Some people live such cold, mundane lives that they believe God is cold and mundane, as well. They do not realize that *"God is Spirit, and those who worship Him must worship in spirit and truth"* (John 4:24). They also do not know that they are surrounded by a vital and active spiritual realm in which both good and evil angels operate.

THE HOUR OF GOD'S VISITATION

We must always keep our eyes on the glory that is being manifested throughout the earth today. This is the hour of God's dispensation; this is the hour of the visitation of the Lord. As the second coming of our Lord Jesus Christ draws closer, I believe that the visible activity of angels will continue to increase here on earth. I have noticed that others have also seen revelations from God and have written books about them. I believe God is preparing international events for the triumph and reign of His Son, Jesus Christ.

I also believe that God is preparing His people for the trouble and turmoil that will come on this earth as Satan attempts a last-ditch but futile effort to prevent the return of our blessed Lord. In this age of uncertainty, upheaval, and loss of control over our daily lives, it is very comforting to know that God has commissioned multitudes of spiritual beings whose principal responsibility is to protect and encourage His people. Jesus is truly the great I Am! Our God is a wonderful God, and He wants us to know how much He loves us, how much He cares for us. Let us ask the Lord to surround us with His holy angels, and let us always persevere in loving and serving Him, for Jesus said,

I am coming soon. Hold on to what you have, so that no one will take your crown. Him who overcomes I will make a pillar in the temple of my God. Never again will he leave it. I will write on him the name of my God and the name of the city of my God, the new Jerusalem, which is coming down out of heaven from my God; and I will also write on him my new name. (Revelation 3:11–12 NIV)

3

WHAT ARE ANGELS LIKE?

Angels are often portrayed today as chubby little cupids who look cute and sweet, but this is not the biblical view. In the Bible, those who saw angels were often amazed or overwhelmed at the sight of these magnificent beings.

The Word of God presents a striking picture of the nature, number, and appearance of angels. In the visions and revelations that God has given me, I have seen the manifestation of many of these characteristics.

THE NATURE OF ANGELS

Angels are a unique creation with specific qualities that reflect who they are and what they were created to do.

ANGELS ARE SPIRIT BEINGS

First, angels are spiritual beings, not flesh and blood (although they can take physical form, as I will discuss presently). God *"makes His angels spirits, His ministers a flame of fire"* (Psalm 104:4; see Hebrews 1:7). There are several qualities of angels as spiritual beings that we should be aware of.

SPIRITS ARE IMMORTAL

Spirits are immortal; they do not die, but live eternally. Jesus said,

> *Those who are considered worthy of taking part in that age and in the resurrection from the dead will neither marry nor be given in marriage; and they can no longer die; for they are like the angels.*   (Luke 20:35–36 NIV)

SPIRITS ARE NOT SUBJECT TO PHYSICAL LIMITATIONS

Angels are not subject to physical restrictions as human beings are. As spirits, they are not limited by time or space. Locked doors and solid walls are no barrier to them, and they can appear and disappear. (See, for example, Acts 5:17–23; 12:5–11.)

SPIRITS HAVE NO GENDER

Although we often think of angels in terms of having male or female characteristics, and although they have often appeared to humans in bodily form, spirits have no gender in the sense that they do not marry and have "baby" angels. *"In the resurrection* [people] *neither marry nor are given in marriage, but are like angels of God in heaven"* (Matthew 22:30).

ANGELS ARE HOLY

Second, the Scriptures teach that angels are holy beings.

> *When the Son of Man comes in His glory, and all the holy angels with Him, then He will sit on the throne of His glory.*   (Matthew 25:31)

> *Whoever is ashamed of Me and My words in this adulterous and sinful generation, of him the Son of Man also will be*

*ashamed when He comes in the glory of His Father with the
holy angels.* (Mark 8:38)

*And they said [to Peter], "Cornelius the centurion, a just
man, one who fears God and has a good reputation among all
the nation of the Jews, was divinely instructed by a holy angel
to summon you to his house, and to hear words from you."*
(Acts 10:22)

*If anyone worships the beast and his image, and receives his
mark on his forehead or on his hand, he himself shall also
drink of the wine of the wrath of God, which is poured out
full strength into the cup of His indignation. He shall be tormented with fire and brimstone in the presence of the holy
angels and in the presence of the Lamb.*
(Revelation 14:9–10)

Angels must be holy because they serve a holy God. This
passage from Isaiah is a compelling picture of how the seraphim
reflect the holiness of the Lord:

*In the year that King Uzziah died, I saw the Lord sitting on
a throne, high and lifted up, and the train of His robe filled
the temple. Above it stood seraphim; each one had six wings:
with two he covered his face, with two he covered his feet, and
with two he flew. And one cried to another and said: "Holy,
holy, holy is the LORD of hosts; the whole earth is full of His
glory!"* (Isaiah 6:1–3)

ANGELS ARE ELECT

Third, the Bible describes angels as *"elect."* In 1 Timothy 5:21,
Paul wrote, *"I charge you before God and the Lord Jesus Christ and
the elect angels that you observe these things without prejudice, doing
nothing with partiality."* The word *"elect"* in the Greek means *"select"*

or "chosen." (See *Strong's* #G1588.) Paul's meaning is not entirely clear, but he may have been referring to the holiness and eternal nature of all God's holy angels, as David Jeremiah wrote in *What the Bible Says about Angels:*

> God's angels are known as the "elect" angels (1 Timothy 5:21), indicating that God chose to let them live eternally in his heaven. Christians are also called "the elect" (2 Timothy 2:10). The angels themselves will be sent by God to "gather his elect from the four winds" (Matthew 24:31), for we too are chosen for eternal life. We and the angels will share permanent citizenship in God's heavenly kingdom forever.
>
> ...C. F. Dickason...says the good angels who did not fall in Satan's rebellion "remain fixed in holiness." They are incapable of sin, just as we will be in eternity. But we will be there in heaven only because the blood of Christ has washed away our sins.

Herbert Lockyer, in *All the Angels of the Bible,* wrote,

> The widely held view is that the elect angels are those who retained their purity and obedience when certain of the angels fell. They are the angels who kept *"their position of authority"* and did not *"abandon their own home"* (Jude v. 6).

ANGELS ARE INTELLIGENT BEINGS, BUT NOT OMNISCIENT

Next, angels are depicted in the Bible as carrying out God's instructions with intelligence, wisdom, and efficiency. Paul even talked about the language of angels. (See 1 Corinthians 13:1.) Yet even though angels have much more knowledge of the spiritual world than we do, they are not all-knowing, as God is. Nothing in Scripture indicates that they are omniscient.

*But of that day and hour [of Jesus' second coming] no one
knows, not even the angels of heaven, but My Father only.*
(Matthew 24:36)

*To [the Old Testament prophets] it was revealed that,
not to themselves, but to us they were ministering the things
which now have been reported to you through those who have
preached the gospel to you by the Holy Spirit sent from heaven;
things which angels desire to look into.* (1 Peter 1:12)

Angels know only what God chooses to reveal to them or
allows them to know. The Bible teaches that angels learn things by
observing God's working in and through His people! Paul wrote
about how God uses the church to reveal certain things to His
holy angels:

*For I think that God has displayed us, the apostles, last, as
men condemned to death; for we have been made a spectacle
to the world, both to angels and to men.*
(1 Corinthians 4:9)

*[The purpose is] that through the church the complicated,
many-sided wisdom of God in all its infinite variety and
innumerable aspects might now be made known to the angelic
rulers and authorities (principalities and powers) in the heavenly sphere.* (Ephesians 3:10 AMP)

I believe the angels were amazed when Jesus came to earth as a
human being to be the Savior of the world. I think they were filled
with wonder to see the extent of Jesus' suffering and the cruelty of
His death on the cross. I think they still marvel today when they
behold the deliverance that God's Son brings to suffering humanity. When God's people come together for a deliverance service,
and His Spirit begins to heal, deliver, and set men and women free,
I believe the angels are astounded at all the miracles of God's grace.

ANGELS HAVE SUPERHUMAN POWER BUT ARE NOT OMNIPOTENT

The apostle Peter said that *"angels...are greater in power and might"* (2 Peter 2:11) than human beings. Paul also referred to angels as *"mighty,"* saying,

> *It is a righteous thing with God to repay with tribulation those who trouble you, and to give you who are troubled rest with us when the Lord Jesus is revealed from heaven with His mighty angels.*   (2 Thessalonians 1:6–7)

Angels are given great strength and ability by God to carry out His will and commands. However, they are not all-powerful, as He is. They don't have unlimited power or authority, but only what God gives them.

The powerful might of angels is demonstrated many times in the Bible in its depictions of angels working on behalf of God's people and fighting God's battles. Here are several examples:

> *The LORD said to Moses, "...And I will send My Angel before you, and I will drive out the Canaanite and the Amorite and the Hittite and the Perizzite and the Hivite and the Jebusite."*   (Exodus 33:1–2)

> *The LORD sent a plague upon Israel from the morning till the appointed time. From Dan to Beersheeba seventy thousand men of the people died. And when the angel stretched out his hand over Jerusalem to destroy it, the LORD relented from the destruction, and said to the angel who was destroying the people, "It is enough; now restrain your hand."*   (2 Samuel 24:15–16)

> *And it came to pass on a certain night that the angel of the LORD went out, and killed in the camp of the Assyrians one hundred and eighty-five thousand.*   (2 Kings 19:35)

Daniel said to the king, "...My God sent His angel and shut the lions' mouths, so that they have not hurt me, because I was found innocent before Him." (Daniel 6:21–22)

He will send His angels with a great sound of a trumpet, and they will gather together His elect from the four winds, from one end of heaven to the other. (Matthew 24:31)

I saw four angels standing at the four corners of the earth, holding the four winds of the earth, that the wind should not blow on the earth, on the sea, or on any tree. Then I saw another angel ascending from the east, having the seal of the living God. And he cried with a loud voice to the four angels to whom it was granted to harm the earth and the sea. (Revelation 7:1–2)

So the four angels, who had been prepared for the hour and day and month and year, were released to kill a third of mankind. (Revelation 9:15)

THE NUMBER OF THE ANGELS

Next, how many angels are there? There are various references in the Bible to numbers of angels. In Matthew 26:53, Jesus referred to *"legions of angels"*: *"Do you think that I cannot now pray to My Father, and He will provide Me with more than twelve legions of angels?"* Again, a Roman legion could be made up of between three thousand and twelve thousand soldiers, including cavalry and support staff. Therefore, Jesus was talking about tens of thousands of angels being readily available to come to His aid.

Daniel had a vision in which he saw *"the Ancient of Days"* (Daniel 7:9), or God Himself, on His throne. Daniel said that *"a thousand thousands ministered to Him; ten thousand times ten thousand stood before Him"* (v. 10). That number comes to more than one hundred million! Yet, even then, apparently not all the angels were present because, in Revelation 5:11, John looked at the angels and elders around God's throne and said that *"the number of them was ten thousand times ten thousand, **and** thousands of thousands"* (emphasis added). In other words, there were even *more* than one hundred million. The writer of Hebrews refers to an *"innumerable company of angels"* (Hebrews 12:22). There are too many angels for us to count!

Another reason we know there are multitudes of angels is that they are referred to as "hosts" of the Lord. In fact, numerous times in the Old Testament (285 times in the King James Version), God is referred to as the *"Lord of hosts"* or the *"God of hosts."* In the New Testament, the angel choir that was praising God at Jesus' birth was called *"a multitude of the heavenly host"* (Luke 2:13). The Hebrew and Greek words that are translated *"hosts"* or *"host"* refer to an army, particularly one organized and ready for war. (See *Strong's* #H6635; #H4264; #G4756.) Consider these Scriptures that refer to the Lord of hosts:

> [Hannah] *made a vow and said, "O* LORD *of hosts, if You will indeed look on the affliction of Your maidservant and remember me, and not forget Your maidservant, but will give your maidservant a male child, then I will give him to the* LORD *all the days of his life."* (1 Samuel 1:11)

> *Then David said to the Philistine, "You come to me with a sword, with a spear, and with a javelin. But I come to you in the name of the* LORD *of hosts, the God of the armies of Israel, whom you have defied."* (1 Samuel 17:45)

> *Then Micaiah said, "Therefore hear the word of the* LORD: *I saw the* LORD *sitting on His throne, and all the host of heaven standing by, on His right hand and on His left."* (1 Kings 22:19)

O LORD God of hosts, who is mighty like You, O LORD?
                                                    (Psalm 89:8)

Bless the LORD, you His angels, who excel in strength, who do His word, heeding the voice of His word. Bless the LORD, all you His hosts, you ministers of His, who do His pleasure.
                                                    (Psalm 103:20–21)

So the LORD of hosts will come down to fight for Mount Zion.   (Isaiah 31:4)

O LORD of hosts, God of Israel, the One who dwells between the cherubim, You are God, You alone, of all the kingdoms of the earth.   (Isaiah 37:16)

For thus says the LORD of hosts: "Once more (it is a little while) I will shake heaven and earth, the sea and dry land; and I will shake all nations, and they shall come to the Desire of All Nations, and I will fill this temple with glory."
                                                    (Haggai 2:6–7)

God saves and delivers through His mighty hosts of angels. There is an innumerable host of angelic beings who surround and worship the Lord day and night and who do His bidding.

THE APPEARANCE OF ANGELS IN THE BIBLE

Third, what do God's angels look like? Angels are choice specimens of beauty and grace, reflecting the glory of their Creator. Sometimes, angels are not visible to the human eye as they go about fulfilling God's Word and purposes. At other times, they are visible to us.

Even though angels are spirits, they can take on various physical forms as they carry out God's will. Humans have observed angels (at least) since the fall of mankind when God placed the cherubim in the garden of Eden to guard the way to the Tree of Life with a flaming sword. (See Genesis 3:24.)

In the Bible, angels did not appear to people as a form of mist or ethereal fog. They sometimes appeared as dazzling, strange, or overpowering entities who could seem frightening, while at other times, they appeared as human beings. These manifestations seemed to be in keeping with the functions and roles they were carrying out. Angels were sometimes seen sitting down, and other times standing up. (See, for example, Judges 6:11; Matthew 28:1–2; John 20:12; Genesis 18:2; Isaiah 6:2; Luke 24:4.) They almost always seemed to inspire awe, however, in those who saw them, as was the case with Samson's parents, who encountered the angel of the Lord:

> *The woman came and told her husband, saying, "A Man of God came to me, and His countenance was like the countenance of the Angel of God, very awesome."...It happened as the flame went up toward heaven from the altar; the Angel of the LORD ascended in the flame of the altar! When Manoah and his wife saw this, they fell on their faces to the ground.*
>
> (Judges 13:6, 20)

SHINING OR DAZZLING APPEARANCE

In the Bible, when the angels appeared in shining or dazzling brightness, they reflected God's own glory. For example, the angel who announced Jesus' birth to the shepherds was accompanied by the glory of God: *"Behold, an angel of the Lord stood before them, and the glory of the Lord shone around them, and they were greatly afraid"* (Luke 2:9). The two angels who appeared at Jesus' empty tomb to announce His resurrection from the dead wore *"shining garments"* (Luke 24:4). When Herod was persecuting the early church and had the apostle Peter imprisoned, *"an angel of the Lord stood by*

[Peter], *and a light shone in the prison*" (Acts 12:7); Peter was led to freedom by this angel. In Revelation 18:1, John wrote, "*I saw another angel coming down from heaven, having great authority, and the earth was illuminated with his glory.*" God declares and reveals His glory through His angels.

STRANGE FORMS OR FEATURES

Sometimes angels in the Bible appeared in strange forms or with unusual features. For example, here is a description of "*four living creatures*" that the prophet Ezekiel saw in a vision. He later identified these beings as cherubim:

Then I looked, and behold, a whirlwind was coming out of the north, a great cloud with raging fire engulfing itself; and brightness was all around it and radiating out of its midst like the color of amber, out of the midst of the fire. Also from within it came the likeness of four living creatures. And this was their appearance: they had the likeness of a man. Each one had four faces, and each one had four wings. Their legs were straight, and the soles of their feet were like the soles of calves' feet. They sparkled like the color of burnished bronze. The hands of a man were under their wings on their four sides; and each of the four had faces and wings. Their wings touched one another. The creatures did not turn when they went, but each one went straight forward. As for the likeness of their faces, each had the face of a man; each of the four had the face of a lion on the right side, each of the four had the face of an ox on the left side, and each of the four had the face of an eagle. Thus were their faces. Their wings stretched upward; two wings of each one touched one another, and two covered their bodies.... As for the likeness of the living creatures, their appearance was like burning coals of fire, like the appearance of torches going back and forth among the living creatures.

> *The fire was bright, and out of the fire went lightning. And the living creatures ran back and forth, in appearance like a flash of lightning.*   (Ezekiel 1:4–11, 13–14)

In Ezekiel 40:3, Ezekiel encountered another angel "*whose appearance was like the appearance of bronze,*" and in Isaiah 6:2, Isaiah described the seraphim as having six wings. In 2 Kings 6:17, angels appeared as a defensive army of fiery chariots and horses surrounding Elisha. Daniel saw this vision of an angel:

> *As I was by the side of the great river, that is, the Tigris, I lifted my eyes and looked, and behold, a certain man clothed in linen, whose waist was girded with gold of Uphaz! His body was like beryl, his face like the appearance of lightning, his eyes like torches of fire, his arms and feet like burnished bronze in color, and the sound of his words like the voice of a multitude.*
> (Daniel 10:4–6)

John gave this description of an angel he saw in the revelation he received:

> *I saw still another mighty angel coming down from heaven, clothed with a cloud. And a rainbow was on his head, his face was like the sun, and his feet like pillars of fire. He had a little book open in his hand, and he set his right foot on the sea and his left foot on the land, and cried with a loud voice, as when a lion roars.*   (Revelation 10:1–3)

In our everyday lives, we can sometimes lose sight of the power and holiness in which God continually dwells. These depictions of angelic beings remind us that God is glorious and omnipotent, and that He is continually working to carry out His purposes in the world.

HUMAN APPEARANCE

Many times, when angels appeared to people on earth, they looked like human beings. For example, in Genesis 18, angels with the appearance of men accompanied the Lord when He spoke to Abraham about the destruction of Sodom and Gomorrah:

> The LORD appeared to [Abraham] by the terebinth trees of Mamre, as he was sitting in the tent door in the heat of the day. So he lifted his eyes and looked, and behold, three men were standing by him; and when he saw them, he ran from the tent door to meet them, and bowed himself to the ground, and said, "My Lord, if I have now found favor in Your sight, do not pass on by Your servant."... Then the men rose from there and looked toward Sodom, and Abraham went with them to send them on the way. And the LORD said, "Shall I hide from Abraham what I am doing, since Abraham shall surely become a great and mighty nation, and all the nations of the earth shall be blessed in him?..." And the LORD said, "Because the outcry against Sodom and Gomorrah is great, and because their sin is very grave, I will go down now and see whether they have done altogether according to the outcry against it that has come to Me; and if not, I will know." Then the men turned away from there and went toward Sodom, but Abraham still stood before the LORD.
>
> (Genesis 18:1–3, 16–18, 20–22)

The angels who came to rescue Lot and his family from Sodom—the same angels who visited Abraham in the above passage—at first seemed like men. (See Genesis 19:1–29.)

In Ezekiel's vision, the angels carrying out God's judgment also looked like men:

> Then He called out in my hearing with a loud voice, saying, "Let those who have charge over the city draw near, each with

a deadly weapon in his hand." And suddenly six men came from the direction of the upper gate, which faces north, each with his battle-ax in his hand. One man among them was clothed with linen and had a writer's inkhorn at his side. They went in and stood beside the bronze altar.   (Ezekiel 9:1–2)

Daniel spoke of his encounter with the angel Gabriel, who had "*the appearance of a man*," at least at the beginning:

Then it happened, when I, Daniel, had seen the vision and was seeking the meaning, that suddenly there stood before me one having the appearance of a man. And I heard a man's voice between the banks of the Ulai, who called, and said, "Gabriel, make this man understand the vision." So he came near where I stood, and when he came I was afraid and fell on my face.   (Daniel 8:15–17)

When angels appeared in human form, they almost always looked like males, but there is a notable exception to this. The Bible tells of two angels who had the appearance of women. Their rank is not mentioned in the biblical account, but they had wings like the wings of a stork, and the wind was in their wings. They performed their mission in a spectacular way, lifting up a basket of wickedness between heaven and earth. (See Zechariah 5:5–11.)

It seems from the biblical accounts that often even the angels who appeared as men had a certain awe-inspiring quality about them that revealed their angelic nature. However, this is not always the case. We are told to be hospitable to strangers because they may be angels disguised as humans. "*Do not forget to entertain strangers, for by so doing some people have entertained angels without knowing it*" (Hebrews 13:2 NIV).

We may see an angel and not recognize him as one! Perhaps, at these times, the presence of angels is hidden from us to prevent us from slipping into the worship of angels and to keep us focused on our true calling. God wants us to love and serve Him not only in the obvious presence of His holy angels, but also in the presence of human beings, who are precious in His sight. The Bible exhorts us in 1 John 4:20, *"If someone says, 'I love God,' and hates his brother, he is a liar; for he who does not love his brother whom he has seen, how can he love God whom he has not seen?"*

ANGELS AMONG US

Friends, the Bible teaches that there are truly angels among us. Sometimes we see them and do not even realize what they are. At other times, we sense their presence and know that they are with us. Then, there are certain times when we think we desperately need them, but they seem to be somewhere else! If we believe the Bible, however, we must understand that angels are always around us. They are helping us, guiding us, and watching over us as they carry out God's will in the earth. Seen or unseen, God's angels always serve Him in love and give Him the glory—and so should we.

I have seen many angels in many different forms. The angels whom God has permitted me to see in the visions and revelations He has given me are amazing creatures to behold. The way they looked always corresponded with the mission they were on. Sometimes I see angels in their spirit forms, and sometimes I see them in "human" form. In their spirit forms, angels appear to me to be transparent, with the outline or shape of a human being. Physical walls are no barrier to them. Light floats around them and through them, and many times this makes it difficult for me to see their facial features distinctly. Often, I see spirit angels like these. Sometimes, however, I see angels with visible wings working with the spirit angels to fulfill the Word of the Lord.

What impresses me about all the angels is that they are continually working for the will and kingdom of God. This is what we must always keep in mind in regard to angels. No matter how magnificent or powerful angels are, we should remember that they are servants of the Most High God, as we are. He alone is worthy to be honored and worshipped.

PART II:
THE ROLE OF ANGELS

4

TYPES AND RANKS OF ANGELS

Are all angels alike, or are there differences among them? The Bible clearly indicates that the angelic realm includes holy beings called "angels," "archangels," "cherubim," and "seraphim." It also suggests there is an organizational hierarchy of angels and even demons.

In referring to *"legions of angels"* in Matthew 26:53, Jesus made an apparent reference to the organization of angels. As I mentioned earlier, a legion was a unit in the organizational structure of the Roman army. When Paul talked about *"the voice of an archangel"* (1 Thessalonians 4:16), he seemed to be alluding to a hierarchy in which some angels have more authority than others, an archangel being higher in rank than an angel. The Lord's brother Jude mentioned the archangel Michael. (See Jude v. 9.)

Over the centuries, church tradition developed this hierarchy of angels, which is made up of nine orders or levels of angelic beings: angels, archangels, principalities, powers, virtues, dominions, thrones, cherubim, and seraphim. We can see how this list was formed in part from several of Paul's writings, in which he gave us a glimpse into the organization of angels:

> *For I am persuaded that neither death nor life, nor angels nor principalities nor powers,...nor any other created thing, shall be able to separate us from the love of God which is in Christ Jesus our Lord.*   (Romans 8:38–39)

> *[God] raised [Jesus] from the dead and seated Him at His right hand in the heavenly places, far above all principality and power and might and dominion, and every name that is named, not only in this age but also in that which is to come.*
>   (Ephesians 1:20–21)

> *God...created all things through Jesus Christ; to the intent that now the manifold wisdom of God might be made known by the church to the principalities and powers in the heavenly places.*   (Ephesians 3:9–10)

> *For by Him all things were created that are in heaven and that are on earth, visible and invisible, whether thrones or dominions or principalities or powers. All things were created through Him and for Him.*   (Colossians 1:16)

Believers have held various opinions about the categories and ranking of angels from the time of the early church fathers up to today. But it seems clear from the Bible that there are different types of angels and that angels have various positions in God's kingdom. Just as it is within the body of Christ, it is true among angels that

> *there are diversities of gifts, but the same Spirit. There are differences of ministries, but the same Lord. And there are diversities of activities, but it is the same God who works all in all.*   (1 Corinthians 12:4–6)

Let's look more closely at what the Bible tells us about archangels, seraphim, and cherubim.

ARCHANGELS

According to Jewish tradition, there are four archangels: Michael, Gabriel, Raphael, and Uriel. However, there are only two places in the Bible where the word *archangel* is mentioned, and only one place where an archangel is explicitly named:

For the Lord Himself will descend from heaven with a shout, with the voice of an archangel, and with the trumpet of God. And the dead in Christ will rise first. Then we who are alive and remain shall be caught up together with them in the clouds to meet the Lord in the air. And thus we shall always be with the Lord. (1 Thessalonians 4:16–17)

Yet Michael the archangel, in contending with the devil, when he disputed about the body of Moses, dared not bring against him a reviling accusation, but said, "The Lord rebuke you!" (Jude v. 9)

MICHAEL, COMMANDER OF ANGELS

Michael is the only angel whom the Scripture specifically calls an archangel. He is also one of only two angels in the entire Bible who are named. The name *Michael* means "Who is like God?" (See *Strong's* #H4317.)

Michael appears in both the Old and New Testaments (Daniel 10:13, 21; 12:1; Jude 1:9; Revelation 12:7). He is always depicted in the Bible in spiritual conflict with evil and wicked powers. Michael appears to be the supreme commander of the angels who do warfare for God—the "hosts" of heaven.

In Daniel 10:13, Michael is called *"one of the chief princes."* In this passage, Daniel told of an angel's appearance to him in response to his prayers, and what the angel said:

> *Then* [the angel] *said to me, "Do not fear, Daniel, for from the first day that you set your heart to understand, and to humble yourself before your God, your words were heard; and I have come because of your words. But the prince of the kingdom of Persia withstood me twenty-one days; and behold, Michael, one of the chief princes, came to help me, for I had been left alone there with the kings of Persia. Now I have come to make you understand what will happen to your people in the latter days, for the vision refers to many days yet to come."*
>
> (Daniel 10:12–14)

Later on in the chapter, we again read that Michael stood with this angel and opposed the spiritual ruler of the kingdom of Persia:

> *And now I must return to fight with the prince of Persia; and when I have gone forth, indeed the prince of Greece will come. But I will tell you what is noted in the Scripture of Truth. (No one upholds me against these, except Michael your prince.)*
>
> (vv. 20–21)

In Daniel 12:1, Michael is called *"the great prince"* who stands guard over the people of God at "the time of the end":

> *At that time Michael shall stand up, the great prince who stands watch over the sons of your people; and there shall be a time of trouble, such as never was since there was a nation, even to that time. And at that time your people shall be delivered, every one who is found written in the book.*

In the New Testament, Jude records the sobering fact that when Moses died on Mount Nebo, the devil came and tried to claim his body. But Michael, God's angelic general, withstood the devil and rebuked him in the name of the Lord:

> *Yet Michael the archangel, in contending with the devil, when he disputed about the body of Moses, dared not bring against*

him a reviling accusation, but said, "The Lord rebuke you!"

(Jude v. 9)

The archangel Michael also battled Satan in the great conflict recorded in the book of Revelation:

And war broke out in heaven: [the archangel] Michael and his angels fought with the dragon; and the dragon and his angels fought, but they did not prevail, nor was a place found for them in heaven any longer. So the great dragon was cast out, that serpent of old, called the Devil and Satan, who deceives the whole world; he was cast to the earth, and his angels were cast out with him. (Revelation 12:7–9)

The mighty archangel Michael is always mentioned with respect and admiration by those in the Bible. He should be an inspiration to us to be faithful and obedient to God as we serve His purposes in His kingdom.

GABRIEL, CHIEF MESSENGER ANGEL

The only other angel mentioned by name in the Bible is Gabriel. *Gabriel* means "man of God." (See *Strong's* #H1403.) Tradition holds that he is an archangel, although, again, the Bible does not specifically say this. However, he is a very important messenger angel *"who stands in the presence of God"* (Luke 1:19) and plays a prominent role in Scripture.

Gabriel appears in the Bible four different times, and each time his appearance is related to the mission of announcing God's purpose and program concerning Jesus the Messiah and *"the time of the end."* Daniel wrote about his encounter with Gabriel after receiving a second vision from God:

Then it happened, when I, Daniel, had seen the vision and was seeking the meaning, that suddenly there stood before me one having the appearance of a man. And I heard a man's voice...who called, and said, "Gabriel, make this man under-stand the vision." So he came near where I stood, and...he said to me, "Understand, son of man, that the vision refers to the time of the end."   (Daniel 8:15–17)

Daniel also told of another visit from Gabriel after Daniel had humbled himself, confessed his sins and the sins of the nation, and interceded with God for the people of Israel:

Now while I was speaking, praying, and confessing my sin and the sin of my people Israel, and presenting my supplication before the LORD my God...yes, while I was speaking in prayer, the man Gabriel, whom I had seen in the vision at the begin-ning, being caused to fly swiftly, reached me about the time of the evening offering. And he informed me, and talked with me, and said, "O Daniel, I have now come forth to give you skill to understand. At the beginning of your supplications the command went out, and I have come to tell you, for you are greatly beloved; therefore consider the matter, and understand the vision."   (Daniel 9:20–23)

Gabriel went on to explain to Daniel the events of the *"seventy weeks"* (v. 24) and that they would be a turning point in Israel's history. He interpreted God's purpose and program for the people of Israel and the Messiah. (See verses 24–27.)

In the New Testament, Gabriel announced the birth of John the Baptist to his elderly parents. Zechariah (or Zacharias), a priest, was burning incense in the temple, when

an angel of the Lord appeared to him, standing on the right side of the altar of incense. And when Zacharias saw him, he was troubled, and fear fell upon him. But the angel said to him, "Do not be afraid, Zacharias, for your prayer is heard; and your wife Elizabeth will bear you a son, and you shall call his name John.... He will turn many of the children of

Israel to the Lord their God. He will also go before Him in the spirit and power of Elijah...to make ready a people prepared for the Lord." And Zacharias said to the angel, "How shall I know this? For I am an old man, and my wife is well advanced in years." And the angel answered and said to him, "I am Gabriel, who stands in the presence of God, and was sent to speak to you and bring you these glad tidings."

(Luke 1:11–13, 16–19)

This same hallowed messenger also announced the birth of Jesus Christ to His mother Mary:

Now in the sixth month the angel Gabriel was sent by God to a city of Galilee named Nazareth, to a virgin betrothed to a man whose name was Joseph, of the house of David. The virgin's name was Mary. And having come in, the angel said to her, "Rejoice, highly favored one, the Lord is with you; blessed are you among women!" But when she saw him, she was troubled at his saying, and considered what manner of greeting this was. Then the angel said to her, "Do not be afraid, Mary, for you have found favor with God. And behold, you will conceive in your womb and bring forth a Son, and shall call His name JESUS. He will be great, and will be called the Son of the Highest; and the Lord God will give Him the throne of His father David. And He will reign over the house of Jacob forever, and of His kingdom there will be no end."

(Luke 1:26–33)

While Matthew, the writer of the first gospel, did not name him by name, it was probably Gabriel who assured Joseph that he should go ahead with his plan to marry Mary:

An angel of the Lord appeared to him in a dream, saying, "Joseph, son of David, do not be afraid to take to you Mary

your wife, for that which is conceived in her is of the Holy
Spirit."   (Matthew 1:20)

It is also likely that it was Gabriel who took messages to Joseph
in order to protect the life of Christ until His time:

Now when [the wise men] had departed, behold, an angel
of the Lord appeared to Joseph in a dream, saying, "Arise,
take the young Child and His mother, flee to Egypt, and stay
there until I bring you word; for Herod will seek the young
Child to destroy Him." When he arose, he took the young
Child and His mother by night and departed for Egypt, and
was there until the death of Herod, that it might be fulfilled
which was spoken by the Lord through the prophet, saying,
"Out of Egypt I called My Son."... When Herod was dead,
behold, an angel of the Lord appeared in a dream to Joseph in
Egypt, saying, "Arise, take the young Child and His mother,
and go to the land of Israel, for those who sought the young
Child's life are dead." Then he arose, took the young Child
and His mother, and came into the land of Israel.
                                        (Matthew 2:13–15, 19–21)

Gabriel is often depicted as a celestial trumpet player. This idea
probably comes from the Scripture about Jesus' return that says,
"For the Lord Himself will descend from heaven with a shout, with the
voice of an archangel, and with the trumpet of God" (1 Thessalonians
4:16). This verse doesn't say that the archangel will sound the
trumpet. However, the archangel does appear to be announcing to
the earth that the Messiah has returned.

Gabriel is God's trustworthy messenger angel who stands in
His presence and brings important news to His people concerning
His plan for the world. This angel's reverence for God, His Word,
and His work should inspire us to love and serve God as He carries
out His purposes in our own lives and in the lives of all humanity.

CHERUBIM AND SERAPHIM

Two special kinds of angels are prominent in the Bible: cherubim and seraphim. Both are connected with the presence of God.

CHERUBIM

Cherubim or cherubs are not at all like today's popular depictions of them as plump little babies with wings. They are powerful and holy beings. The first time the Bible mentions cherubim is in Genesis 3:24 when Adam and Eve were banished from the garden of Eden because of their rebellion against God: *"So He drove out the man; and He placed cherubim at the east of the garden of Eden, and a flaming sword which turned every way, to guard the way to the tree of life."*

The origin of the name *cherubim* is unknown, but these angels are closely associated with God. In seven different places in the Bible, we read that our great Lord is the God who *"dwells between the cherubim"* (1 Samuel 4:4; 2 Samuel 6:2; 2 Kings 19:15; 1 Chronicles 13:6; Psalm 80:1; Psalm 99:1; Isaiah 37:16). In 2 Samuel 22:11, David said that when God answered his prayer and came to his rescue, *"He rode upon a cherub, and flew; and He was seen upon the wings of the wind."* (See also Psalm 18:10.)

When God gave Moses the plans for the ark of the covenant, or ark of testimony, in the tabernacle, He instructed Moses to place replicas of two cherubim on each end of the mercy seat, upon which the blood of atonement would be sprinkled:

You shall make a mercy seat of pure gold; two and a half cubits shall be its length and a cubit and a half its width. And you shall make two cherubim of gold; of hammered work you shall make them at the two ends of the mercy seat. Make one cherub at one end, and the other cherub at the other end; you shall make the cherubim at the two ends of it of one piece with the mercy seat. And the cherubim shall stretch out their wings above, covering the mercy seat with their wings, and they shall face one another; the faces of the cherubim shall be toward the mercy seat. You shall put the mercy seat on top of the ark, and in the ark you shall put the Testimony that I will give you. And there I will meet with you, and I will speak with you from above the mercy seat, from between the two cherubim which are on the ark of the Testimony. (Exodus 25:17–22)

God's presence dwelt between these cherubim in the tabernacle, and from that place, He also spoke to Moses. (See also Numbers 7:89.) The Bible says that curtains and the veil in the tabernacle were decorated with cherubim, as well. (See Exodus 26:1, 31; 36:8, 35.)

When Solomon built the temple in Jerusalem, he decorated it with elaborate and elegant carvings, engravings, and sculptures of cherubim, and he had the temple curtain embroidered with cherubim. (See 1 Kings 6:22–35; 7:29, 36; 2 Chronicles 3:7, 10–14.) In exile in Babylon, Ezekiel saw a vision of the future temple, and it still contained rich carvings of cherubim. (See Ezekiel 41:18–20, 25.)

What are cherubim like? Ezekiel mentioned them in chapter 1 of his book, but he described them in detail in chapter 10:

And I looked, and there in the firmament that was above the head of the cherubim, there appeared something like sapphire stone, having the appearance of the likeness of a throne. Then He spoke to the man clothed with linen, and said, "Go in among the wheels, under the cherub, fill your hands with coals of fire from among the cherubim, and scatter them over the city." And he went in as I watched. Now the cherubim were standing on the south side of the temple when the man went in, and the cloud filled the inner court. Then the glory of the LORD went up from the cherub, and paused over the threshold of the temple; and the house was filled with the cloud, and the court was full of the brightness of the LORD's glory. And the sound of the wings of the cherubim was heard even in the outer court, like the voice of Almighty God when He speaks. Then it happened, when He commanded the man clothed in linen, saying, "Take fire from among the wheels, from among the cherubim," that he went in and stood beside the wheels. And the cherub stretched out his hand from among the cherubim to the fire that was among the cherubim, and took some of it and put it into the hands of the man clothed with linen, who took it and went out. The cherubim appeared to have the form of a man's hand under their wings. And when I looked, there were four wheels by the cherubim, one wheel by one cherub and another wheel by each other cherub; the wheels appeared to have the color of a beryl stone. As for their appearance, all four looked alike; as it were, a wheel in the middle of a wheel. When they went, they went toward any of their four directions; they did not turn aside when they went, but followed in the direction the head was facing. They did not turn aside when they went. And their whole body, with their back, their hands, their wings, and the wheels that the four had, were full of eyes all around. As for the wheels, they were called in my hearing, "Wheel." Each one had four faces: the first face was the face of a cherub, the second face the face of a man, the third face the face of a lion, and the fourth the face of an eagle. And the cherubim were lifted up. This was the living creature I saw by the River Chebar. When the cherubim went, the wheels went beside them; and when the cherubim lifted their wings to mount up from the earth, the same wheels also did not turn from beside them. When the cherubim stood still, the wheels stood still, and when one was lifted up, the other lifted itself up, for the spirit of the living creature was in them. Then the glory of the LORD departed from the threshold of the temple and stood over the cherubim. And the cherubim lifted their wings and mounted up from the earth in my sight. When they went

*out, the wheels were beside them; and they stood at the door
of the east gate of the LORD's house, and the glory of the God
of Israel was above them..., and I knew they were cherubim.
Each one had four faces and each one four wings, and the
likeness of the hands of a man was under their wings.*

(Ezekiel 10:1–21)

Imagine these magnificent beings connected with God's presence, purity, and glory that reflect the majesty of the Lord!

Yet there is a sober note related to cherubim, as well. As I wrote earlier, Lucifer was apparently a cherub before he fell and became Satan. In Ezekiel 28, the prophet was probably referring to the devil when he said he was *"the anointed cherub who covers"* and who was *"on the holy mountain of God"* (v. 14). Because of Lucifer's sin, God said, *"I destroyed you, O covering cherub, from the midst of the fiery stones"* (v. 16). It is almost unimaginable to think of how low Satan fell when he succumbed to pride, rebelled against God, and was cast out of heaven. He went from being an *"anointed cherub"* to *"the dragon, that serpent of old"* (Revelation 20:2) who will be *"cast into the lake of fire and brimstone"* (v. 10). What a terrible fall!

This is a grave reminder to us of the consequences of sin, if even a cherub can have such an end. Yet it is also a reminder of Christ's great sacrifice on our behalf that restores us to the very presence of God as if we had never sinned! As Hebrews 2:16 says, *"For indeed He does not give aid to angels, but He does give aid to the seed of Abraham."*

SERAPHIM

Seraphim or seraphs are mentioned directly in only one passage of the Bible. Isaiah vividly described these heavenly creatures:

*In the year that King Uzziah died, I saw the Lord sitting on
a throne, high and lifted up, and the train of His robe filled
the temple. Above it stood seraphim; each one had six wings:*

with two he covered his face, with two he covered his feet, and
with two he flew. And one cried to another and said: "Holy,
holy, holy is the Lord *of hosts; the whole earth is full of His*
glory!" And the posts of the door were shaken by the voice of
him who cried out, and the house was filled with smoke.

(Isaiah 6:1–4)

(The angels we read about in Revelation 4:8 who surrounded
the throne and cried continuously, "Holy, holy, holy, Lord God
Almighty, *who was and is and is to come!"* may be either seraphim or
cherubim since they seem to have features of both.)

Seraphim are closer than all the other angels to their Creator
and Maker, hovering above the throne of God. These attendants
at God's throne seem to dwell in the midst of His holiness. The
sight of God on His throne with the seraphim above Him filled
Isaiah with a sense of his own sin and unworthiness, and one of the
seraphs was sent by God to touch Isaiah's mouth with a purifying
live coal from the altar of heaven:

[Isaiah] *said: "Woe is me, for I am undone! Because I am*
a man of unclean lips, and I dwell in the midst of a people
of unclean lips; for my eyes have seen the King, the Lord *of*
hosts." Then one of the seraphim flew to me, having in his
hand a live coal which he had taken with the tongs from the
altar. And he touched my mouth with it, and said: "Behold,
this has touched your lips; your iniquity is taken away, and
your sin purged."   (Isaiah 6:5–7)

Of the seraphim's six wings, two pairs cover their faces and
feet in the presence of God's brilliant glory, while only one pair is
used for flying. In the Hebrew, the word *seraphim* means "burning"
or "fiery." (See *Strong's* #H8314.) In the visions and revelations I
have received, when I see angels as spirits (rather than in a human
form), they always look like fire to me. I believe this is because
angels, and especially the seraphim, stand before the One of whom

it is written, *"Our God is a consuming fire"* (Hebrews 12:29). In one of his visions, Daniel said, *"[God's] throne was a fiery flame, its wheels a burning fire; a fiery stream issued and came forth from before Him"* (Daniel 7:9–10). Moses reported that *"the sight of the glory of the LORD was like a consuming fire"* (Exodus 24:17). In Psalm 104:4, we read that *"[God] makes His angels spirits, His ministers a flame of fire."*

Seraphim are intelligent beings who celebrate the Holy One of Israel. They are aflame with love for God. Their devotion should inspire deep love for God in us, as well.

ANGEL OF THE LORD

I would like to say a brief word here about the term "angel of the Lord" or "Angel of the Lord," which occurs frequently in Scripture. (See, for example, Genesis 16:7–11; Exodus 3:1–6; 2 Samuel 24:16; Zechariah 3:1–7; Acts 12:21–23.) At various times, this term may be referring to one of God's angels, to God Himself, or to the Lord Jesus Christ in what is often called a pre-incarnate appearance. Either way, a reference to such an angel in Scripture clearly deserves our attention and respect.

SENT TO SERVE

We have seen that there are different types of angels who serve God, and that angels have various positions in His kingdom. All God's angels reflect His greatness, power, and holiness. The amazing thing is that they work on our behalf! Again, Hebrews 1:14 says, *"Are not all angels ministering spirits sent to serve those who will inherit salvation?"* (NIV).

In the next chapter, we will look at some of the specific roles that God's angels fulfill.

5

MINISTERING SPIRITS

According to the Bible, angels have spheres of authority and certain duties to perform in the heavens and in the universe at large. While the earth is not their native habitat, they do conduct active operations here. Angels travel back and forth between heaven and earth as they do God's will. Jacob saw a vision of a ladder reaching from heaven to earth on which angels ascended and descended. (See Genesis 28:12.) In part 3, I will talk about what I have seen of the activity of angels through the visions and revelations God has given me. These revelations illustrate God's continuing presence and work among His people today.

Yes, my dear friend, angels are in action around us all the time. Things are happening in the spiritual realm that our physical senses cannot detect; these things have to be spiritually discerned.

A story in 2 Kings 6 illustrates this truth. The king of Syria was puzzled and perplexed because the king of Israel always seemed to know his plans ahead of time. When he invaded Israel, God's people were always able to defeat him. The Syrian king thought that there was a spy among his associates, but someone told him that there was a prophet in Israel, Elisha, who knew even *the words that you speak in your bedroom* (v. 12).

> *Therefore* [the king of Syria] *sent horses and chariots and a great army there, and they came by night and surrounded the city. And when the servant of the man of God arose early and went out, there was an army, surrounding the city with horses and chariots. And his servant said to him, "Alas, my master! What shall we do?" So he answered, "Do not fear, for those who are with us are more than those who are with them." And Elisha prayed, and said, "LORD, I pray, open his eyes that he may see." Then the LORD opened the eyes of the young man, and he saw. And behold, the mountain was full of horses and chariots of fire all around Elisha.*   (2 Kings 6:14–17)

With a whole universe of celestial beings, both seen and unseen, surrounding and helping us, we can be both comforted and strengthened. We should have respect for these agents of God, these created beings we call angels. God puts them in our lives to minister to our needs. Their works and their actions toward God's people should inspire us to persevere in our daily walk with Him.

WORSHIPPERS OF GOD

The primary role of all angels is to praise and exalt God and His Son, Jesus Christ. This is because *everything* God has created—angels, people, even nature—was created for the purpose of glorifying Him. The Scriptures tell us:

> *Praise the LORD! Praise the LORD from the heavens; praise Him in the heights! Praise Him, all His angels; praise Him, all His hosts! Praise Him, sun and moon; praise Him, all you stars of light! Praise Him, you heavens of heavens, and you waters above the heavens! Let them praise the name of the LORD, for He commanded and they were created.*
> (Psalm 148:1–5)

When [God] again brings the firstborn into the world, He says: "Let all the angels of God worship Him [Christ]."

(Hebrews 1:6)

[John] heard the voice of many angels around the throne, the living creatures, and the elders; and the number of them was ten thousand times ten thousand, and thousands of thousands, saying with a loud voice: "Worthy is the Lamb who was slain to receive power and riches and wisdom, and strength and honor and glory and blessing!" (Revelation 5:11–12)

All the angels stood around the throne and the elders and the four living creatures, and fell on their faces before the throne and worshiped God, saying: "Amen! Blessing and glory and wisdom, thanksgiving and honor and power and might, be to our God forever and ever. Amen." (Revelation 7:11–12)

When I had a revelation of heaven, the presence of the Lord was so awesome. No matter what activity the various angels there were engaged in, they were singing to the Lord and praising Him. Angels by the seeming millions continually worshipped Him. There were also, at intervals, times of silence, times of meditation.

The atmosphere around the throne of God is always filled with glories, honor, and amens. The writer of Hebrews said, "*You have come to Mount Zion, to the heavenly Jerusalem, the city of the living God. You have come to thousands upon thousands of angels in joyful assembly*" (Hebrews 12:22 NIV). The four living creatures at God's throne (perhaps seraphim or cherubim) "*do not rest day or night*" because they are saying, "*Holy, holy, holy, Lord God Almighty, who was and is and is to come!*" (Revelation 4:8).

There are endless reasons for the angels to praise and worship God. For example, when God created the world, the angels must have gazed with excitement and fascination on God's mighty acts of creative genius. Job 38 says of that significant occasion that "*the morning stars sang together and all the angels shouted for joy*" (v. 7 NIV). Through their worship of God, the angels inspire us to appreciate God's beauty and majesty and the glory of His creation, as well as all His other wondrous works.

MINISTERS OF GOD'S PEOPLE

Angels not only worship God, but are also His willing servants. They are God's active agents who do His will day and night as they minister to Him and His people.

Again, the first chapter of Hebrews tells us, "*Are not all angels ministering spirits sent to serve those who will inherit salvation?*" (v. 14 NIV). Angels are servants of the kingdom of God, and they work for all of us who are heirs of God's salvation, as they are directed to by the will and Word of God. If you are a child of God, angels have worked for you, whether you were aware of it or not. Angels will sometimes appear to believers during times of special need. Their protecting presence shows us how much God cares about us. Here are several of the ways in which angels minister to believers.

BRINGING MESSAGES FROM GOD

First, angels are couriers from God who bring special messages to His people. Let's look at a few biblical examples of this. In Genesis 18:9–14, the angel of God's presence announced to Abraham that his wife, Sarah, an elderly, barren woman, would become pregnant and give birth to a child. The angel of the Lord also reaffirmed to Abraham that through his lineage all the nations of the earth would be blessed. (See Genesis 22:11–18.)

An angel of the Lord appeared to Gideon and told him that he would save Israel from the hand of the Midianites. (See Judges 6:11–14.)

As we saw earlier, the angel Gabriel announced to Zechariah that his wife Elizabeth would give birth to John the Baptist in her old age. (See Luke 1:11–17.) Gabriel also announced to Mary that she would conceive a child through the power of the Holy Spirit who would be the Messiah. (See verses 28–35.) An angel appeared to Mary's fiancé, Joseph, in a dream, assuring him that the baby was conceived of the Holy Spirit and encouraging him to go ahead with his plan to take Mary as his wife. (See Matthew 1:20–21.)

On the night of the blessed Savior's birth, a single angel appeared to the shepherds in nearby fields, bathing them in a glorious light and saying, *"Behold, I bring you good tidings of great joy"* (Luke 2:10). Then, as the angel announced the birth of Jesus,

> *suddenly there was with the angel a multitude of the heavenly host praising God and saying: "Glory to God in the highest, and on earth peace, goodwill toward men!"*   (vv. 13–14)

An angel appeared to Cornelius in a vision and told him to send for Peter so that Peter could preach the gospel to him. (See Acts 10:1–6.) Philip was instructed by an angel to go to Gaza for the purpose of meeting an Ethiopian eunuch and explaining to him the message of salvation through Christ. (See Acts 8:26–39.)

We can see from these examples that angels bring important news to God's people of His activity in their lives and His plan for the salvation of the world.

DELIVERING GOD'S WORD

In a related role, angels deliver God's Word to people and also help them to understand it. For instance, angels were involved when God gave the Ten Commandments and the sacred Law on Mt. Sinai:

> *The LORD came from Sinai and dawned over them from Seir; he shone forth from Mount Paran. He came with myriads of holy ones from the south, from his mountain slopes. Surely it is you who love the people; all the holy ones are in your hand. At*

*your feet they all bow down, and from you receive instruction,
the law that Moses gave us.*   (Deuteronomy 33:2–4 NIV)

In his address before the Sanhedrin court in Acts 7, Stephen said that Israel had *"received the law by the direction of angels"* (v. 53). The *New International Version* reads, *"The law...was put into effect through angels"* (v. 53). Paul echoed this truth when he wrote:

What purpose then does the law serve? It was added because of transgressions, till the Seed should come...and it was appointed through angels by the hand of a mediator.

(Galatians 3:19)

Angels are always true to Scripture in word and in action. The angel in Daniel 10 stood for the truth of God's Word. He told Daniel, *"But I will tell you what is noted in the Scripture of Truth"* (v. 21). Paul told us, *"But even if...an angel from heaven, preach any other gospel to you than what we have preached to you, let him be accursed"* (Galatians 1:8). He knew that if an "angel" begins to tell you things contrary to God's Word, he is not a holy angel from God, but a demon spirit who has disguised himself as one. Remember that Satan misquoted the Scripture to Jesus during the Temptation, and he still pretends to be an *"angel of light"* (2 Corinthians 11:14) in order to deceive people.

When God has shown me His angels in action, He has always pointed me to Scripture that confirms what I just saw. An angel from God will never give you instruction or guidance that deviates from what God has already said in His Word. I will talk more about the role of angels and God's Word in chapter 7.

BRINGING GOD'S GUIDANCE

God's angels also direct people's steps and clear the path before them as they do His will. For example, in Genesis 24, Abraham told his servant that an angel would lead him to the young woman who would be the right wife for his son Isaac. *"The LORD God of heaven...will send His angel before you, and you shall take a wife for my son from* [the land I came from]*"* (v. 7).

In Genesis 31, an angel told Jacob that it was time for him to return home after many years of running from God and his brother Esau. Jacob reported, *"Then the Angel of God spoke to me in a dream, saying, 'Jacob.' And I said, 'Here I am.' And He said,... Now arise, get out of this land, and return to the land of your family"* (vv. 11–13).

The angel who spoke to Philip guided him to the right person at the right time who needed ministry:

> Now an angel of the Lord spoke to Philip, saying, "Arise and go toward the south along the road which goes down from Jerusalem to Gaza." This is desert. So he arose and went. And behold, a man of Ethiopia, a eunuch of great authority under Candace the queen of the Ethiopians, who had charge of all her treasury, and had come to Jerusalem to worship, was returning. And sitting in his chariot, he was reading Isaiah the prophet. Then the Spirit said to Philip, "Go near and overtake this chariot." So Philip ran to him, and heard him reading the prophet Isaiah, and said, "Do you understand what you are reading?" And he said, "How can I, unless someone guides me?" And he asked Philip to come up and sit with him.
>
> (Acts 8:26–31)

An angel gave Philip specific direction on what to do and where to go, but the Holy Spirit was with him and continued to guide him on his mission. It is always God whom we are to look to for guidance. Once again, we are to pray only to God, not to the angels, even though He will sometimes use His angels to guide us.

During services, I have sometimes seen, in the spiritual realm, angels go up and put crosses on certain people's shoulders. God showed me that this means He has called these people for special tasks, that they have been chosen of the Lord. Sometimes the Lord will allow me to call them up to where I am ministering and tell them that God has called them for a purpose. Often, they will say, "Yes, I know that, but I haven't done it yet." I respond, "Well, seek the Lord. He will surely direct your path. He will not forget you."

As we trust in God, He guides all our paths, and one way He does this is through His angels. The Scripture says, "*Trust in the* LORD *with all your heart, and lean not on your own understanding; in all your ways acknowledge Him, and He shall direct your paths*" (Proverbs 3:5–6).

COMFORTING AND ENCOURAGING GOD'S PEOPLE

God's angels also comfort and encourage people during difficult times in their lives. For example, in Genesis 16, the Angel of the Lord gently comforted Hagar when she fled from the harsh treatment of Sarah (Sarai):

> *Now the Angel of the* LORD *found her by a spring of water in the wilderness, by the spring on the way to Shur. And He said, "Hagar, Sarai's maid, where have you come from, and where are you going? She said, "I am fleeing from the presence of my mistress Sarai." The Angel of the* LORD *said to her, "Return to your mistress, and submit yourself under her hand." Then the Angel of the* LORD *said to her, "I will multiply your descendents exceedingly, so that they shall not be counted for multitude." And the Angel of the* LORD *said to her: "Behold, you are with child, and you shall bear a son. You shall call his name Ishmael, because the* LORD *has heard your affliction."*
>
> (vv. 7–11)

In Genesis 21, "*the angel of God*" (v. 17) comforted Hagar when she and Ishmael were sent away from Abraham and Sarah, and Hagar thought they would die in the desert. (See verses 9–21.)

In Genesis 28, Jacob had a dream in which angels were climbing up and down a ladder from heaven to earth. Through this dream, God used angels to help assure Jacob that he was in the presence of God, that he was at the very gates of heaven. (See verses 11–15.)

On board ship during a violent storm at sea, Paul received encouragement from an angel that God would save his life and the lives of everyone on the boat, and that God would be with him when he was on trial before Caesar in Rome. Paul said,

> There stood by me this night an angel of the God to whom I belong and whom I serve, saying, "Do not be afraid, Paul; you must be brought before Caesar; and indeed God has granted you all those who sail with you." (Acts 27:23–24)

Second Corinthians 7:6 says that "God... comforts the downcast," and at times He uses His angels to bring that comfort to His people. On one occasion, I was going through several crises in my life. I was praying as an intercessor and faithfully preaching the gospel under a heavy anointing, and I read in the Word about the special ministry of angels to God's people.

I was staying in a hotel, and as I went to bed that night, I heard what seemed to be angels singing above my head. These were beautiful voices singing praises to God, and as I lay there, I joined in worship with them. As we praised and worshipped the Lord, the Holy Spirit began to comfort me. He truly is a faithful comforter. There is a verse that says, "The LORD your God in your midst, the Mighty One, will save; He will rejoice over you with gladness, He will quiet you with His love, He will rejoice over you with singing" (Zephaniah 3:17).

Suddenly, I realized my room was filled with angels! God is a comforter, and angels are in action around us doing His bidding all the time. If we will be open and see with spiritual eyes, we will know that we are blessed by God in this way.

SUSTAINING GOD'S PEOPLE

Next, God sometimes sends His angels to strengthen and sustain people. Often, this serves to encourage them, as well.

In Genesis 21, the angel of God who appeared to Hagar in the wilderness showed her where to find water for herself and her dying son. (See verse 19.)

When Elijah the prophet was frightened and running for his life from Jezebel, God used an angel to physically sustain him:

> *Jezebel sent a messenger to Elijah, saying, "So let the gods do to me, and more also, if I do not make your life as the life of one of* [the executed prophets of Baal] *by tomorrow about this time." And when he saw that, he arose and ran for his life, and went to Beersheba, which belongs to Judah, and left his servant there. But he himself went a day's journey into the wilderness, and came and sat down under a broom tree. And he prayed that he might die, and said, "It is enough! Now, LORD, take my life, for I am no better than my fathers!" Then as he lay and slept under a broom tree, suddenly an angel touched him, and said to him, "Arise and eat." Then he looked, and there by his head was a cake baked on coals, and a jar of water. So he ate and drank, and lay down again. And the angel of the LORD came back the second time, and touched him, and said, "Arise and eat, because the journey is too great for you." So he arose, and ate and drank; and he went in the strength of that food forty days and forty nights as far as Horeb, the mountain of God.* (1 Kings 19:2–8)

At Horeb, Elijah encountered God in the *"still small voice"* (v. 12), and the Lord encouraged him and told him what he should do next. (See verses 9–18.)

In the New Testament, we see that God sent angels to strengthen and sustain His Son Jesus while He was on earth. For instance, at the beginning of our Lord's ministry, after He had withstood the devil's temptation in the wilderness, *"the devil left Him, and behold, angels came and ministered to Him"* (Matthew 4:11). Perhaps they also sustained Him because of the presence of wild beasts in that wilderness. (See Mark 1:13.) Near the close of Jesus' ministry, after He had earnestly prayed to the Father in the Garden of Gethsemane that God's will be done, *"an angel appeared to Him from heaven, strengthening Him"* (Luke 22:43).

As it was with Jesus, so it is with us! Remember that God sent manna or *"angels' food"* to sustain the Israelites when they were wandering in the wilderness: *"Men ate angels' food; He sent them food to the full"* (Psalm 78:25). Whether the need is for spiritual or physical nourishment, or both, God always comes through for His children and sustains them in times of need.

PROTECTING AND DELIVERING GOD'S PEOPLE

God's angels also protect and deliver those who belong to Him. As we have already seen, the Bible assures us that angels guard the righteous: *"He shall give His angels charge over you, to keep you in all your ways. In their hands they shall bear you up"* (Psalm 91:11–12). *"The angel of the LORD encamps all around those who fear Him, and delivers them"* (Psalm 34:7).

Let's look first at some biblical examples of God's protection. Lot, who is called a *"righteous man"* in 2 Peter 2:8, and his family were protected by angels and kept from perishing with the people of Sodom and Gomorrah:

> *Now the two angels came to Sodom in the evening, and Lot was sitting in the gate of Sodom. When Lot saw them,...he said, "Here now, my lords, please turn in to your servant's house and spend the night, and wash your feet; then you may rise early and go on your way."... Then the men said to Lot, "Have you anyone else here? Son-in-law, your sons, your*

daughters, and whomever you have in the city; take them out
of this place! For we will destroy this place, because the outcry
against them has grown great before the face of the LORD,
and the LORD *has sent us to destroy it."... But to his sons-in-*
law he seemed to be joking. When the morning dawned, the
angels urged Lot to hurry, saying, "Arise, take your wife and
your two daughters who are here, lest you be consumed in the
punishment of the city." And while he lingered, the men took
hold of his hand, his wife's hand, and the hands of his two
daughters, the LORD *being merciful to him, and they brought*
him out and set him outside the city. So it came to pass, when
they had brought them outside, that he said, "Escape for your
life! Do not look behind you nor stay anywhere in the plain.
Escape to the mountains, lest you be destroyed."... And it came
to pass, when God destroyed the cities of the plain, that God
remembered Abraham, and sent Lot out of the midst of the
overthrow, when He overthrew the cities in which Lot had
dwelt.   (Genesis 19:1–2, 12–17, 29)

In Exodus 14:19–20, we read that the Angel of God protected
His people from the Egyptian army:

The Angel of God, who went before the camp of Israel, moved
and went behind them; and the pillar of cloud went from
before them and stood behind them. So it came between the
camp of the Egyptians and the camp of Israel. Thus it was a
cloud and darkness to the one, and it gave light by night to the
other, so that the one did not come near the other all that night.

Daniel was protected by an angel after being falsely accused
and thrown into a den of fierce lions with no way of escape. When
King Darius went to discover Daniel's fate, Daniel testified to him,
"My God sent His angel and shut the lions' mouths, so that they have
not hurt me, because I was found innocent before Him; and also, O
king, I have done no wrong before you" (Daniel 6:22).

Jesus indicated that some angels are assigned to watch over little children. He said, *"Take heed that you do not despise one of these little ones, for I say to you that in heaven their angels always see the face of My Father who is in heaven"* (Matthew 18:10).

Second, the Bible tells us that angels not only give protection, but also provide deliverance for God's people. In Matthew 26:53, Jesus said He could have asked the Father to send twelve legions of angels to deliver Him from the Romans when they came to arrest and crucify Him. However, He allowed them to crucify Him so that He could provide atonement for the sins of the world—for your sins and mine. (See verse 54.)

In Acts 5, when some of the apostles were jailed, an angel opened the prison doors without the guards even realizing it and freed the apostles so they could continue preaching the gospel to the people:

> *Then the high priest rose up, and all those who were with him (which is the sect of the Sadducees), and they...laid their hands on the apostles and put them in the common prison. But at night an angel of the Lord opened the prison doors and brought them out, and said, "Go, stand in the temple and speak to the people all the words of this life."...But when the officers came and did not find them in the prison, they returned and reported, saying, "Indeed we found the prison shut securely, and the guards standing outside before the doors; but when we opened them, we found no one inside!"*
> (Acts 5:17–20, 22–23)

In Acts 12, an angel intervened in Peter's imprisonment and led him in another clandestine jailbreak so that the guards Peter had been chained to didn't even wake up!

> *That night Peter was sleeping, bound with two chains between two soldiers; and the guards before the door were keeping the*

prison. Now behold, an angel of the Lord stood by him, and a light shone in the prison; and he struck Peter on the side and raised him up, saying, "Arise quickly!" And his chains fell off his hands. Then the angel said to him, "Gird yourself and tie on your sandals"; and so he did. And he said to him, "Put on your garment and follow me." So he went out and followed him, and did not know that what was done by the angel was real, but thought he was seeing a vision. When they were past the first and the second guard posts, they came to the iron gate that leads to the city, which opened to them of its own accord; and they went out and went down one street, and immediately the angel departed from him. And when Peter had come to himself, he said, "Now I know for certain that the Lord has sent His angel, and has delivered me from the hand of Herod."   (Acts 12:6–11)

Through the visions and revelations God has given me, I have come to understand the subtle difference in the roles of what I call "defensive angels" and "offensive angels." Defensive angels protect us from harm and danger and all kinds of evil devices of Satan. They serve as guardian angels. They protect us even when we don't know they are there. Offensive angels wage active war against strongholds, principalities, demons, forces of darkness, and everything else that opposes the work of God. We'll look at the role of offensive angels in more detail shortly.

PROMOTING THE GOSPEL

God's angels are also active in promoting the gospel. They are very interested in the salvation of the lost. In Luke 15, after Jesus told the parable of the lost sheep, He said, *"I say to you that likewise there will be more joy in heaven over one sinner who repents than over ninety-nine just persons who need no repentance"* (v. 7). Jesus repeated this idea after telling the parable of the lost coin: *"Likewise, I say* to you, there is joy in the presence of the angels of God over one sinner who repents" (v. 10).

During the great tribulation that will come upon all the earth, a mighty angel will proclaim the blessed gospel to the nations of the world. John wrote,

> Then I saw another angel flying in the midst of heaven, having the everlasting gospel to preach to those who dwell on the earth; to every nation, tribe, tongue, and people; saying with a loud voice, "Fear God and give glory to Him, for the hour of His judgment has come; and worship Him who made heaven and earth, the sea and springs of water."   (Revelation 14:6–7)

We saw earlier that an angel of God appeared to Cornelius and instructed him how to find Peter, who would tell him the truth about salvation through Jesus. (See Acts 10.) In his conversation with Cornelius, Peter referred to the Scriptures, saying, "To [Christ] all the prophets witness that, through His name, whoever believes in Him will receive remission of sins" (v. 43).

This is an important passage of Scripture that again emphasizes for us a key truth about angels. We know from the Bible that a true angel will always promote a message found in God's holy Word. I can't stress this point enough because, again, Satan will try to deceive you and draw you away from the truth of salvation through Christ. Cornelius had a true angelic visitation, and it led to salvation in Jesus for him and all his household.

Let us thank God for the salvation He has provided for us through the Lord Jesus Christ, and for the ministry of His angels in helping to bring the message of the gospel to those who are lost.

CARRYING GOD'S PEOPLE TO HEAVEN

Another role of angels is that they are spiritual "pallbearers" at the death of God's saints. Believers do not have to transition from life to afterlife alone. Even in our deaths, angels are ministering to us by the will of God. When our pilgrimage on this earth is over, the angels will carry our spirits away to glory, just as they did for Lazarus. Jesus said,

> *There was a certain rich man who was clothed in purple and fine linen and fared sumptuously every day. But there was a certain beggar named Lazarus, full of sores, who was laid at his gate, desiring to be fed with the crumbs which fell from the rich man's table. Moreover the dogs came and licked his sores. So it was that the beggar died, and was carried by the angels to Abraham's bosom.* (Luke 16:19–22)

In a vision of heaven that God gave me, I saw what happens to believers when they reach heaven's gates. If you are a believer, when you die, your soul will leave your body, and angels will convey you to heaven. A book will be opened, and angels will welcome you. Then you will be dressed and prepared by the angels to stand before God.

By the time you are presented to Him, you will be like a perfect young person—even if you were one hundred years old when you died. Who would not want to serve the God who can do this? He will give you back your youth, and He will give you life eternal so that you will never again die.

I also saw that when babies and young children die, their souls are taken to heaven. There they become grown-up, mature, and complete—perfect! God showed me that when babies are killed through abortion, He breathes eternal life into the little ones so that they become complete in Him. I saw angels transporting the souls of aborted babies to heaven, and I saw God making them perfect on heaven's altar. How awesome is our God!

CONTINUALLY ACTIVE

God's angels continually carry out His will, including ministering on behalf of His people. In the revelations God has given me, the angels are always working, but they never seem to toil or sweat. As they work, they show a keen interest in what humans are doing for God and His cause. Let us commit ourselves to loving and serving the Lord with the same zeal and devotion that the angels have. Let us also appreciate the help God sends through His angels to enable us to serve Him as He carries out His purposes in this world.

DEFENDERS OF GOD'S GLORY AND HONOR

We have seen that celestial beings worship God and assist His people. A third major role of angels is to help fight God's battles and execute His judgments in the world. I believe that the angels involved in these activities are the "offensive angels" that I mentioned earlier in this chapter. Angels can be fierce warriors who oppose demons and fight individual battles with them, bring divine judgment on people who defy the Lord, and fight physical battles for God's people. There are many biblical examples of angels fighting on God's behalf. For example, we just read how angels were active in the judgment and destruction of the cities of Sodom and Gomorrah. (See Genesis 19.)

Angels were also involved in both the protection and defense of the Israelites when they left Egypt. The psalmist wrote of the Exodus, "[God] *cast on* [the Egyptians] *the fierceness of His anger, wrath, indignation, and trouble, by sending angels of destruction among them*" (Psalm 78:49). In Exodus 33, God said His Angel would defeat Israel's enemies as they conquered the promised land:

> *The* LORD *said to Moses, "...I will send My Angel before you, and I will drive out the Canaanite and the Amorite and the Hittite and the Perizzite and the Hivite and the Jebusite."*
>
> (vv. 1–2)

Joshua encountered the help of the commander of God's heavenly army when the Israelites were going up to fight against Jericho:

> *And it came to pass, when Joshua was by Jericho, that he lifted his eyes and looked, and behold, a Man stood opposite him with His sword drawn in His hand. And Joshua went to Him and said to Him, "Are You for us or for our adversaries?" So He said, "No, but as Commander of the army of the LORD I have now come."*   (Joshua 5:13–14)

A single angel helping to defend God's people in Jerusalem killed 185,000 soldiers of the mighty Assyrian empire in one night. (See 2 Kings 19:8–35.) The archangel Michael and other angels fought the devil and his demonic spirits. (See Daniel 10:12–13, 20–21; Jude 1:9.)

Angels were sometimes involved in the punishment of God's people when they disobeyed Him. In 2 Samuel 24, God sent an angel to execute a plague on Israel because David had sinned by trusting in the number of his fighting men instead of the Lord. At least seventy thousand people died before the Lord commanded the angel, *"It is enough; now restrain your hand"* (v. 16). David actually saw this destroying angel. First Chronicles 21 tells us what a terrifying sight that was:

> *Then David lifted his eyes and saw the angel of the LORD standing between earth and heaven, having in his hand a drawn sword stretched out over Jerusalem. So David and the elders, clothed in sackcloth, fell on their faces.*   (v. 16)

The plague ended when David took responsibility for his sin, built an altar to the Lord, and sacrificed offerings to God, as God commanded him. (See 2 Samuel 24:17–25.)

God's holy angels are zealous for His glory, and they work on His behalf to defeat disobedience and evil in the world. This is a prelude to their role in helping to defeat evil in the end times.

PARTICIPANTS IN END-TIME EVENTS

Fourth, at the end of the age, angels will help bring this world to a culmination as the old heavens and earth pass away and the new heavens and earth come into being.

Angels will, first of all, accompany Jesus when He returns to the earth.

For the Lord Himself will descend from heaven with a shout, with the voice of an archangel, and with the trumpet of God.
(1 Thessalonians 4:16)

For the Son of Man will come in the glory of His Father with His angels, and then He will reward each according to his works. (Matthew 16:27)

Second, angels will harvest the disobedient for the Day of Judgment. Jesus explained the parable of the tares (Matthew 13:24–30) with this sobering application:

He who sows the good seed is the Son of Man. The field is the world, the good seeds are the sons of the kingdom, but the tares are the sons of the wicked one. The enemy who sowed them is the devil, the harvest is the end of the age, and the reapers are the angels. Therefore as the tares are gathered and burned in the fire, so it will be at the end of this age. The Son of Man will send out His angels, and they will gather out of His kingdom all things that offend, and those who practice lawlessness, and will cast them into the furnace of fire. There will be wailing and gnashing of teeth. Then the righteous will shine forth as the sun in the kingdom of their Father. He who has ears to hear, let him hear! (Matthew 13:37–43)

Third, angels will gather together all the righteous for eternal life:

> *He will send His angels with a great sound of a trumpet, and*
> *they will gather together His elect from the four winds, from*
> *one end of heaven to the other.*   (Matthew 24:31)

> *They will see the Son of Man coming in the clouds with great*
> *power and glory. And then He will send His angels, and*
> *gather together His elect from the four winds, from the far-*
> *thest part of earth to the farthest part of heaven.*
>   (Mark 13:26–27)

What a glorious day it will be when Jesus returns, and we are gathered by His angels to live with Him forever! Angels are with us while we live on this earth, they will be with us when we die, and they will be with us at the end of the age. Blessed be God, He truly sends His angels as *"ministering spirits sent to serve those who will inherit salvation"* (Hebrews 1:14 NIV)!

GOD'S REVELATIONS

In parts 1 and 2, we have looked at the nature and role of angels as they are revealed in the Word of God. In part 3, I want to share with you some experiences I have had in seeing the angels of God in action in my own life. God's angels continue to minister to His people today. Again, their activity is not for Bible times alone. It is for you and for me right now as we love the Lord and do His will.

PART III:
REVELATIONS OF
ANGELS TODAY

INTRODUCTION TO PART III

God began to show me the work of angels among His people many years ago when He first called me into ministry. I was in my car ready to go to the veteran's hospital to pray for my brother-in-law. He had had a massive heart attack, and our church was praying for him. The "wind of God" blew, and the pages of my Bible opened up to Isaiah 6:8: "*Whom shall I send, and who will go for Us?*"

I knew God was speaking to me, and I began to weep. In my heart, I understood that God wanted to use me (this was a long time before I saw the revelations of hell and heaven), and I said, "God, I'll go; send me."

At the veteran's hospital, I prayed for my brother-in-law, and I also ended up praying for many of the patients there. God did a creative miracle and gave my brother-in-law a new artery; he lived twenty more years. Because of this miracle, several were saved that day. Truly, the wind of God had directed me.

One day, I began to seek God about the wind, asking, "What is this wind, Father? May I please see it?" God opened my eyes, and I saw what looked like a vapor mixed with glory—a whitish, living wind, a living light. Words were flowing in the wind.

In the old days, Native Americans communicated with each other using smoke signals. The wind of God reminded me of this, as it seemed like a smoke or mist. I could see angels in the wind, and they were carrying scrolls containing the messages God had given them. Some contained orders that God had commanded the angels to carry out. It was awesome to see.

I began to see this manifestation in church services. I'd feel the wind blow. Sometimes, something like a misty rain would come down, and I would know the miraculous was about to happen. I would see angels coming into the sanctuary. Some would come in with scrolls, some with bows, and others with swords. They would stand all around the church and on the platform. As the minister would begin to speak, the angels would stand guard by him. Then I would see things begin to happen in the Spirit. It was almost as if I was looking at a television show or a movie.

Oh, how I love to see the wind of God in action! It is so exciting to see God working in these ways. Truly, His wind is moving all over the land. I believe that God's angels of deliverance are "invading" our cities, our churches, and our homes today with His power.

In the next few chapters, I will share with you some of the things I've seen in the spiritual realm concerning God's angels, along with a few stories of others who have experienced angels in action in recent years. I believe God gave me these revelations to strengthen and comfort His people, to let them know that He is with them. Invariably, people are encouraged when I share these experiences. I know that you, too, will be blessed when you read them. Through His angels, God guards and protects us. Even though we live in an age of uncertainty and upheaval, God is showing us that His Word holds true: "*For He Himself has said, 'I will never leave you nor forsake you.' So we may boldly say, 'The* LORD *is my helper; I will not fear. What can man do to me?'*" (Hebrews 13:5–6).

I also believe that, through these visions and revelations, God is revealing some important truths for the church, such as the role of God's Word in our lives; the purifying, healing, and judging fire of God; the necessity of intercessory prayer; and the power of God to deliver His people. We must understand these important truths as we draw nearer to end-times events and the second coming of our Lord and Savior Jesus Christ. To Him be all the glory and praise!

6

ANGELS AND PROTECTION

Angels are our spiritual guardians. None of us will ever know, this side of eternity, what miracles God has performed through the angels whom He has sent to protect and care for us. This is the promise God gives us:

> Because you have made the LORD, who is my refuge, even the Most High, your dwelling place, no evil shall befall you, nor shall any plague come near your dwelling; for He shall give His angels charge over you, to keep you in all your ways. In their hands they shall bear you up, lest you dash your foot against a stone. You shall tread upon the lion and the cobra, the young lion and the serpent you shall trample underfoot. "Because he has set his love upon Me, therefore I will deliver him; I will set him on high, because he has known My name. He shall call upon Me, and I will answer him; I will be with him in trouble; I will deliver him and honor him. With long life I will satisfy him, and show him My salvation."
>
> (Psalm 91:9–16)

We are kept by God's power; we are safe and secure in the hands of our mighty Savior! The angels cover us, watch over us, and guard us from countless evils. Angels also protect our children; mine have been protected many times through the power of almighty God. What amazing things angels do to protect God's people! They keep us from more foes than we could ever imagine. As Psalm 91 encourages us, let us be sure to set our love upon God and know His name, for He honors those who honor Him.

PROTECTION FROM INJURY

I have seen God's angels protect my family from injury. One time, my son traveled to work on his motorcycle. At about two o'clock that afternoon, I wasn't even thinking of him as I prayed in my house. Suddenly, the Spirit prompted me to intercede in a special way, and I began to really pray in earnest in the Holy Spirit. I didn't understand all of what I was praying, only a part of it.

At about five o'clock, my son pulled up in the yard on his motorcycle and said, "Mom, have you been praying for me?"

I said, "I have been praying for somebody. I didn't know specifically that it was for you; God just prompted me to intercede."

"Well, Mom, I just want you to know this. About an hour and a half ago, I was driving down Tropical Trail at fifty to sixty miles per hour on my motorcycle. As I came around a corner, a large semi truck turned across the street in front of me. Mother, I'm telling you that God was with me. As the semi turned, I realized I had to do something or I would crash into it. So I turned my bike on its side and *went underneath the semi!* I then rode off into a field unharmed!"

"Oh!" I gasped.

He said, "The only thing that happened was that my mirror came off my bike, and I hurt my leg a little bit. But it's okay."

I began to cry. I hugged him and thanked God for him. I have beautiful sons, and I have found that, many times, our children's safety depends on us. If we will press into God in prayer, He is right there for us. We need to pray for our children that God will manifest Himself to them. I rejoice in the protection my family has received from His angels in action. I am thankful that the angels shielded my son that day so many years ago. To God be the glory, and praises be to His righteous and holy name.

PROTECTION FROM PERSECUTION

Angels often come to us in unassuming ways and in unexpected works. At times, we don't even realize that a heavenly visitor is protecting us. Dr. Billy Graham, in his book *Angels*, relates a story first told by his wife's father, Dr. L. Nelson Bell, a missionary doctor, of a Chinese bookstore operator and his encounter with an angel:

> The incident occurred in 1942, after the Japanese had won control of certain areas of China. One morning around nine o'clock, a Japanese truck stopped outside the bookroom. It was carrying five marines and was half-filled with books. The Christian Chinese shop assistant, who was alone at the time, realized with dismay that they had come to seize the stock. By nature timid, he felt this was more than he could endure.
>
> Jumping from the truck, the marines made for the shop door; but before they could enter, a neatly dressed Chinese gentleman entered the shop ahead of them. Though the shop assistant knew practically all the Chinese customers who traded there, this man was a complete stranger. For some unknown reason the soldiers seemed unable to follow him, and loitered about, looking in at the four large windows, but not entering. For two hours they stood around, until after eleven, but never set foot inside the door. The stranger asked what the men wanted, and the Chinese shop assistant explained that the Japanese

were seizing stocks from many of the book shops in the city, and now this store's turn had come. The two prayed together, the stranger encouraging him, and so the two hours passed. At last the soldiers climbed into their truck and drove away. The stranger also left, without making a single purchase or even inquiring about any items in the shop.

Later that day the shop owner, Mr. Christopher Willis (whose Chinese name was Lee), returned. The shop assistant said to him, "Mr. Lee, do you believe in angels?"

"I do," said Mr. Willis.

"So do I, Mr. Lee." Could the stranger have been one of God's protecting angels? Dr. Bell always thought so.

PROTECTION IN MINISTRY

Many times, God protects His people as they minister the gospel. In an earlier chapter, we read how the apostles were delivered from prison so they could continue preaching God's Word.

I know the angels protect me as I am ministering. One time, a little boy came up to me after a service and said, "Mary, I saw an angel standing by you—a huge angel. He was standing behind you, on the back of the platform. He was so big that he was taller than the ceiling."

I looked at the ceiling, and it had to be thirty feet high.

"Although he was tall, I could see his head," the little boy continued, "which looked as if it was going through the ceiling. His arms were crossed, and he had a very determined look on his face. The angel had a sword of fire by his side, and if the devil or any of the spirits tried to come near you, he would pull out the sword and would *cremate* them."

Cremate is the word the little boy used to describe what he saw. It reminds me of the Scripture, *"You shall trample the wicked, for they shall be ashes under the soles of your feet"* (Malachi 4:3).

PROTECTION FROM OUR ENEMIES

Sometimes, God sends His angels to protect us when we feel most vulnerable. Corrie ten Boom, a spiritual hero of the twentieth century, spent many years after World War II traveling around the world telling about her sufferings and witness for Christ in a Nazi concentration camp. God often intervened in difficult situations by sending angels in answer to her prayers. One of those times was when she was being processed into the camp at Ravensbruck, as she described in her book *Tramp for the Lord:*

> It was the middle of the night when Betsie and I reached the processing barracks. And there, under the harsh ceiling lights, we saw a dismaying sight. As each woman reached the head of the line she had to strip off every scrap of clothes, throw them all onto a pile guarded by soldiers, and walk naked past the scrutiny of a dozen guards into the shower room. Coming out of the shower room she wore only a thin regulation prison dress and a pair of shoes.
>
> Our Bible! How could we take it past so many watchful eyes?
>
> "Oh, Betsie!" I began—and then stopped at the sight of her pain-whitened face. As a guard strode by, I begged him in German to show us the toilets. He jerked his head in the direction of the shower room. "Use the drain holes!" he snapped.
>
> Timidly Betsie and I stepped out of line and walked forward to the huge room with its row on row of overhead

spigots. It was empty, waiting for the next batch of fifty naked and shivering women.

A few minutes later we would return here stripped of everything we possessed. And then we saw them, stacked in a corner, a pile of old wooden benches crawling with cockroaches, but to us the furniture of heaven itself.

In an instant I had slipped the little bag over my head and, along with my woolen underwear, had stuffed it behind the benches....

Of course when I put on the flimsy prison dress, the Bible bulged beneath it. But that was His business, not mine. At the exit, guards were feeling every prisoner, front, back, and sides. I prayed, "Oh, Lord, send your angels to surround us." But then I remembered that angels are spirits and you can see through them. What I needed was an angel to shield me so the guards could not see me. "Lord," I prayed again, "make your angels untransparent." How unorthodox you can pray when you are in great need! But God did not mind. He did it.

The woman ahead of me was searched. Behind me, Betsie was searched. They did not touch or even look at me. It was as though I was blocked out of their sight.

A PROTECTIVE COVERING OF BLOOD

There is something we must realize about calling on God for protection: Our salvation in Christ includes the protective covering of His precious blood. I have learned that when we are praying for people, and God impresses upon us to cover people with the blood, we should say, "I cover you with the blood of Jesus, the covenant of God!" This means that Jesus Christ is the Son of God who was sent from heaven. He knew His purpose and His destiny. He was sent to give His life on a cruel cross for you and me, so that we could have eternal life. He died so that our sins could be washed away. God has shown me the importance of the cross and the blood covenant with its accompanying covering.

When we pray or command a covering of His blood, we are affirming that we believe Jesus provided a covering for us and our families through the atonement. The angels go to us immediately and seal and protect us. Through the blood covenant, we build a hedge of protection around our families and ourselves!

Another thing was revealed to me. When we dedicate someone or something to the Father, the Son, and the Holy Spirit—when we really mean this and anoint the person or thing with oil—we are saying, "This is God's territory." In the Spirit, I've seen that angels fly down from heaven and erect crosses when we do this. When spiritual enemies try to come, they have to back up when they confront the crosses because that territory has been dedicated to God.

LOOK WITH EYES OF FAITH

Rejoice, saints! God sends His angels to protect you when the devil would try to do you harm. *"He has delivered us from the power of darkness and conveyed us into the kingdom of the Son of His love"* (Colossians 1:13). Look with eyes of faith and see the spiritual bodyguards God has placed around you. Believe in God and call on His name!

7

ANGELS AND GOD'S WORD

When a believer is true to the Word and to the Lord's witness, God sends His angels, in answer to prayer, to help and rescue him. Remember that Psalm 91:14–15 says, *"Because he has set his love upon Me, therefore I will deliver him; I will set him on high, because he has known My name. He shall call upon Me, and I will answer him."*

The following visions and revelations illustrate how angels affirm God's Word and how God helps us when we believe and obey His commands. In a previous chapter, we saw how the angels took part in the giving of the Ten Commandments and the sacred Law on Mt. Sinai. The Bible says that Israel *"received the law by the direction of angels"* (Acts 7:53) and that *"the law...was appointed through angels"* (Galatians 3:19). In the Scriptures, the angels have a special role in honoring God's Word and conveying it to His people. Angels are involved in helping us to understand the Scriptures, as well.

GOD'S WORD IS TRUE

On one occasion, I saw a vision of a large, white table way off in the distance. It was about six feet by twelve feet in dimension, and it was suspended in the air. I could see people standing all around the table, looking at it. The table itself was higher than the people were tall, so that some of those looking at it were standing on their tiptoes. Others were sitting in high chairs, gazing at the table; but they were all asking questions of one another.

As I drew closer to them, I could see angels standing behind them. Drawing closer still, I could suddenly see the vision clearly. I could see that the big table was an open Bible. The huge Bible represented the Word of the living God. The Lord explained to me that the various people looking at it had different views of what the Bible meant. One person would say one thing, and someone else would say another.

They were all curious about the Bible, and I was glad to see that. Many questions arose among them about certain things in the Word, and they were looking for answers. The angels standing behind the people seemed to be guiding them in their search for the truth. But the vision represented the fact that what God said, He means. We cannot change or alter His Word.

PULPITS OF FIRE

Often, in a church service, I will see angels writing in large books. Sometimes the angels are standing by individuals and sometimes they are not. At times, they are standing beside the minister who is prophesying, and they're recording what he says. I will see an image of a Bible superimposed on the minister's chest. I believe this means that the Word of God, the open Bible, is in his heart.

In the places where I have preached during the past few years, I have seen, in the spiritual realm, pulpits that had God's fire upon them and pulpits that looked dirty and unclean. I have observed that behind the pulpits that were full of fire were holy men and women of God who revered and honored Him and who wanted things *"done decently and in order"* (1 Corinthians 14:40). These men and women had a holy fear of doing anything against God. They were afraid to harm or hurt Him or His cause deliberately in any way. These men and women truly exhibited the love of Christ. They were so wonderful to the servants of God who came in to minister with them. They would take good care of them and encourage them.

It also seemed that, in every place where I saw God's fire on the pulpit, I would see angels touching the pulpit at various times and worshipping God. Often, I would see them holding one hand to heaven (sometimes both of them) as they magnified the Lord.

I kept returning to churches like this, and one day, during a service, the glory of God rolled in with a mighty revelation. I saw angels come into the church with a large cross that looked about fifteen feet high. They went to the pulpit, which appeared to be on fire. The angels seemed to dig around in the floor, and then they anchored the cross in front of the pulpit. The cross was solid, but fire shot out of both ends and the top of it. I saw this revelation several times, and each time, there would be a great deliverance. Many people would come to the altar, get saved, and be delivered in a marvelous way. It was an awesome sight.

I wondered about what I had seen, so I began to ask the Lord, "God, what is all of this? What does this mean in the holy Word of God?" He said to me,

> These pulpits that you see with the fire upon them represent pulpits where My true Word is being preached. These holy, anointed ministers are purifying the flock with the Word of God and the cross that you see. Therefore, I have established the cross there, and the Spirit is with them for the purposes of deliverance and for the Word of God to be fulfilled. This is a sign that things will happen that they have been asking Me to do, and it means they are

preaching the pure, holy Word of God through the eternal and mighty power of the cross.

All over the land, I would see the same revelation. Again, as I observed the angels in action, it was almost like watching a movie screen. In many places, I would see angels come in like a cleanup crew and begin to sweep evil powers out of the churches. They would break the bonds of people and liberate them. At one service, some people took pictures, and when they were developed, you could see fire around the people we were praying for. It was a brilliant red in color, and I was excited because it showed the revelation knowledge of the blood of Jesus Christ. It was awesome for me to see these angels working in the spirit realm for God. While it excited me to see these things happen, they did not occur in all the churches or all the meetings.

THE ALTAR OF THE HEART

One time, I was on a ministry trip with a friend who is a preacher and has the gift of prophecy. We stopped for the night at a motel in a small town. She quickly fell asleep, and I began to seek God. The glory of the Lord came in the room like a fire, and I sat up in bed. Suddenly, I saw an old-time altar, a stone altar, such as people built in Bible days. It was high and obviously designed for offering sacrifices.

The altar was suspended about two feet in the air, and it was on fire. Flames were visible all around the approximately four-foot-wide structure, but it wasn't being burned up. I got out of bed, and as I looked at the altar, I saw a vision of the presence of God. Books were open in front of Him as He spoke to me:

> My child, I've called you and chosen you to have dreams, visions, and revelations in order to show you mysteries. I have shown you heaven. I have shown you what happens to people when they go to hell. All over the land, I have

shown you these things; yet all over the land, many places are not preaching the truth. They do not tell the truth to the people. They have polluted altars. I have appointed you to go through the land and rebuild the altars. "Stand in the ways and ask for the old paths, where the good way is, and walk in it." [See Jeremiah 6:16.] You are to rebuild the old ways and reopen the old paths. You are to rebuild the altars of God.

As God spoke to me, the appearance of His presence kept flaming up, and I thought, *The altars of God can never be burned up. They can never be destroyed. The wicked altars will fall. They are tempered with inferior mortar and bad bricks, and they are going to crumble.*

God began dealing with me about the altars of the heart. He said that when people kneel in church and seek God for themselves, each person is all alone with God and is saying, "God, here I am at the altar; this is me, Lord. I have these problems. I am a sinner. I've done this; I've done that." Then God said to me,

As they pour out their hearts to Me at the altar, they are making themselves an altar to Me. This is the altar of the heart. I want to clean out the altars in the hearts—the idolatry, the witchcraft, the sorcery, whatever evil they are doing. I want it out of them. I want those who seek Me to tell Me the truth because truth and righteousness can meet together. I want them to tell Me the truth so I can set them free through My Son, Jesus Christ.

As they begin to confess these things to Me and make a new commitment to Me, I will wash away the debris by My fire, by My Spirit, by My Word. They will feel light and happy because deliverance will have come in the name of My Son, Jesus Christ. When they arise from that physical altar, they will have built a new altar to Me.

When you go over the world and talk about hell, the judgment of God, the fierceness of God, and what happens to people when they go to hell, this helps them to understand that they must be sincere with Me and with their souls. This helps them to understand who I am and what I mean. I'm a holy and righteous God, and they shall have no other gods before Me.

Child, many people are never taught these truths. They have ears to hear but do not hear, and eyes to see but do not see. But to you revelations, mysteries, knowledge, and truth shall be revealed. The Scriptures will back up the revelations I will give you, and these Scriptures shall be very important to the world. The Word of God is in action, and this book on angels in action shall bless many to give them strength and encouragement.

In the Bible, God wanted people to repent and tear down the unclean altars in their lives. I began to understand that this is exactly what the visions are all about. God is calling His people to tell the truth and tear down the altars of idolatry.

This is God's divine purpose for all ministries. All ministers, in particular, are called to do this—to obey God and His Word, to go forth and speak His judgments in right ways, and to be faithful in telling people to repent and get right with Him. May this book accomplish what God intends!

THE POWER OF THE WORD

Another phenomenon I saw in my travels really amazed me. I would see a true prophet of God speak, and he would be covered with a transparent flame of fire. I would see an image of the Bible opened up in his heart, with the Word written there. An angel would be by his right shoulder, and this angel would pour fire on the prophet's head. The fire would go down to the Word in his heart, and he would begin to prophesy. As the Word came out of his mouth, it would turn into a sword. (See Ephesians 6:17; Hebrews 4:12.) Inside the sword was the written Word of God.

When the prophet of God spoke, the Word would shoot out into the congregation, and the congregation would become alive and animated. The Lord showed me that when He speaks, He speaks things into existence, and things begin to happen.

For example, I saw a prophet prophesying, saying,

I am the Lord thy God who healeth thee; I, the Lord, am here to do great works with thee. I am here for thee, to set you free, to undo your burdens. I am here to rebuke thee, to love thee, to lift thee up.

Everything the prophet said would move out over the congregation and fall on the people. Truth and righteousness had met together, and things began to happen. Angels appeared all around and began ministering to the people, some of whom would fall down under the power of God.

On some of the people, I saw black spots. The angels took the power to these afflicted people. They would lay the fire on the black spots, and it would burn out the sicknesses. People were healed, and people were "slain in the Spirit." Through these experiences, I began to understand revelation knowledge of God's Word in 1 Corinthians about the gifts of the Spirit. (See chapter 12.)

It was wonderful to see what God did—and *is* doing. It is awesome when the joy bubbles up in us and the laughter begins to come as we see the acts of almighty God and those of His angels at work. The Word and the Spirit work together with the vessels God chooses to minister through.

In a service in Ohio, some people took pictures of me while I was preaching about the living Word of God. I reminded the people that we must believe God's Word, repent of our sins, and turn back to God—that we must believe the blood of Jesus will cleanse us if we've sinned.

When one of the photos was developed, you could see the outline of a large open book in the picture. It was huge—it looked as if it were about ten feet high. The book was pure white, and it was lifted up over the heads of the people in the congregation. I knew that it represented the living Word of God.

I also have a photo of a little girl from Big Piney, Wyoming, who was about twelve years old and who wanted the baptism in the Holy Spirit. We actually captured on film a white cloud rolling in over this little child, coming near her as she was baptized in the Holy Spirit.

When the cloud came over her, she was lying on the floor, praying. Her little friend was sitting beside her and praying with her. She seemed to go to sleep in the Lord for quite a while. When she got up, she came to me and said, "Mrs. Baxter, can I preach?"

I saw the glory of the Lord upon her, and I asked, "What is it, honey?"

She said, "Well, when I was down there, Jesus came and talked to me. He took me and showed me hell. He showed me how awful hell was, and how we have to believe. We've got to believe it because it's real. It's a true story."

She began to weep, and all the other children began to cry with her. The Holy Spirit fell on them, and they began to groan and travail in the Spirit, praying for people to be saved and to be born again. I could see angels above and around the children.

As we witnessed the works of God, I knew that we were to give God all the glory and praise for them, and to understand that His Word is still marching on, no matter what!

THE WORD AND SALVATION

One time, I had been praying to the Lord concerning my family members who were unsaved. Perhaps you, too, have family members who are not ready to meet the Lord, and you are concerned about their souls. While I was seeking God that day, He gave me a special revelation.

I could see sacred books. The angels would open up a book and turn a page, and I could see the written Word of God on it. Flames came out of the book, along with what looked like a mist. It seemed as if glory and power were intermingling with white and red flickers of fire. I knew this meant that I was seeing the living Word of God.

I believe the purpose of this revelation was to convey that what God has said in His Word, He *will* accomplish. He has promised us, *"Great shall be the peace of your children"* (Isaiah 54:13). He has said that He will *"love you and bless you and multiply you; He will also bless the fruit of your womb"* (Deuteronomy 7:13). That is exactly what my blessed Lord does! Keep believing that God will save your loved ones, and give Him the glory for it.

THE WORD'S POWER OVER SATAN

I have seen visions in which demon powers and evil spirits were fighting with angels. The angels would always win because they would quote the Word of God. The Word is *"the sword of the Spirit"* (Ephesians 6:17) and defeats the enemy. Remember that Jesus quoted the truth of the Scripture to Satan during His wilderness temptation. The devil had no more ammunition and had to leave Him.

The following is an experience I had in which God taught me the power of the Word over Satan. One time, I went to Miami with a few others to a Christian convention. There was great oppression in the area; evil powers could be felt in certain parts of the city, and

I was grieved. We could feel the oppression mostly when we were eating dinner or at nighttime. I wondered, *God, why do we feel such evil when the power of God is so great here in the convention?*

There was a woman at the convention who had been scheduled to share a room with me, but for some reason did not. One evening, she came up to me and said, "I'm a witch. I came to your Christian convention acting like a Christian so I could find out what all you Christians are doing. I want to take it back into the coven so we can work witchcraft against this atmosphere and stop what you are doing."

I said, "Oh, really." Then I began to quote God's Word to her. I said, "Listen, lady, there's nothing you can do to harm me or to harm this meeting. 'God is for us, who can be against us?' (Romans 8:31)."

She became angry at me and stormed away. I thanked God that she was prevented from staying in my room. I was in a room alone so I could have a quiet place and the time to better understand the oppression and what we were feeling.

On the way back home, we had to travel by car, and I got into the back seat. I thought I would rest for a while, so I began to pray to God about this situation. As I looked up into heaven, first the glory came, and then I saw a mighty vision of the Lord. He was in the middle of a brilliant white light, with glory and power all around Him. The white light symbolized purity; God is so pure and holy.

I saw Him step out of the heavens and into the sky, and I saw His right hand go down. From each of His fingertips I saw power like I had never seen before; this power turned into swirls of energy and fire. Then he put down His left hand. Again, from His fingers and even His thumb, fire shot out. It also came from the palm of His hand and went through the universe like a river of fire.

He said to me, "I have destroyed their works through this fire and My Word. At times, I will step out and fight for My children Myself." I began to shout aloud and praise the Lord. He said to me,

Child, when you pray, curse the works of darkness. There will be witchery, sorcery, and other evil things planted against people and their works. I want you to pray for their souls to be saved. Ask Me to have mercy on them and save their souls. You never curse the people, just the works of darkness and their activities. Stand on My Word, and My power and might will fulfill it. Believe Me, and I will send forth this fire, and I will cause the wicked to be ashes under your feet. [See Malachi 4:3.]

I praised Him more! I thanked Him and rejoiced. I could feel a lifting and the presence of God that was so joyful. Then I saw an army of angels coming down from heaven with flags and banners and crosses. They were putting up crosses and claiming the land back for the Lord. I thought, *Wow, Lord, how beautiful to behold!*

THE WORD IS ALWAYS ACCOMPLISHING SOMETHING

On another occasion, I had a vision in which I saw the angels holding up the Word of God—a large, complete, open Bible—in the universe. Flames were coming out of it. It was so large and beautiful! "The Word of God" was written in big letters inside the flames on the pages. One of the pages turned into a picture, and what looked like power radiated from it. Then the pages turned into a large horn (it looked like a trumpet) that stretched out a long way. I could see power, glory, and honor coming from the end of the horn. I knew this meant that it was the living Word of God. I thought, *Oh, God, You are so wonderful! You are the Word.*

I believe that, through this vision, God was telling me to *"blow the trumpet in Zion"* (Joel 2:15), to *"cry aloud, spare not; lift up your voice like a trumpet; tell My people their transgression, and the house of Jacob their sins"* (Isaiah 58:1), so that they will return to Him.

I have seen this large book with its pages open many times in the Spirit. Out of this book would come the Word of God in action. The Word was always accomplishing something for the Lord. Truly, the Word of our God is powerful:

> *For I am the LORD. I speak, and the word which I speak will come to pass.*   (Ezekiel 12:25)

> *For the word of God is living and powerful, and sharper than any two-edged sword, piercing even to the division of soul and spirit, and of joints and marrow, and is a discerner of the thoughts and intents of the heart.*   (Hebrews 4:12)

We often don't realize the power of God's Word. God wants to accomplish many things *"by the word of His power"* (Hebrews 1:3). We should reverence His Word, as His angels do, believing and obeying it, so that He will bring it to pass in our lives and the lives of those we minister to.

8

ANGELS AND GOD'S FIRE

Recently, I have been seeking God about His fire—the fire of the Holy Spirit. I have learned that it is both a fire of revival, purification, and healing for His people—and a fire of judgment for those who reject Him. John the Baptist said,

> I indeed baptize you with water unto repentance, but He who is coming after me is mightier than I, whose sandals I am not worthy to carry. He will baptize you with the Holy Spirit and fire. His winnowing fan is in His hand, and He will thoroughly clean out His threshing floor, and gather His wheat into the barn; but He will burn up the chaff with unquenchable fire. (Matthew 3:11–12)

A FIRE OF REVIVAL, PURIFICATION, AND HEALING

The prophet Joel prophesied of the baptism with the Holy Spirit:

> Then you shall know that I am in the midst of Israel: I am the LORD your God and there is no other. My people shall never be put to shame. And it shall come to pass afterward that I will pour out My Spirit on all flesh; your sons and your

daughters shall prophesy, your old men shall dream dreams, your young men shall see visions. And also on My menservants and on My maidservants I will pour out My Spirit in those days.... And it shall come to pass that whoever calls on the name of the LORD *shall be saved. For in Mount Zion and in Jerusalem there shall be deliverance, as the* LORD *has said, among the remnant whom the* LORD *calls.*

(Joel 2:27–29, 32)

This prophecy was fulfilled when Jesus' followers were baptized with the Holy Spirit at Pentecost and "tongues of fire" rested on each one of them:

When the Day of Pentecost had fully come, they were all with one accord in one place. And suddenly there came a sound from heaven, as of a rushing mighty wind, and it filled the whole house where they were sitting. Then there appeared to them divided tongues, as of fire, and one sat upon each of them. And they were all filled with the Holy Spirit and began to speak with other tongues, as the spirit gave them utterance.

(Acts 2:1–4)

In the revelations and visions I have seen, angels seem to be connected with the fire of the Spirit of God. Once I saw a great angel flying in the heavens. He had a scroll in one hand and a bowl of fire in the other. As I watched, he came down to where I was and said, "God wants to put fire upon His children to purge them and to purify them so they can be cleansed." I thought, *Glory to God, hallelujah!* My prayer is, "How I thank You for the fire, God, and the purging and the cleansing. Anoint us with the fire of the Holy Spirit, Father."

God is sending His fire to purge His children and to take the old leaven (sin and disobedience) out of those who will allow Him. First Corinthians 5:7–8 says,

Purge out the old leaven, that you may be a new lump, since you truly are unleavened. For indeed Christ, our Passover, was sacrificed for us. Therefore let us keep the feast, not with old leaven, nor with the leaven of malice and wickedness, but with the unleavened bread of sincerity and truth.

As I relate these stories of angels in action, God continues to open my eyes. I'm beginning to learn more fully what it means to experience the ministry of angels. I have seen angels being dispatched all over the earth with God's fire. They put it in people who were open to God.

One night, I was preaching at a women's convention, and I had about twenty minutes to finish my message before I had to leave for the airport. Suddenly, God gave me a vision of about seven women in the congregation, and they were all full of fire. As I watched, they turned into skeleton-like forms, and I could see hell beneath them. I said to the congregation, "Let us pray." Immediately, we stood to our feet to pray. As I began to seek God, I related the vision I had seen, and the women ran to the altar and got saved.

Remember, this happened just twenty minutes before I was to leave. Naturally, those leading the convention would have continued the meeting after I left and would have given an altar call. But God wanted that altar call done then, at that time!

Lately, I have been seeing much of the fire of God. I see it in church services—fire around people and on people. Heat from the power of almighty God is "burning out" diseases and sicknesses, such as cancer. I have witnessed angels with bowls of fire, and I have seen them pouring this fire on people. Often, I hear people say, "I feel hot. I feel heat," as they are ministered to by the Lord. Because of this, I have been seeking more understanding about the fire of the Holy Spirit.

A FIRE OF JUDGMENT

One thing I have learned is that God's fire is one of judgment as well as one of cleansing and healing. In chapter 5, we saw that the angels have a role in executing God's judgment in the world. In the Old Testament, God announced through the prophet Amos that He would send fire *"upon the wall of Gaza"* (Amos 1:7), *"upon the wall of Tyre"* (v. 10), and *"upon Teman"* to *"devour the palaces of Bozrah"* (v. 12). *"This is what the Sovereign* LORD *showed me,"* the prophet further declared. *"The Sovereign* LORD *was calling for judgment by fire"* (Amos 7:4 NIV). The same fire of purification that brings us joy, peace, and healing will punish the wicked and bring His judgment on them. This fire is from heaven and will fulfill its intended purpose. We all must wake up to this truth. God means what He says.

Once, when I was in prayer, God permitted me to see into the heavenlies. I saw what looked like a rope of fire—it was always aflame—and the angels used it as a measuring line. It reminds me of when the prophet Amos saw a plumb line in the hand of the Lord. (See Amos 7:7–8.) A plumb line has a weight at one end and is used to measure whether a wall is completely straight up and down. The plumb line was a symbolic way of showing that God was measuring the lives of the Israelites to see if they were spiritually upright.

Similarly, I believe that God's judgment is with us today. I really believe that God has, in effect, dropped a plumb line from heaven to separate the righteous from the wicked. We need to be devoted to God with all our hearts. God says, *"I will make justice the measuring line, and righteousness the* [plumb line]" (Isaiah 28:17).

Judgment has been going on for quite a while. God wants us to turn to Him before it is too late. How would your life measure up before God? Too many times, the devil brings a spirit of distraction to keep us from hearing the truth. Our lives can be measured as straight and sound only as we receive the Lord Jesus Christ and His righteousness through the atonement He provided for us when He died on the cross, and as we remain in His righteousness through faith and obedience to Him. We are not to take sin lightly.

Not long ago, I was awakened during the night, and I saw a mighty revelation of a huge angel. He had a large scroll in his hands, which he kept turning. Then he opened up the scroll, unrolling it from both ends. The angel looked at me and said, "Thus saith the Lord: The archives of time are opened in heaven." He repeated this three times and then flew away.

I began to seek God about what this meant. The Holy Spirit brought to my mind thoughts about the judgment that has been established for the earth. We are in a time like we have never had before. Yet with troubles and the judgments of God in the land, we are also seeing a mighty outpouring of His Spirit. Again, God does not want people to experience judgment, but to repent and turn to Him through Christ.

Let us allow Him to purge us with that fire and to cleanse us by His holy Word. Many times, in prayer, I have seen God's angels using this plumb line full of fire. I read a book by another person who had seen heaven, and the writer also saw this plumb line on fire. God is drawing the plumb line, saints. We need to get ready for the coming of the Lord.

A PERIOD OF GRACE

I have seen some ministers and preachers who have preached the gospel of Jesus Christ and done His will, but who have then fallen into adultery or some other sin. I have noticed that God will give them a space of time to repent, a period of grace. God deals with them, and the angels try to get them back on the right way.

Conviction grips the erring ones' hearts, but if they resist, they start to harden their hearts. In the beginning, they had the glory of the Lord around them. They had the fire of God in them and about them. This fire was like a hedge of protection for them, but as they fell into the errors of sin and lies, they allowed openings to be created in that protection. Their falling into sin also created openings in their anointing from God, and, pretty soon, they became corrupt, with the enemy attacking them every way he could. They became filled with lies and sin.

Yet God's grace still deals with them. He still draws them toward Himself. God's mercy is still calling; He desires them to repent and turn back to Him. Thankfully, many do repent and return to God and His true anointing.

I believe that the revelation God gave me of hell was for a purpose. I am convinced that God gave me the things I have seen and heard so that, as I go and tell them to others, scales will come off people's eyes, and the light of the gospel will come in. For if they continue in their sins, essentially rejecting Christ, and then die, they will go to hell.

Yet Jesus was manifested to deliver us from sin and save us from eternal punishment. He came to the earth to keep us from a burning hell. Saints, I'm telling you now, we're serving a mighty God who loves us and cares about us.

HOW WILL YOU RESPOND?

God's fire is for renewal and judgment. With it, He refreshes and revives His people and punishes the wicked. How will you respond to God's fire? Allow God to purify you and renew you in His love and truth as you *"serve the living and true God, and...wait for His Son from heaven, whom He raised from the dead, even Jesus who delivers us from the wrath to come"* (1 Thessalonians 1:9–10).

9

ANGELS AND DELIVERANCE

In times of danger and distress, the Lord has impressed upon me, *"Call upon Me in the day of trouble; I will deliver you, and you shall glorify Me"* (Psalm 50:15). Many times, I've called upon the Lord *"in the day of trouble."* I've prayed in the Holy Spirit for hours, and the Scriptures have become real and powerful to me. The Lord has said to me, "No matter what you see, no matter what you feel, you must believe in My Word. Believe in what I have promised you. My promises are true." Here are some promises of deliverance from God's Word that we can fill our hearts and minds with and use as the basis of our prayers:

> *Like birds flying about, so will the LORD of hosts defend Jerusalem. Defending, He will also deliver it; passing over, He will preserve it.* (Isaiah 31:5)

> *Even to your old age, I am He, and even to gray hairs I will carry you! I have made, and I will bear; even I will carry, and will deliver you.* (Isaiah 46:4)

> *"Do not be afraid of their faces, for I am with you to deliver you," says the LORD.* (Jeremiah 1:8)

[Christ] *has made* [you] *alive together with Him, having for-*
given you all trespasses, having wiped out the handwriting of
requirements that was against us, which was contrary to us.
And He has taken it out of the way, having nailed it to the
cross. Having disarmed principalities and powers, He made a
public spectacle of them, triumphing over them in it.

(Colossians 2:13–15)

And the Lord will deliver me from every evil work and pre-
serve me for His heavenly kingdom.   (2 Timothy 4:18)

The Lord knows how to deliver the godly out of temptations.
(2 Peter 2:9)

There are many wonderful assurances of God's deliverance in
the book of Psalms, as well. Here are several of them:

The Lord *is my rock and my fortress and my deliverer; my*
God, my strength, in whom I will trust; my shield and the
horn of my salvation, my stronghold.   (18:2)

You are my hiding place; You shall preserve me from trouble;
You shall surround me with songs of deliverance.   (32:7)

I sought the Lord, *and He heard me, and delivered me from*
all my fears.   (34:4)

The angel of the Lord *encamps all around those who fear*
Him, and delivers them.   (34:7)

Blessed is he who considers the poor; the Lord *will deliver him*
in time of trouble. The Lord *will preserve him and keep him*
alive, and he will be blessed on the earth; You will not deliver
him to the will of his enemies. The Lord *will strengthen him*

on his bed of illness; You will sustain him on his sickbed.

(41:1–3)

You called in trouble, and I delivered you.　　(81:7)

Because he has set his love upon Me, therefore I will deliver him; I will set him on high, because he has known My name. He shall call upon Me, and I will answer him; I will be with him in trouble; I will deliver him and honor him. With long life I will satisfy him, and show him My salvation.

(91:14–16)

He sent His word and healed them, and delivered them from their destructions.　　(107:20)

GOD'S PRESENCE BRINGS DELIVERANCE

The presence of the Lord Himself brings us deliverance. In visions God has given me, I have seen angels coming into churches from the outside, usually through the front door that faces the pulpit in many sanctuaries. When Christ was going to come down, they would begin to sweep with their wings—like a huge fan. They would fan the floor, and a royal red carpet would be laid out for Christ to walk upon.

Then I would see the angels form two parallel rows down the middle aisle of the church. The people in the congregation wouldn't be able to see the angels, but the heavenly messengers would lift their trumpets and blow them as if a king or queen were about to arrive. Then I would see a large chariot come to the main doors at the front of the church. Huge angels would open the doors—they were spiritual doors—and Christ would come in.

Oh, my, He was so beautiful! Angels were always with Him to escort Him and bring messages in books and scrolls. Some of the angels carried horns of fire. Others carried swords or other things.

When Christ would come in, the minister would say, "Oh, I feel the presence of the Lord." I would see clouds appear over the congregation. (Similarly, when I'm preaching in home meetings, often the presence of the Lord will begin to roll in, and I'll see what looks like a mist or a cloud hovering over the people. Many will begin to raise their hands and say, "I feel the presence of the Lord.") It seemed as if there were hundreds of angels working with the Lord. They also worked with the ministers to bring the healing of Jesus to people, and they worked when prophecy was given. Through all this, I knew God was telling me that angels are with us.

I have seen this mighty vision many, many times during my travels over the past ten years. Whenever I see it, souls are always saved. There is such a great move of God that people repent of their sins when I preach on hell. I see the angels go to work in the congregation, and sometimes I see people who are bound in chains, really black chains. The angels torch the chains with fire as the people repent before God. I see people forgiving completely those who have hurt them. They raise their hands and praise the mighty King of Kings and Lord of Lords.

During these mighty visitations, the Lord will get out of His chariot and walk through the church. He will touch certain people on the head. The anointing of God, the covenant of God, is so real! Believe that Jesus died to make us whole. Believe that He is coming back. Believe that He will manifest His glory in our services if we will let him, if we will believe Him.

Satan wants to cause us to doubt in order to hinder us. He wants to interject unbelief into all of us. Yet hallelujah, our God has paid the price for our deliverance! Our Lord Jesus did it for us! If we will only join with Him, if we will only forgive one another, we will receive absolute forgiveness. (See Matthew 6:14–15.) Let there be no blockage in that joining. Let us be healed of our infirmities, our sicknesses, and our diseases.

THE POWER OF THE CROSS IN DELIVERANCE

On another occasion, I was preaching in a church service, and I was under a heavy anointing. Suddenly, I saw a vision of angels carrying a huge white cross across the front of the church. As the people were prayed for by another minister, I could see power come out of the end of the cross and go onto the person being prayed for. Each one was healed or delivered as they were touched by the power coming from the cross.

I have seen the same thing many other times. As I preach the living Word of God, I can see the cross over my head. Power always comes from the cross. It is through the power of the cross that deliverance is accomplished and salvation is possible. We can be delivered today if we will only claim for ourselves what Jesus Christ paid for on Calvary. The secret is in the atonement. We must believe in Jesus, and we must believe in His miracles.

Again, one of the greatest tricks of the devil is to bring doubt and unbelief to us. God wants to bring us joy, happiness, and fulfillment, but the devil wants to bring us pain, sorrow, and grief. God is greater than all these things, however, and we must look to Him. Deliverance is possible through the power of the cross.

GOD'S COMPASSION LEADS TO DELIVERANCE

I was flying on an airplane one day, thinking about a crisis someone in my family was having, when I started crying, and the tears began to flow down my face. Thank the Lord, I had some privacy: I was wearing sunglasses, and there weren't many people in the section of the plane I was in. It was a long flight, so I just curled up in the corner next to the window as I wept.

As the tears streamed down my face, I looked out the window and was amazed to see a beautiful rainbow! Immediately, I remembered the promises of God. When He put the first rainbow in the sky, He promised Noah that He'd never destroy the earth with a flood again. (See Genesis 9:8–17.) Seeing the rainbow that day encouraged my heart because I was reminded of the precious promises of God.

Then, as if affirming what I had seen in nature, I saw a beautiful, glorious, overwhelming vision. I saw what appeared to be a huge red fire in the sky and a resemblance of God on His throne. It is difficult to describe what I saw next, but it looked like a trail leading from the earth up to God's throne. There, in the trail, I saw tears, and immediately I thought of Jesus.

My thoughts of Jesus coincided with my memory of a historical event. In one of the saddest episodes of American history, some of the Cherokee Indians were taken from their land, herded into makeshift forts with minimal facilities and food, then forced to march a thousand miles. (Some made part of the trip by boat in equally horrible conditions.)

About four thousand Cherokee people died during this removal from the Southeast to government reservations in Oklahoma Territory. The route they traveled and the journey itself became known as "The Trail of Tears." The literal meaning of the Cherokee words *Nunna daul Tsuny* is "The trail where they cried."

When I saw this vision of the throne and the trail of tears leading to it, I thought of this historical event, but my most vivid thoughts were of Jesus. I remembered how Jesus walked the *Via Dolorosa*, the Way of Sorrow, climbing up that hill to Calvary. I remembered the tracks of God, the pain and suffering. Then I remembered the pain, suffering, and sorrow that the saints of God still go through at times. As a sign that He was with me, God gave me a poem that I call "In the Tracks of God's Tears."

> In the tracks of God's tears were many written words,
> Many messages unto God of sorrow and grief.
> In the tracks of these tears, the enemy has done great harm.
> To many people on the earth, he's inflicted great harm.
> The tracks of these tears are cries unto God
> Mixed with doubt and unbelief of God's covenant promise.
> Such sorrow, such grief of heart as, you see,
> The enemy kills and wounds our children,
> And others we love.
> But yet there's hope in the tracks of God's tears.
> Yet there's life, there's peace, in the tracks of God's tears.

As I continued looking out the window, it seemed as if tears were falling from heaven. Each teardrop had a divine message in it, leaving a trail down to the earth. I knew that God had heard my cries; He is truly touched by the things we go through.

There are many stories in the tracks of God's tears. His teardrops come down like rain and mix with our tears. My tears and yours are a language unto God.

> *You number my wanderings; put my tears into Your bottle; are they not in Your book? When I cry out to You, then my enemies will turn back; this I know, because God is for me. In God (I will praise His word), in the LORD (I will praise His word), in God I have put my trust; I will not be afraid. What can man do to me?* (Psalm 56:8–11)

The revelation that day gave me even greater respect for what Jesus went through and for the love of our great God. He loves us so much that He sent His Son Jesus to give us life eternal so that we may never die. Yet while we are on this earth, we have to continue to tear down Satan's kingdom through the Word of God. We have to continue to do the things that God would have us to do.

The vision also gave me unbelievable joy. Through it, God dried my tears, reminding me that "*surely He has borne our griefs and carried our sorrows*" (Isaiah 53:4). He assured me that my relatives could be set free, and so can you and yours. "*Believe on the Lord Jesus Christ, and you will be saved, you and your household*" (Acts 16:31).

When the plane landed, I continued on to my destination strengthened in the Lord. That night, I ministered at a service where I saw many hurting and sad people. I gave them words of comfort, encouragement, and hope in the Word of the living God. I told them that, truly, the tears Christ shed for us are as powerful today as they were the day He shed them.

You, too, have probably cried many tears because you have not understood some of the things that have happened to you. Just remember that we can never understand everything in this life. But the holy Word was written to us and given to us by God. The Holy Spirit inspired men of old to write the Scriptures. (See 2 Peter 1:20–21.) Believe it—believe all of it! "*Jesus Christ is the same yesterday, today, and forever*" (Hebrews 13:8). He is the One we are to look to. He is the One we can have hope in. He is the One who gives us delight and joy.

I challenge you today to be encouraged and to know that there is a God who is always taking care of you and your family. He sends His angels to watch over you. They are always ready to work for you and to help you. Be aware of angels and know that they have been sent to you by God.

CRIES FOR DELIVERANCE

In an earlier chapter, we saw that angels fight against the devil on God's behalf. God employs His angels to deliver people from demons, sickness, and disease. In many deliverance services, I have heard people cry out, "God, help me. God, set me free." It was obvious that they really desired deliverance. As they cried out to God, I would see angels appear and firmly touch their hearts. I could see things, or objects, break off the people, and evil spirits would actually come out of their mouths. The angels would bind these evil spirits with chains and take them to the "dry places." (See Matthew 12:43–45.) I have seen some evil spirits shoot through the roof and disappear; others seem to burst into flames.

One night, I was praying diligently in the Holy Spirit for God to deliver people from drugs. From midnight until 6:00 a.m., I interceded with God because I was determined not to rest until I received an answer from Him. Early the next morning, God sent an angel to give me a vision.

As I was caught up in the Spirit, I saw beams of light shoot like arrows from my home straight into heaven. Then I saw the gates of heaven open up, and I saw an army of huge horses. The backs of the horses were approximately four feet wide, and their hooves were about a foot wide. These majestic animals were pure white in color and had skin like satin. They were beautiful, and they were outfitted in armor, ready for battle.

Then I saw those who were riding the horses. They were angels who looked as if they were twelve feet tall or even taller. They were very broad shouldered and wore what looked like big army boots. Pieces of a metal-like substance were strapped around their knees and shins, covering the lower half of their legs. From their waists to their knees, they wore long garments of metal. They had on breastplates of iron, and their sleeves were made of material I have never seen before, but which looked like silver mixed with gold. Each angel had a large sword hanging at his side. Flames shot out from the bottoms and tops of the swords. The angels also wore fierce-looking helmets. Their faces were covered, but there were holes in the helmets that they could see through. Fire came from their mouths, and their eyes were flames of fire. If you saw them on earth, you might think the devil was coming after you; however, I knew that they were coming from heaven to help us.

These angel warriors were riding in formation, rank upon rank, just like an earthly army that is getting ready for battle. It was obvious that they were prepared. Stern-faced and powerful, the angels headed straight for the earth on those mighty horses.

When they reached the earth, the Lord showed me a vision of the horses and riders going into the cities. They rode into the nighttime streets where the drug dealers, murderers, prostitutes, gay bars, and nightclubs were—the streets of pain and sorrow. I saw them go into homes and other places where people were being tormented spiritually. At first, I prayed in alarm, "Oh, my Lord!" Then it occurred to me that they were going in with a powerful deliverance, not a fierce judgment. I saw them walk up to people on the street who were spiritually bound and who didn't even know the angels were there.

On the bound people, I could see spirits—dark shapes, like monkeys or demons. The evil tormentors had wings on their shoulders. Around their heads or their bodies were serpents. What I was seeing was real people who were being attacked by invisible evil spirits.

I saw the warrior angels go up to the evil spirits and cast off the serpents. The angels then seemed to turn the evil spirits into ashes—fire came out of the angels' hands and appeared to cremate the demons. The angels would also touch some of the street people's heads and pull oppressive, evil-looking things off them. I knew they were unclean spirits. The people would shake their heads in relief right there on the street as they were being delivered.

I saw the warrior angels do these things in many locations. For example, I watched the angels go into a place that looked like a nightclub. They went to a man who was sitting in a bar and crying because he had a dark spirit on his shoulder. An angel jerked the monster off him (it was bigger than the man himself), and the thing was turned into ashes. The man shook his head, dried his tears, stood up, and walked out the door. The Holy Spirit said to me,

> A change is coming. A deliverance is coming. I am deliver-ing many from the trickery and bondage of sin and Satan. You will see a big move of my Spirit in the lands, and I will deliver many through the prayers of the saints. I am anointing you for this ministry because you've been crying out to Me for the deliverance of the people. I will do this thing for you.

Then I saw the angels go into hospitals and other places, deliv-ering people from sicknesses and diseases. It was awesome to see the mighty works of these warrior angels. Demons fled from them. They trembled because they knew they were being destroyed.

For several weeks, I saw this as a recurring vision. I'd be caught up in it and see the angels and the Word. The Bible would open up at times—I would see the scrolls—as the angels worked with the Word of God and the Holy Spirit.

God showed me that, all over the world, deliverance had come in the name of the Son, the Lord Jesus Christ. What an awesome sight it was!

In her book *Marching Orders for the End Battle*, Corrie ten Boom wrote about an experience in the Congo during a rebel uprising that further illustrates how God sends angels to deliver His people:

> When the rebels advanced on a school where two hundred children of missionaries lived, they planned to kill both the children and teachers. Those in the school knew of the danger and therefore went to prayer. Their only protec-tion was a fence and a couple of soldiers, while the enemy,

who came closer and closer, amounted to several hundred. When the rebels were close by, suddenly something happened: they turned around and ran away! The next day the same thing happened, and again on the third day. One of the rebels was wounded and was brought to the mission hospital. While the doctor was busy dressing his wounds, he asked him: "Why did you not break into the school as you planned?" "We could not do it. We saw hundreds of soldiers in white uniforms and we became scared." In Africa soldiers never wear white uniforms, so it must have been angels. What a wonderful thing that the Lord can open the eyes of the enemy so that they see angels! We, as children of God, do not need to see them with our human eyes. We have the Bible and faith, and by faith we see invisible things.

STREAMS OF DELIVERANCE

In another revelation God gave me, the Holy Spirit came like a divine wind. He began to flow through towns and cities. As the wind blew, balls of fire began to appear, going up and down and sweeping all over. It was as if the Holy Spirit was preparing the way for something.

Then I saw what looked like large doors opening up into heaven, and I could feel the power of God coming through the doors. It seemed as though the doors were in the universe and heaven was high above them. Through the doors came angels on horses dressed for battle—just as I described earlier. Here again came those spiritual warriors from heaven, full of God's glory, power, might, and majesty!

The angels rode over the land where the wind of the Holy Spirit had flowed, and I could see rivers of white and light and glory moving along. These rivers would move through the mountains and the valleys—they were little rivers and streams of deliverance. Everywhere they flowed, demons by the seeming millions would run away, trying to escape from them. Evil spirits were running and running, and as they ran, fire came out of the angels' swords and appeared to cremate them.

God's Word confirms that the wicked will be consumed. Again, in Malachi 4:3, God says, *"You shall trample the wicked, for they shall be ashes under the soles of your feet."* I firmly believe that God has to send us delivering angels from heaven because of the abundance of attacks we face from Satan and his cohorts.

STAYING DELIVERED

In one service where miracles were taking place, a young man who was about twenty-five years old came into the service crying. He had a wild and desperate look on his face. You could tell he had been drinking and was high on drugs. He said to me, "Please, please help me. Won't someone help me? I want to be delivered so badly. I'm tired of this life; I'm tired of this addiction. Help me. Help me!"

The compassion of the Lord swept over the room. Filled with this compassion, we began to pray for the young man and to cast out evil spirits from him in Jesus' name. We anointed him with oil. Then we led him in the sinner's prayer, and immediately he began to shake his head. He was totally set free; when he stood up, his eyes were completely clear. This young man raised his hands in the air. Soon, he began to magnify and praise the Lord. God had totally transformed him in about fifteen minutes!

Then a little twelve-year-old boy came over and said to him, "Can I tell you something? Do you know what I saw as the people were praying for you?"

The man answered, "No."

"I saw when the demons left you, and they were standing around, trying to go back into you. But all the people were around you, praying. Then I saw an angel with a sword come and chase them away. They couldn't come back!"

The young man praised the Lord, and we were so happy that God had reached out and saved and delivered him. This man is now with good Christian people and is going to church.

God has revealed many things to me about deliverance. Some of the people we have prayed for truly wanted deliverance, but six weeks later, they had the same demons of lust or addiction. We have to continue to pray for them. We also have to counsel them. We have to teach them that, after a person is delivered, he can't be involved any longer with the things that bound him in the first place.

If you want to taste the goodness of God and the world at the same time, there is a fatal conflict in your heart that has to be resolved. It is very important to stay delivered after God has changed you. Find a good church that believes in Jesus Christ and His deliverance. Obey the Word of God. Keep away from those sinful things that drag you down. Stay close to the heart of God.

These truths are essential because, if you have been delivered, you want to stay delivered! You have to make up your mind which way you are going. Do you really want to adore Jesus and serve Him? Or do you want to follow the things of the world and the devil? If you have been set free from evil things, God brings you to a place where you have to choose.

God is truly a deliverer, and those whom the Lord delivers are delivered, indeed. (See John 8:36.) Therefore, when you cast out Satan, say, "Satan, you must go in the name of Jesus." When demons are cast out of people, angels stand with chains ready to drag these evil powers away. But there is something we must do for the Lord as we commit our lives afresh to Him.

He expects us to worship Him, to serve Him, to praise Him, and through every situation to believe that He will bring us out. I know and believe that He will. Every minister of the gospel should believe this. When we do, Jesus will go through the lands demonstrating His power. The Holy Spirit will come and, with the angels, will minister in every service to those who really love God and keep His commandments. You will see a move of God in the lands like you have never seen before.

God is preparing a people for this end-time movement. He is looking for a people who will simply trust Him and love Him for who He is and who will believe what the Word says. I fully believe that God is getting ready to do some really great and mighty things in our lands.

THE ANOINTING DESTROYS THE YOKE

One time, during a service when many people were coming up for prayer, I began to see, in the Spirit, a white light mixed with black in a circle around the seekers' necks. I knew that this circle represented a bondage. The Lord spoke to me and said, "I'm going to break the yoke; the anointing shall destroy the yoke." Then I remembered that the Bible says, *"It shall come to pass in that day that...the yoke shall be destroyed because of the anointing"* (Isaiah 10:27 KJV).

As the people repented of their sins and asked God to forgive and help them, I could see the angels go to work. With their hands, they broke the yokes of bondage right off the people's necks. Serving Satan causes spiritual bondage as well as natural bondage. The people had been under spiritual bondage because they had been serving sin and the devil.

The angels of God do His will and break these yokes through the Word of God and in the power of the Spirit of God. The reason people say, "I feel lighter; I feel better," after they are prayed for is that their bondage has been broken in the spiritual realm. When you get serious with God, when you are real and open before Him, He delivers you. He sets you free!

The main thing is to stay honest in your soul before Him. Second, be sure to forgive other people for any wrongs they have committed against you. By the Word of God, you must forgive anyone who has harmed you and hurt you. Unforgiveness is a horrible thing. You *must* forgive so that the heavenly Father can forgive you. Jesus said in Matthew 6:14–15,

> For if you forgive men their trespasses, your heavenly Father will also forgive you. But if you do not forgive men their trespasses, neither will your Father forgive your trespasses.

DELIVERANCE FROM SATAN'S CONTROL

Once I was going to another country, and I knew the people in that land worshipped many false gods and idols. However, I also knew that God loved the souls of the people there and wanted to save them. While I was there, the Holy Spirit anointed me to prophesy against their idols and their witchery. I knew, and prophesied, that God's presence and His Word had come into the country to save to the uttermost. (See Hebrews 7:25.) He had come to set the captives free, to undo the heavy burdens, and to take the "scales" off people's eyes so they could receive God's truth. (See Isaiah 61:1; Acts 9:1–18.)

In the spiritual realm, God permitted me to see many faces whose eyes had been shut and whose ears had been closed. Then I saw a visible outline of hands pulling layers of scales off these eyes and ears. Those who were delivered would shake their heads in freedom. They would shout with joy and say, "Oh, I see now. I understand now." It was as though a darkness had blinded their minds, but when God touched them, the blindness that Satan had put there was removed. I knew this vision meant that the gospel was to go forth to every nation and every country.

In this same country, a pastor's wife and I prayed for many hours over two days. In the middle of the night, I saw a vision of a cart rolling through the city. Everywhere it rolled, it would cut off the heads of thousands of snakes that were stretched out all along the way. As the cart went through the valley killing the snakes, I prayed to God and saw the moving of the Holy Spirit.

Suddenly, it was as if the gates of heaven itself opened up. Armies of angels came sweeping down in majesty. I could see manifestations of the power, the glory, and the might of God. He had sent His angels to earth to deliver the city!

Then I saw the angels go into an opening in the earth. From the darkened depths, they pulled out a round, ugly monster with a horrible-looking head. First they chained the monster; then they began to uproot it. This thing was miles long and had wrapped up the entire city. It had permeated the earth, the streets, the houses, and the atmosphere. But the monster was helpless against the power of God. I watched the angels delivering the city from this evil force for what seemed like hours, and I knew God had liberated the city completely from demon powers.

I told my friend, "You should see what God is doing for this country." Since then, we have heard many good reports of the gospel moving in that nation. Wonderful things are happening, and churches are being established. But God in His mercy dealt with the devils first and delivered that country from the demon of idolatry and the worship of idols. God says the following in His Word:

> By the blessing of the upright the city is exalted, but it is overthrown by the mouth of the wicked.　(Proverbs 11:11)

Righteousness exalts a nation [or city], but sin is a reproach to any people.   (Proverbs 14:34)

It is an abomination for kings to commit wickedness, for a throne is established by righteousness. Righteous lips are the delight of kings, and they love him who speaks what is right.
(Proverbs 16:12–13)

The LORD will enter into judgment with the elders of His people and His princes: "For you have eaten up the vineyard; the plunder of the poor is in your houses."   (Isaiah 3:14)

God will answer the prayers and intercession of those who are devoted to Him, and He will uproot the evil that is present in their communities and nations.

THE POWER OF JESUS' NAME

Something that I have come to expect, but which still constantly amazes me, is the reaction of evil angels—demon spirits—when I rebuke them in Jesus' name. As I have cast out devils in Jesus' name, I have seen angels open up the Bible and shove it in Satan's face; the Word of God becomes a sword that goes after him. I've seen Satan when he looked like a serpent, I've seen him when he looked like a man, and I've seen him when he looked like an angel in disguise. Whatever form he takes, I always recognize that it is the devil. When God's servant or the angels begin to speak the Word of God, the devil backs up and releases his victim. He goes because God's Word stands against him.

It's important for us to have an honest and close relationship with the Lord before we cast out demons in Jesus' name. In the Bible, the sons of Sceva attempted to use the name of the Lord without having a true relationship with Him:

Some of the itinerant Jewish exorcists took it upon themselves to call the name of the Lord Jesus over those who had evil spirits, saying, "We exorcise you by the Jesus whom Paul preaches." Also there were seven sons of Sceva, a Jewish chief priest, who did so. And the evil spirit answered and said, "Jesus I know, and Paul I know; but who are you?" Then the man in whom the evil spirit was leaped on them, overpowered them, and prevailed against them, so that they fled out of that house naked and wounded. This became known both to all Jews and Greeks dwelling in Ephesus; and fear fell on them all, and the name of the Lord Jesus was magnified.

(Acts 19:13–17)

Jesus' name is not a gimmick. He is our powerful Savior, and He is worthy to be worshipped and honored. His name is not to be used lightly. Yet when we use Jesus' name with true reverence and faith, Satan cannot stand against it.

GOD HAS THE VICTORY

It is very important to remember in regard to deliverance that Satan is only a created being. He is neither omnipotent, omniscient, nor omnipresent, as God is. Our Lord Jesus Christ is *always* stronger than the devil or any of his demons. *"Jesus Christ...has gone into heaven and is at the right hand of God, angels and authorities and powers having been made subject to Him"* (1 Peter 3:21–22).

In addition, God has multitudes of angels to carry out His works and plans. Regardless of how many demons the devil has, God's holy angels are more in number. God always has the victory, and He will bring deliverance. *"The LORD is my rock and my fortress and my deliverer; my God, my strength, in whom I will trust; my shield and the horn of my salvation, my stronghold"* (Psalm 18:2).

10

ANGELS AND PRAYER

In this chapter, I want to mention two areas in which the angels are involved in our prayers: in our worship and in our intercession. When we understand the activity of angels in answer to our prayers, we will be encouraged to pray and intercede on behalf of ourselves, our families, and others who need God's help and deliverance.

ANGELIC ACTIVITY IN WORSHIP

First, the angels join us in worshipping the Lord. The Bible says,

Praise the LORD! Praise the LORD from the heavens; praise Him in the heights! Praise Him, all His angels; praise Him, all His hosts! Praise Him, sun and moon; praise Him, all you stars of light! Praise Him, you heavens of heavens, and you waters above the heavens! Let them praise the name of the LORD, for He commanded and they were created.

(Psalm 148:1–5)

In the visions and revelations God has given me, I have seen the activity of angels as God's people worship Him. For example, I have seen the following vision many times during church services.

As different groups of people come to worship and praise God, I have watched as the Holy Spirit has moved over the congregation. Suddenly, above the pulpit and behind the choir area, high and between curtains, I will see a large door in a wall. Through the door will come rows of angels with fluttering wings. They are dressed in glistening white garments.

Dozens of angels sweep through the door and look over the situation. It is so beautiful and awesome to see these angels in action. They hold something in their hands, and with it they fan the air as if they are cleansing it. Then a great cloud appears, and on the cloud is the throne of God. The brilliant white throne has glowing colors all around it.

I have also seen this likeness of the throne of God suspended in the air behind the pulpit where an anointed minister was preaching. Angels on both sides of the servant of God would write down what the preacher was saying, what he was doing, and how he or she prayed for the people. Everything was recorded.

On one occasion, I had been to London, England, with my sister to preach the gospel. When we were returning on the airplane, I was very tired because I had ministered in a number of churches and we had had to deal with many people, some who were Christians and some of who were not. It was a long flight back home, and I was totally exhausted, so I fell asleep.

As I slept, I was suddenly transported into the heavenlies. I could see what appeared to be a large ballroom with curtains such as I had never seen before. The curtains formed a huge circle, and the tops of them were pulled up, like you would hold up a balloon. The bottoms of the curtains were suspended, swinging in the air.

The front of the curtains opened up, and inside I could see scenery. In this ballroom, there were crystal chandeliers, but nothing was holding them up. They just hung in the air. Then I could hear music that was accompanying praise. I could see that worship was taking place. As the front of the drapes opened up, I saw that people and angels were sitting at tables inside and carrying on conversations.

Excitedly, I thought, *O, God, these things were never dreamed of. They are things I never even thought of.* It seemed that redeemed believers and angels were praising God and enjoying fellowship together. Splendor and glory and riches were everywhere. I thought, *Oh, my God is so unique. He is so wonderful,* and I began to praise Him.

One day, in prayer, I had a vision of heaven's throne room with Jesus sitting on the throne. He was no longer suffering and bleeding, as He had been on the cross; instead, He was being worshipped by what seemed to be millions of angels. The throne He was sitting on was enormous and beautiful. Jesus was dressed in marvelous royal apparel that had long, full sleeves and was interwoven with pure gold and silver. A robe made of another piece of material was draped around His shoulders. It was the most beautiful garment I have ever seen, and it had a wide sash on it.

When I looked up at Christ's face, I saw that He was wearing a crown mixed with green, red, and gold velvet. Diamonds, sapphires, and other jewels glittered all over the crown. I thought, *O my Lord, how beautiful!*

Jesus had a scepter lying across His lap, which He gently tapped with His hand. Fire was on the end of the scepter. Jesus was looking intently at me and smiling. I was on my knees before Him, lifting up my hands and worshipping Him. Then He took the scepter and touched me on the top of my head, blessing me. I looked up, and He touched my heart with a flame of fire. As the fire warmed my heart, I felt tremendous love for God.

The love! The purity! The wholesomeness! As I bowed and worshipped Him, I began to praise Him with all my heart. I thank Jesus for that mighty visitation with the Lord.

It is important for us to realize that our worship of God is made possible only through sacrifice. We can worship because of Jesus' sacrifice on the cross, through which He has reconciled us to God and restored our relationship with Him. In addition, worship is possible only as we offer the Lord our own sacrifices—sacrifices of praise. *"Therefore by [Jesus] let us continually offer the sacrifice of praise to God, that is, the fruit of our lips, giving thanks to His name"* (Hebrews 13:15). Because of what Jesus has done for us, we can join with the angels and worship Him with joy:

> *Thus says the* LORD: *"Again there shall be heard in this place...* *the voice of joy and the voice of gladness, the voice of the bridegroom and the voice of the bride, the voice of those who will say: 'Praise the* LORD *of hosts, for the* LORD *is good, for His mercy endures forever.'"*   (Jeremiah 33:10–11)

ANGELIC ACTIVITY IN INTERCESSION

Second, angels are especially near to God's saints when they pray. Remember that angels went to Jesus twice and strengthened Him—and He was praying both times! The Bible gives this teaching from heaven's viewpoint:

> *Then another angel, having a golden censer, came and stood at the altar. He was given much incense, that he should offer it with the prayers of all the saints upon the golden altar which was before the throne. And the smoke of the incense, with the prayers of the saints, ascended before God from the angel's hand.*   (Revelation 8:3–4)

Many times, in the spiritual realm, I have seen angels gathering the prayers of God's saints at a church altar. They have taken them and gone straight to heaven, where they have presented their prayers before Jesus and the heavenly Father. One time, I saw stairs going up into heaven, and angels carrying our prayers to God like beams of light. Some of the angels flew and some climbed the stairs; some had wings, and some didn't. In addition, at times, I have been awakened and prompted to pray, and I have seen by my bedside a spiritual being writing in a scroll. The angel would be recording my prayers to take them to heaven.

Besides carrying our prayers to heaven, angels are God's messengers who bring answers to prayers. I often see angels answering the prayers of God's saints. I am going to share with you some of what I have seen because I want you to have the same insight that I have been given regarding the involvement of angels in our intercession.

ANGELS AND PRAYER FOR SALVATION

Many times, in visions, I have seen angels come into a church, or another place where I was ministering, carrying spiritual crosses. These crosses were huge and pure white, symbolizing wisdom and power. They also emitted a brilliant light, and some had fire coming out of them. The angels would point these crosses toward a backslider or sinner in the room, and the flames of the Holy Spirit would come out from the crosses and envelop the person, who would begin to shake. Then the individual would get up, come to the altar, and repent.

The angels were working with the Spirit of truth and righteousness to encourage people to give their lives to the Lord. It is always a beautiful thing for me to behold. The Lord has revealed to me that He sends His angels to work with us because of the prayers of mothers, fathers, brothers, sisters, pastors, laymen, evangelists, and teachers.

Seeing God do His work of salvation in the lives of men and women is marvelous, indeed, and His angels are active in promoting this work. I remember asking a neighbor, who is also an intercessor, to pray for my work in a particular city. The neighbor said,

"When you preach there, God is really going to save souls in that city."

God gave me a vision that confirmed what He was going to do. I saw the heavens open. A large door in heaven swung wide, and many angels riding on horses began coming down to where I was. They came to prepare the way for the work of God. It excited me to see the workings of God in action. I saw books open up, and I recognized the writings in the books. God was promising success for His work. I often see this same scene when I go into towns for services.

In a service one evening, I was preaching on hell and what God had revealed to me about that place. I told the people how we must get right with the Lord, and the church altar filled with people who came forward for prayer. I saw the glory of the Lord coming down around them; God's arms were stretched out to receive them.

It was such a beautiful scene. Many people don't understand that once you surrender to God, He is right there to help you and encourage you. He who calls you will bring you forth. He loves you so much that He shows His mighty mercy to you.

In one vision God gave me, I saw many angels who held crosses in their hands. They would stand the crosses up by some of the people in the meeting, or they would put the crosses on people's shoulders. There was a huge cross, and I understood it to symbolize Christ's cross.

The people who had been given the crosses began to place them at the base of Christ's cross. In the middle of His cross, there was a brilliant light, and it seemed as though the nearer they got to His cross and the light, the closer they got to God. It pays to seek God's face and continue on with Him!

In the visions, Jesus would often say, "Souls, souls, come forth," and angels would spring into action. They would touch some sincere soul who was seeking God. Some of the people had black bands—indicating sin—fastened around them. As the angels would touch the people, I would see them raise their heads in the service and say, "O God, please forgive me. I'm a thief," or "Forgive me; I'm a liar," and so forth. Then the angels would touch these dark bands of bondage and the bands would burst into flames.

Some of the people's hearts looked as black as coal. But as they confessed their lying, cheating, stealing, adultery, witchcraft, or whatever bondage they were in, the blackness would appear to boil out of their hearts. The angels would touch their hearts, and their hearts would become beautiful and pink. It reminded me of the Scripture, "*Then I will...take the stony heart...and give them a heart of flesh*" (Ezekiel 11:19).

To receive this kind of change in our lives, we must totally repent before God. We have to turn to God with all our hearts, all our minds, all our souls, and all our spirits. We are to do all these things in the name of Jesus.

ANGELS AND PRAYER FOR HEALING

About five years after the Lord showed me the revelations of hell and heaven, one of my children—who were all still young— became sick. I had been praying for them, and the Lord began to speak to me, saying,

Child, when I took you into hell, I held your left hand. A few times, you thought I had left you, but I hadn't. I was right there. I revealed to you much of the depths of the torments of hell, but I also gave you a great gift of the working of miracles in your left hand. It is a gift from Me to you, especially for the suffering and grief you are seeing. It is My gift so that you can help others on the earth. When the appointed time comes, I will magnify that gift and manifest it to heal the sick.

Use the gift on your children. Use it and pray for them, and they will be healed.

The gift of the working of miracles is listed in 1 Corinthians 12 along with the other gifts of the Spirit. (See verses 8–10.) I began to exercise the gift that God had given me, and God started to train me in it; later on, I would see angels coming into services to assist me as I ministered in this gift.

God began to tell me many things about what He wanted to do in my ministry with healings, signs, wonders, and miracles. Angels were always there, carrying out the orders of God. When I would see them in my services, I would tell the people, "God wants to heal you," and many people were healed. Signs and wonders continue to be manifested in my services today. I see the Lord doing great and mighty things. He is healing the sick and performing marvelous miracles. I know that the day is coming when God is going to pour out more oil and more power upon me so that I can continue to work for Him, exalt Him, and obey His Word to take the message of the gospel to others in a greater way.

Let me tell you of two other circumstances in which I have witnessed the angels of God participating in healing. At times, when a servant of God is praying over an infant who is critically ill, I have seen angels with scrolls and pens standing in the room, writing down what the minister is saying. Understand, please, that infants are too young to apply faith in such a situation. The minister exercises faith on the infant's behalf, believing that the child is being healed by God's Word and Spirit. He or she may pray, "In Jesus' name and by Jesus' stripes, this child is healed. I cast out the spirit of infirmity in Jesus' name. Spirit of infirmity, you must go. I take dominion over you in the name of Jesus!" I have seen how, as the minister lays his hands on a child's head and anoints him or her with oil, praying according to God's Word (see James 5:14–15), an angel will place his hands on the afflicted one's little legs. Other angels sometimes just stand there, perhaps in support of the healing.

The second circumstance was a very personal one. On May 3, 2001, my son Scott had a grand mal seizure. At the time, I was in Michigan preaching the gospel, and I was staying at the home of my sister. I was unaware that Scott had had a major seizure, but I had a vision of angels coming down from heaven and getting ready to do something on the earth. They were mighty, warrior angels. Then, as I was walking up the stairs at my sister's house, I clearly heard the words, *"I am the resurrection and the life"* (John 11:25).

A few hours later, my daughter Teresa called and told me about Scott's grand mal seizure. She said the paramedics had taken him to a hospital, but she didn't know which one. As I tried to find out where my son was, I still did not know the whole story and what a terrible thing had happened to him.

I called some people in Michigan and other states and asked them to pray. A man in Michigan who has the gift of prophecy called me and said, "Mary, I want to tell you what I see. I see your son in a vision, and I see God connecting the soul and the spirit back together in the brain. I see the brain, and I see the Lord healing this child." And he began to prophesy and pray.

This man is a good friend of mine, and when he had finished praying, I said, "Brother, I know that you're a prophet and a man of God, but I don't really believe Scott's situation was that tragic. I think it was just a normal seizure."

I am telling you this story so you may know how important it is to believe in God and serve Him, to keep His commandments and know that He is the Word of God. He is the Healer and Deliverer. He is the same God *"yesterday, today, and forever"* (Hebrews 13:8).

When I finally contacted Scott, I asked him, "Son, how are you? What has happened to you?" As he began to tell me, he could hardly talk. He said he'd had a horrible seizure and had been in the hospital. He had gotten home about four o'clock that morning. I said, "You need to really praise God that you didn't die."

He said, "Mom, I did die."

"What are you talking about?" I asked. "What happened?"

Scott told me that he had been about to go into a grocery store when, suddenly, he had felt a lot of pain in his shoulder. Right there, he had a seizure, and that was all he remembered. When he woke up, he was in the hospital. The paramedics told him that when they first arrived, he wasn't breathing and showed no vital signs. They said they had brought him back to life with electric shock and other emergency procedures and then taken him to the hospital.

The paramedics were astonished at Scott's good condition because, given the severity of his seizure, he should have been brain-dead and on life-support machines. But by a miracle of God, Scott was raised up—at the very time I heard the voice of God at my sister's house saying, *"I am the resurrection and the life"* (John 11:25). The warrior angels I had seen coming down from heaven in the vision had apparently come to fight for Scott's life.

ANGELS AND PRAYER FOR MIRACLES

When I lived in Michigan, I led a prayer meeting that met in my home. One day, I was leaving my house to run some errands in town with several believers who had been with me in the prayer meeting, when a storm quickly arose, and rain started pouring down.

As we got into the automobile, the winds and the rain seemed to get worse, so we sat in the car praying in the Spirit. Suddenly, we heard sirens and saw an ambulance. We knew that something had happened, such as an automobile accident, so we proceeded to the store with caution and completed our errands.

We were taking a different route on the way back when we saw another ambulance's light flashing. There had been a car wreck. We saw a stretcher beside the road with someone lying on it. A white sheet covered the victim, so we knew the person was dead. The police pulled us over to wait by the side of the road while they got the other people out of the wreckage. It was still raining hard—just pouring.

As we waited, the Holy Spirit fell on us and impressed us to pray. As we prayed in the Spirit, we began, under the Spirit's direction, to command life to come back into the victim. As the Holy Spirit prompted us, we remitted the person's sins in the name of Jesus. (See John 20:23.) In a few minutes, we saw that white sheet raise up. Then the person on the stretcher lifted up his hands and pulled the sheet away from himself.

All at once, one of the paramedics turned around, saw what was happening, and ran over to work with the injured man. The paramedic was happy because God had put life back into the victim. We never even touched the man, but the angels did. We didn't even get out of the car, but the Word of God was in action to save that person's life.

ANGELS AND PRAYER FOR DELIVERANCE

A few years ago, my family was going through an especially rough time. A family member had disappeared and had not been seen for almost six months. No one could find him. This was one of the most difficult crises my family had ever faced. We had to believe God with everything in us. In addition to this crisis, other blows constantly rained on us. It seemed that the old enemy was hammering us first on one side and then on another.

I'm sure many of you can understand how hard this time was for us because you've gone through similar experiences. Perhaps the devil is hitting your bank account, taking money that doesn't belong to him, and you wonder where it is all going. Maybe he is causing your automobiles to break down or your appliances to stop working. When he isn't doing that, you are getting sued for something. Everything in your life seems to be in an uproar because there is always some problem. That's exactly what we were going through. Troubles and difficulties were constant in our family at that time in our lives. I thought, *O Lord, haven't I prayed enough? Haven't I stood on Your Word enough?* I went to God in prayer because I was so deeply grieved over the situations that were occurring.

During this difficult time, the Lord would send His angels, and His peace would come upon us. God promised us peace, deliverance, and help. (See, for example, John 14:27; Psalm 34:7; Isaiah 41:10, 13–14.) So we began to stand on the Word of God, no matter how hard the waves hit.

One day I would have to be the strong one; the next day I would be weak and one of my children would have to be strong. It was awesome to see God's angels ministering to us. Someone with the gift of prophecy would call me, or a friend would call me, or I would call them, and we would encourage one another in the Lord. It is so important for us to encourage one another, especially during difficult times.

In the midst of this trial, I saw a mighty vision in which God assured me that He is the Deliverer. The vision seemed to last for hours! It was a revelation of how the Lord brings deliverance to the lands through His angels! In the vision, I observed angels going into houses. The houses looked as though they were way back in a forest, and darkness was all around.

Suddenly, I saw witches and warlocks having séances. I also saw devil worshippers. Then I saw the angels of God shake the places where they were. When the angels did this, the witches, warlocks, and devil worshippers ran out of the buildings. They got into their cars and drove away with the fear of the Lord upon them. It was an awesome sight to see.

I have seen this kind of vision many times in the past fifteen years or so. I see it at least twice a year—usually when I am in intercessory prayer. I know that God is the Deliverer and that He sends His angels to His children on errands of mercy. He intervened in the situation my family was going through. Our family member was found and, though he had been ill, God restored him to health!

On another occasion, I had been in deep prayer and meditation. As I ministered at a church service that night, I saw angels everywhere. Every angel had a golden sword in his hand. The Spirit of the Lord spoke clearly to me in an unmistakable voice:

> Child, when prayer time comes for the people, I want to heal certain physical problems. I want this to be a sign in your ministry that the testimony of hell that I gave you is true. I have given My word that I will give signs and wonders and work miracles as the gospel of the Lord Jesus Christ is preached.

I became so excited! In my spirit, I could see an angel with a large book writing things down as I preached. The ceiling seemed to open up, and I could see a vision of the throne of God. Angels were rejoicing all around it and praising God.

When it was time for the altar call, I saw angels going among the congregation, nudging people to go to the altar and give their hearts to the Lord. When the angels touched the hearts of individuals, the blackest sins began to churn up from their hearts as they knelt and prayed to God. It was so beautiful to see God working in their lives!

In the Spirit, I could see chains wrapped around the people. As they received forgiveness, angels seemed to break the bondage, to shatter the chains, to cast them off. The bands broke as people began to raise their hands and confess their sins to the Lord.

Cries and shouts went up all around from souls who were being delivered. It was wonderful. In many of my services all over the world, God provides great miracles like these, and wonderful deliverances happen. I praise God for His signs, wonders, and miracles. I know that the angels are at work helping me with the ministry of the Lord Jesus Christ, which He has given me.

One day, I was in prayer when the Lord began to talk to me about the revelations He was giving to me:

> My child, you must learn that many times I will open up a vision to you, and what I'm showing you is not present right there before you. It will be for the future, or it will be happening in another part of the world. You were given the vision so that you can intercede. Listen to Me, and I will give you instructions on how to pray.
>
> Sometimes, people will receive a revelation, and they will think that what is happening is right there beside their beds. They will think that what they are seeing is there in the room with them, but it is not so. I am a holy God, and I am protective of my children. I am revealing truth and mysteries to you so you can reveal them to the world.
>
> I'm showing you one of the workings of the enemy, Satan, so that you can pray; and the blood that I shed— the blood covenant—will come and stop the flow of these channels, these avenues, of the devil.

I was so excited! I said, "Okay, Lord."

Time went by, and one day, I was in Phoenix to preach the gospel. Some of us had been in intercessory prayer for the city. We had prayed and gone to sleep, but I awoke at three o'clock in the morning. I felt as though I had been awake for hours.

I looked at the ceiling, and I could see something appearing before my eyes. A manifestation of a spiritual object came through the ceiling and hovered around in a circle. At one end of the object,

I could see a small opening that measured about eight inches by twelve inches. I saw that the tiny opening was a door.

As I looked through this door, I could see a witch with a crystal ball sitting at a table. I knew that she could see from the crystal ball into the place where I was. I also knew that God had allowed me to see what I was seeing, and that He had allowed her to be able to do this in order to show me how to pray. I took in this whole scenario very quickly. Then the door shut, and the thing moved right out of the room.

I got up and said, "Lord, what in the world was that?" God said to me,

I'm showing you strategy of the devil. Many witches and warlocks work for the devil in this area, and they have these crystal balls. They have figured out how to go through the airways and spy out the land in certain areas where My blood does not provide a covering. A blood covering can be provided only through prayer and through believing in Me and the covenant of God. Many do not believe in My protection as you do.

When My righteousness covers my children and they are living holy lives before Me, when they are doing the best they can, My covenant—the atonement—stands for them and their families. No matter where they are, no matter where their children are, a hedge of protection surrounds them.

Many do not believe this, but I know you do. I've proven this to you many times over with your own children and your family. Many times, I've saved your family from harmful things that crossed their paths.

My covenant—the atonement for the healing of the body, the blood that I shed over two thousand years ago—still stands today. My covenant promises are for you and your children.

What I'm revealing to you is a message for you to tell to other people. It is to protect the innocent and the guilty. My desire is to save the guilty and weak. I desire this, and this is why I'm telling you these things—so that you can tell the world.

The armlike object you saw, with the opening and a small door at the front of it, was a passageway from the crystal ball through the spirit realm to where you are in this home.

I allowed you to see this hovering in the atmosphere in order to teach you to pray. Watch closely, and I'll show you something else.

God then showed me what looked like a huge television screen. I could see a woman's face, and I would recognize her now if I could see her in the flesh. She was clearly visible, and she was hovering over a crystal ball and screaming in a loud voice. Then the devil came roaring and screaming into the place where she was. "Why did you let her see you?" Satan yelled. "Why did you let her see you?"

The woman and the devil began arguing. This led to fighting and more yelling. I heard the devil tell this wicked woman that she had a big mouth and would tell everybody. The devil—his form was huge—grabbed the wall and started roaring and screaming in anger. Then he went through the door, and the Lord suddenly spoke to me,

Plead My blood! Plead the blood of Jesus! Plead the blood that I shed. The life and the power of the blood of Jesus that was shed two thousand years ago has never lost its power over situations like these. The blood has power over those crystal balls that are the spirit realm's venues of sin; it can shut those doors.

I did just as the Lord said because I believed Him. When I began to pray, I saw fire mixed with blood. I saw vapors of smoke. I saw the power of God shoot through the atmosphere and explode the woman's crystal ball. She screamed and ran all over the room; as the power of God hit again, she ran out of the room.

The Lord told me, "Pray in every area where I send you as you have just done here. Pray right now for others who have these crystal balls."

So I prayed for a long time. He showed me how to pray. His angels taught me how to pray through the Scriptures, how to bind and loose (see Matthew 18:18), how to plead His precious blood, and how to rely on the Word of God. Every time I would do these things, there would be a great deliverance among the people. In the spiritual realm, I saw the angels scatter many of the enemies of God's people. In one vision, I saw what looked like about ten thousand scattered at one time.

I also saw people delivered who were in supernatural bondage. It was as though ropes and vines had grown around them, but when the fire hit them, the shackles would explode. I knew that God was showing me these mighty revelations through the power of His Holy Spirit. I thought, *God, You are such a wonderful God.*

Then I saw the dove of the Holy Spirit soaring through the heavens. God began to draw people by His Spirit. People started coming to the Lord, and I was so happy and excited to see the blessings and joy of the Lord. I truly began to understand that we are in a spiritual war where good is fighting against evil.

THE PRAYER OF BELIEVERS

I thank God for these revelations and for the angels that I have seen. I believe God wants us to understand that the prayers of believers are very important. We are called to pray. Yet we shouldn't pray just once a day and then forget about it. When the Holy Spirit prompts us to pray, we should pray right then, regardless of where we are. Paul taught us to *"pray without ceasing"* (1 Thessalonians 5:17) in the Spirit.

Through the prayers of those who believe His Word, God commissions His angels to come and work with us, and He brings salvation, healing, and deliverance to people. Let the Lord's words to Jeremiah when he was in exile be an encouragement to you as you pray for yourself and others:

> For I know the thoughts that I think toward you, says the LORD, thoughts of peace and not of evil, to give you a future and a hope. Then you will call upon Me and go and pray to Me, and I will listen to you. And you will seek Me and find Me, when you search for Me with all your heart. I will be found by you, says the LORD, and I will bring you back from your captivity.   (Jeremiah 29:11–14)

THE MEANING OF ANGELS

I am so grateful that God has anointed me as His servant and has allowed me to see these supernatural visions in order to communicate the message He wants His people to know. I have shared with you only a part of the things I have encountered in the revelations God has given to me. But I want to assure you that the work of God's angels is all found in His Word, and it is wonderful!

The purpose of this book is to encourage you in your faith. The study of angels provides us with a wonderful opportunity to come to know God and His ways better. As we learn about angels, we are not to place our focus on celestial beings themselves but on almighty God and the power and grace He manifests through His servants, the angels. Our knowledge of God's special messengers and how He works through them can help to enlighten our doubts, solidify our beliefs, comfort us in sorrow, and give us peace. The ministry of angels on our behalf reveals that God loves us and is continually working to help us. What a comfort and joy that knowledge is to us!

One of the messages of *A Divine Revelation of Angels* is that God has angels for every need you have. You may not always see them, but God sends His angels to go before you, stand behind you, walk beside you, and be solid ground underneath your feet.

There are hosts and legions of angels whom He can send to give you strength or any other blessing you may need. Believe what God says in His Word! He cares about you! *"Casting all your care upon Him, for He cares for you"* (1 Peter 5:7).

Another message of this book is that the Word of God and the angels are always in action accomplishing His purposes. God is continually working out His plan of salvation, redemption, and judgment for the world. He wants us to know this and to participate in His purposes with Him. How can we best do this? The biblical examples of the nature and role of angels and the visions and revelations I have shared with you reveal these important truths, among others, for loving and serving God.

THE IMPORTANCE OF WORSHIP

The angels' adoration of God underscores His majesty. Angels are an example to us of how we should reverence and worship God. As all of heaven and the universe echo with the praises of God's angels, let us remember to honor and praise God, too. Heaven gives us this model for our worship:

> *The four living creatures, each having six wings, were full of eyes around and within. And they do not rest day or night, saying: "Holy, holy, holy, Lord God Almighty, who was and is and is to come!" Whenever the living creatures give glory and honor and thanks to Him who sits on the throne, who lives forever and ever, the twenty-four elders fall down before Him who sits on the throne and worship Him who lives forever and ever, and cast their crowns before the throne, saying: "You are worthy, O Lord, to receive glory and honor and power; for You created all things, and by Your will they exist and were created."* (Revelation 4:8–11)

Amen and amen! Blessed be the Lord God Almighty!

THE IMPORTANCE OF BELIEVING

Second, learning about the ministry of angels on our behalf should give us confidence in God's love and power and encourage our hearts that God is with us, no matter what we're going through. Let us remember the words of Psalm 91:14–15:

> *Because he has set his love upon Me, therefore I will deliver him; I will set him on high, because he has known My name. He shall call upon Me, and I will answer him.*

We need to trust God in all things and concentrate on loving and serving Him, for He is worthy of all our trust. Hebrews 11:33–35 encourages us that the saints of Bible times

> ***through faith*** *subdued kingdoms, worked righteousness, obtained promises, stopped the mouths of lions, quenched the violence of fire, escaped the edge of the sword, out of weakness were made strong, became valiant in battle, turned to flight the armies of the aliens. Women received their dead raised to life again. And others were tortured, not accepting deliverance, that they might obtain a better resurrection.*

(emphasis added)

First Peter 1:5 says that we are *"kept by the power of God through faith for salvation ready to be revealed in the last time."* Let us exercise that faith in our daily lives so that we may accomplish all that God wants to do through us in the ministries and gifts He's given us to build up His kingdom.

THE IMPORTANCE OF DISCERNMENT

Today's "angel mania" and the false ideas about angels that are being circulated in both religious and nonreligious circles show us the importance of using discernment when it comes to the use of spiritual gifts and encounters with spiritual beings. We should always remember that the devil is able to transform himself *"into an angel of light"* (2 Corinthians 11:14) in order to deceive us. Therefore, we must fill our hearts and minds with God's Word as we test the spirits.

> *We should no longer be children, tossed to and fro and carried about with every wind of doctrine, by the trickery of men, in the cunning craftiness of deceitful plotting, but, speaking the truth in love, [we should] grow up in all things into Him who is the head; Christ.* (Ephesians 4:14–15)

> *Beloved, do not believe every spirit, but test the spirits, whether they are of God; because many false prophets have gone out into the world. By this you know the Spirit of God: Every spirit that confesses ["acknowledges" NIV] that Jesus Christ has come in the flesh is of God, and every spirit that does not confess ["acknowledge" NIV] that Jesus Christ has come in the flesh is not of God. And this is the spirit of the Antichrist, which you have heard was coming, and is now already in the world.* (1 John 4:1–3)

THE IMPORTANCE OF OBEDIENCE

As I wrote earlier, God wants us to tear down the unclean altars in our lives and make ourselves altars of holiness to Him as we make a new commitment to love and serve Him. This means that we must repent of our sin, come before God in humility, and ask Him to cleanse and restore us through Christ. We must remember that His judgment is going forth in the world. Let us allow Him to discipline us by purging us with His fire and cleansing us by His holy Word.

Once, when I was in prayer, an angel brought me this vision. I saw two huge spiritual faces looking at each other—face-to-face and eye-to-eye. The faces had no bodies; they were just faces. Then, one of the faces kissed the other softly on the lips. I thought of the Word of God: "*Mercy and truth have met together; righteousness and peace have kissed*" (Psalm 85:10). In the book of Psalms, God has much to say about mercy and truth:

> *The* LORD *is good; His mercy is everlasting, and His truth endures to all generations.*   (100:5)

> *But You, O Lord, are a God full of compassion, and gracious, longsuffering and abundant in mercy and truth.*   (86:15)

> *Righteousness and justice are the foundation of Your throne; mercy and truth go before Your face.*   (89:14)

> *All the paths of the* LORD *are mercy and truth, to such as keep His covenant and His testimonies.*   (25:10)

> *God shall send forth His mercy and His truth.*   (57:3)

Then the angel took me back in time, and the Lord showed me another vision that I had seen years ago. God was sitting on His throne. Now, I didn't see God; I just saw the outline of God. I saw the glory of God and the fire of God and the outline of a form sitting on a large throne somewhere in the universe. In each of His hands—His very large hands—was a large rope and a type of round object.

I couldn't see what the ropes were fastened to, but they were in His hands, and He was trying to pull them together. It was as if a tug-of-war was going on between the two. Every time they nearly met, it seemed as if something would struggle against Him and something would pull the opposites apart. Just as He was getting ready to join them together, an invisible force always opposed Him.

Then I saw faces on the ends of the two round objects, and they were the same faces I had seen in the other vision—mercy and truth. I began to understand that, in this symbolic vision, God was trying to get mercy and truth to meet together in our hearts. God desires us to worship Him with integrity. Jesus said,

> But the hour is coming, and now is, when the true worshipers will worship the Father in spirit and truth; for the Father is seeking such to worship Him. God is Spirit, and those who worship Him must worship in spirit and truth.
>
> (John 4:23–24)

God wants our hearts and our minds to be holy and clean. In the vision, the angels seemed to be encouraging me in this truth. Suddenly, this Scripture came to me: "*Love the* LORD *your God with all your heart, with all your soul, with all your strength, and with all your mind*" (Luke 10:27). I thought,

> O Lord, the enemy is planting so much unbelief and doubt in Your body all over the world. It's almost as if, when You get us to join together in the heart, something happens to take away some truth or mercy You've given us. This is why we've got to dig in Your Word and believe Your Word, no matter what we get hit with. No matter what we think in opposition to Your Word, we must go forth and believe Your Word.

Truly, when mercy and truth meet together, how precious and wonderful the Lord is! God is calling you to a special place in Him. As you yield to Him and live a holy life (see 1 Thessalonians 5:23), He will use you mightily—and His angels will go with you continuously!

Once I was praying in preparation for preaching at a service, when I saw many large angels in the sky. They were working diligently at some task. It seemed to me that they were pulling a rope-like vine through a door into heaven.

Doors were open in the sky, and the vine went through one of the doors and up onto a table. Many angels were sitting at the long table examining the vine. If they found bad places in it, they would take a big knife and trim off the contaminated part before it did any further damage. I thought of how God prunes us, and I remembered Jesus' words:

> I am the vine, you are the branches. He who abides in Me, and I in him, bears much fruit; for without Me you can do nothing. If anyone does not abide in Me, he is cast out as a branch and is withered; and they gather them and throw them into the fire, and they are burned. If you abide in Me, and My words abide in you, you will ask what you desire, and it shall be done for you. By this My Father is glorified, that you bear much fruit; so you will be My disciples.   (John 15:5–8)

The vine of the Lord goes all over the earth. Some people are grafted into it, but some are cut off. It is very important for us to love the Lord and keep His commandments as best we can. It is essential that we obey Him, regardless of what He asks us to do.

Be encouraged in the work of God that you are doing. Knowing that angels are around you to assist and bless you will give you encouragement to hear from God. As you are strengthened in the work of God, He will begin to reveal special things to you. Ministers of the gospel must believe that while Jesus is working through His Holy Spirit and through manifestations of power, angels are present to minister in the services and to the servants who really love God and keep His commandments.

Obey Him, and you will see a move of God in the land like you have never seen before. God is looking for a people who will love Him enough to obey Him and trust Him for who He is, and who will believe what the Word says. He is preparing just such a people. It is His will that we walk close to Him. God is getting ready to do some really great and mighty things in our lands. We have much work to do before Jesus comes again.

This is the hour for us to get ready for a move of God like we've never had before. The Lord imparts His gifts to His people. He gives freely and liberally to His own. God's precious gifts are for the holy people of God so that they can train others to do the works of the Lord. I believe that He is preparing all who are open to Him, so that they can teach people and help them to understand how much God loves them.

THE IMPORTANCE OF PERSEVERANCE

God's holy, elect angels persevered in loving and serving Him even when Satan and many other angels rebelled against Him. They are a model for us of everlasting devotion to God and His ways. Let us take their example and persevere in our dedication and loyalty to God and in our work for Him. The Bible assures us that

> God is not unjust to forget your work and labor of love which you have shown toward His name, in that you have ministered to the saints, and do minister. And we desire that each one of you show the same diligence to the full assurance of hope until the end, that you do not become sluggish, but imitate those who through faith and patience inherit the promises.
> (Hebrews 6:10–12)

Remember what happened when Jesus battled Satan in a titanic struggle with temptation in the wilderness. Jesus faced His temptation alone, quoted the truth of the Scripture to the enemy, and defeated Satan. It was *then* that the angels came and ministered to Him.

Likewise, you and I often have to face our temptations without any human help. Many times, we do not have anyone to stand with us in the crucial hour. Yet God's Word lets us know that the Lord never leaves us and that, when the battle is won, we will be ministered to by His angels. What a lesson we can learn from this! We do not go through dark days and trying times in vain. God has deliverance for us, and He will send His angels to strengthen and encourage us. Blessed be our God!

THE IMPORTANCE OF PRAYER

Finally, in chapter 10, we saw the role that angels have in answering our prayers and the importance of our intercession for God's work of salvation and deliverance to go forth. God will deliver many through the prayers of the saints. Paul taught us in Ephesians 6:18 to pray *"always with all prayer and supplication in the Spirit, being watchful to this end with all perseverance and supplication for all the saints."*

Ask the Holy Spirit to guide you in your prayers. Romans 8:26–27 says,

> *The Spirit also helps in our weaknesses. For we do not know what we should pray for as we ought, but the Spirit Himself makes intercession for us with groanings which cannot be uttered. Now He who searches the hearts knows what the mind of the Spirit is, because He makes intercession for the saints according to the will of God.*

Let us seek God's will and ask Him to bring salvation, healing, and deliverance as we intercede for our families, communities, and nations.

THE GOD OF ANGELS AND MEN

Through our study of angels, we have seen that the Lord of Hosts is a mighty God who accomplishes His purposes in heaven and on earth. The verse that strengthens my heart and can strengthen the heart of every true believer is found in Daniel 4:35: *"He does according to His will in the army of heaven and among the inhabitants of the earth. No one can restrain His hand."* He is the God of both angels and men. He is our God! Let our prayer ever be, *"Your kingdom come. Your will be done on earth as it is in heaven"* (Luke 11:2)!

NOTES

FOREWORD

Sir Francis Bacon, *Oxford History of Quotations*, 3rd ed. (Oxford: Oxford University Press, 1980), 27.

CHAPTER 1: ARE ANGELS REAL?

Nancy Gibbs, "Angels Among Us," *Time* (December 27, 1993): 56.

CHAPTER 2: THE TRUTH ABOUT ANGELS

Billy Graham, *Angels: God's Secret Agents* (Nashville: W Publishing Group, 1995), 30.

CHAPTER 3: WHAT ARE ANGELS LIKE?

Dr. David Jeremiah, *What the Bible Says about Angels* (Sisters, Ore.: Multnomah Books, 1996), 116.

Herbert Lockyer, *All the Angels in the Bible* (Peabody, Mass.: Hendrickson Publishers, Inc., 1995), 114.

CHAPTER 6: ANGELS AND PROTECTION

Billy Graham, *Angels: God's Secret Agents* (Nashville: W Publishing Group, 1995), 137–39.

"A Strange Place to Hope" by Corrie ten Boom reprinted with permission from *Guideposts*. Copyright 1972 by *Guideposts*, Carmel, New York 10512. All rights reserved.

CHAPTER 9: ANGELS AND DELIVERANCE

Corrie ten Boom, *Marching Orders for the End Battle* (Fort Washington, Pa.: Christian Literature Crusade, 1969), 112–13.

A DIVINE REVELATION
OF DELIVERANCE

CONTENTS

PREFACE

Jesus never promised that our lives would be void of challenges and trials. Some of our challenges come from God to test our faith and perfect our character. At other times, our trials are a decisive ploy by the enemy to catch us off guard and cause us to stumble from the foundation of God's Word. Often, many of the difficulties we encounter in the natural world are really a manifestation of the clash between the kingdom of God and the kingdom of darkness that is taking place in the invisible spirit realm.

For instance, all too often, members of the body of Christ and society in general suffer in silence as they struggle with habitual acts over which they feel they have no control, unaware of the root cause that drives their behavior. That cause is unseen evil forces from hell, which daily seek to influence our decisions and outlook on life.

Sometimes, when these forces fail to affect our own behavior, they resort to more cunning strategies, such as attacking our family members and others close to us in order to invade the purity of our thoughts and distract us from our calling in Christ. In addition, generational curses may continue in families for decades due to territorial demonic influences that have staked their claims over groups of people.

This is why we must truly understand how to exercise our spiritual authority and power. The only way to stop these toxic cycles is to take authority over them through Christ and fight against them vigilantly through prayer and the Word of God. Regardless of what assaults you face, when you remain steadfast in your faith and use the spiritual knowledge and weapons God has provided for you, you can counteract the enemy's attacks against you and your family. When you are armed with a divine revelation of who you are in Christ Jesus, it becomes increasingly impossible for the forces of evil to prevail against you, even in the midst of turmoil and adversity.

Those who have developed a close relationship with God through Christ are rarely caught off guard by Satan's attacks. By the time an attack manifests, they have already prayed and sought the Lord, and God's angels are standing guard to protect them as their deliverance begins to unfold.

Regardless of the circumstance, Jesus assures us that we hold the power, through His name, to persevere in times of testing and to overcome every attack the devil strategically sets for our demise. It is our desire to equip you with knowledge concerning both Satan's domain and the powerful deliverance of God, through Jesus Christ, which He has made available to all who believe.

INTRODUCTION
BY MARY K. BAXTER

In my first book, *A Divine Revelation of Hell*, I revealed how the Lord showed me life-altering visions of hell and the reality of that hideous place. When Jesus took me on my journey into hell, He said, "The day will come when you can reveal the things that I show you." From that time until the present, I have continued to see visions of God's miraculous power in operation and what is taking place behind the scenes in the spirit realm. I have described a number of these visions in my previous books. God has commissioned me by His power to reveal these visions to the body of Christ. I am also to share these powerful encounters with those who do not know Jesus as Lord and Savior, so that they may receive Him in the excellence of His power.

The ministry of deliverance manifests through a variety of gifts that the Lord has given to the body of Christ. My particular gift is dreams and visions. Visions are God's way of allowing us to take a glimpse into the miraculous world of His omnipotent power. As I have shared my visions and revelations, God has used them to loosen the devil's chains, to cast down demonic strongholds, and to set many people free in salvation and deliverance.

A DIVINE ENCOUNTER

After revealing my dreams and visions in my first book, I began traveling extensively, sharing with others these amazing encounters and encouraging men and women to come to Jesus Christ. It was during these travels that God's divine destiny caused the paths of Bishop George Bloomer and myself to cross. Since that time, we have ministered together on many occasions by the power of God so that thousands have been delivered and set free from years of torment, bondage, and demonic strongholds.

I identify our meeting as a *divine* encounter because God, knowing the gifts of the Spirit He has endowed within us both, saw fit to bring together our gifts in ministry. For years, Bishop Bloomer has been noted for his boldness in delivering the Word of God without hesitation. As we minister together, the power of the ministry of binding and loosing in Jesus' name is shown to be a powerful reality. (See Matthew 16:19; 18:18.)

REVELATIONS FOR TODAY

People's urgent need for deliverance and for a clearer understanding of God's power is what led us to expose more of Satan's tactics and deeds of darkness in this book. *A Divine Revelation of Deliverance* will reveal a number of real-life encounters and visions—some from years ago, some more recent—that the Lord has released me to share now with people throughout the world. We explain the reality of the gates of hell upon the earth (see Matthew 16:18 KJV), which are avenues of demonic attack, and which are also used to transport lost souls to an eternity without God. Most importantly, we share how to overcome demonic attacks through our Deliverer, the Lord Jesus Christ. Our prayer is that many more who are oppressed by the enemy will experience spiritual freedom.

RECOGNIZING SATAN'S DEVICES

Many of the hardships you are experiencing may have been inflicted upon you by the enemy, who seeks to destroy your confession of faith. The revelations that I received from God will help you to become aware of the devices of Satan. With this knowledge, you can properly invoke the power of Jesus Christ to overcome the invisible or hidden traps that have kept you bound.

These traps come by way of Satan's demonic forces. Each demon has been assigned certain duties to fulfill on the face of the earth to promote the ungodly and tragic reign of the *"ruler of this world"* (see John 12:30; 14:30; 16:11)—the devil's kingdom on earth. We are not powerless against these attacks, but we must realize their presence in order to destroy their existence.

God has given us the free will to make our own decisions. Yet the devil seeks to use our minds, wills, emotions, and bodies against us for his own tainted glory. Your choices do not have to be steered by the manipulative influences of Satan's domain. Regardless of how you may struggle with fear, rage, lust, addictions, or pain, your will to call upon the name of the Lord still remains. He will give you an answer if you will wait upon Him, continue seeking Him diligently in prayer, rely on His Spirit, and take action according to His Word.

Jesus promised that the gates of hell would not prevail over the church—over those who know God and have received Him as personal Lord and Savior. *"On this rock I will build My church, and the gates of Hades [hell] shall not prevail against it"* (Matthew 16:18). I have prayed against demonic strongholds, and I have witnessed, right before my very eyes, the miraculous hand of God to set people free. I have seen people healed of physical ailments and delivered from demonic possession and oppression.

EXPOSING SATAN AND THE SINFUL NATURE

With all the authority and power God has made available to the body of Christ, there is no need for a believer to suffer from anything that is not according to God's will. This is why Bishop Bloomer and I thought it not only timely, but also imperative, to expose the lies that keep so many bound, while also uncovering God-ordained ways of escape from Satan's designs and the sinful nature.

God has given you the power to speak the Word of God against demonic forces, and they have no choice but to flee. (See James 4:7.) *"The Lord knows those who are His"* (2 Timothy 2:19). He has made a covenant with all who call upon the name of Jesus. Through this covenant, we have the authority to rebuke the enemy when we are attacked by his ungodly influences, and to be set free when we are taken captive by his schemes. God has also given us the resurrection power of Jesus to overcome our sinful nature, which wages war against the nature and Spirit of God within us.

Our prayer is that you will discover your doorway to deliverance and that the chains of darkness, which have been keeping you bound, will be loosed. As the enemy's hidden hindrances are revealed, and as the workings of the sinful nature are exposed, may you learn to walk in the freedom and liberty God has ordained for your life.

INTRODUCTION
BY GEORGE G. BLOOMER

For years I have preached a message of deliverance, revealing to those who are oppressed their right to live in freedom by the power of God. I have slept in the jungles of Africa, preached in the bush of the Philippines, ministered in India, and seen Muslims and Hindus give their lives to Christ. I have been on rescue trips with the Red Cross and have seen things that could torment you for the rest of your life. I have seen unexplainable phenomena in Haiti, such as levitations and the dead walking in the marketplace three days after their funerals. I have seen faces become contorted and heard several voices come out of one person's mouth while his tongue was not even moving.

Now I realize that all my studying, all my travel, and all those horrific things I saw and experienced were for such a time as this. They have enabled me to contribute to the writing of this book, which explains to you how the power of God delivers those who are bound by Satan. As you read *A Divine Revelation of Deliverance*, you can discover how to be set free from the bondages and strongholds the enemy has been holding over you.

TAKING A SPIRITUAL STAND

Today, more than ever, there is an urgent need within the body of Christ for the people of God to remain cognizant of their ability to have dominion over the things which have kept them bound. No longer can we sit idly by as observers. We must now take a spiritual stand against the havoc that is fighting against God's people.

God commanded mankind to have dominion over everything on the face of the earth. (See Genesis 1:26–28.) He also gave believers authority over Satan, in Jesus' name. (See, for example, Luke 9:1.) In order to activate your rights as a child of God, however, you must understand and apply them through His Word. If you do not know your authority, you will not be able to invoke it when faced with life's adversities and trials.

It is my responsibility as a spiritual leader in the body of Christ to reveal the truth concerning both the insidious deception of the demonic realm and the magnificent truth of God's deliverance. Yet choosing deliverance remains a decision only you can make. You no longer have to tolerate ungodly influences in your life; rather, you can learn to take dominion over the evil forces that have been attempting to overpower you!

A REVELATION OF GATES AND KEYS

This message of dominion is vividly presented in an exchange between the Lord Jesus and His disciple Peter. Peter answered the question that Jesus posed to His disciples, *"Who do men say that I, the Son of Man, am?"* by responding, *"You are the Christ, the Son of the living God"* (Matthew 16:13, 16). Jesus told him this fact could only have been revealed to him by the Father. He then equipped Peter with a truth that would forever secure his spiritual stand in glory:

> *And I also say to you that you are Peter, and on this rock I will build My church, and the **gates of Hades** ["hell" kjv]*

*shall not prevail against it. And I will give you **the keys of
the kingdom of heaven**, and whatever you bind on earth will
be bound in heaven, and whatever you loose on earth will be
loosed in heaven.*   (Matthew 16:18–19, emphasis added)

Peter received a divine revelation that there are gates of hell,
and that Jesus would give him keys—concepts, ideas, authority,
insight, foresight, and the power to bind and loose—for overcoming them. The implication here is that hell does not start in the
abyss, but that there could possibly be gates, or portals, of hell
upon the earth. Moreover, whatever we bind on earth and whatever we loose on earth is bound and loosed in heaven. What is
done on the earth can directly affect the heavenly realm.

Perhaps you are thinking, *So, you're telling me, Bishop, that
you believe that hell's gates are on earth?* Yes, I do. I believe this in
two ways. Not only are there actual invisible gates of hell on the
earth that transport lost souls to hell, but there are also sensory
"gates" in our lives that the devil uses in his schemes against us.
In other words, he uses our senses—sight, hearing, touch, smell,
and taste—to tempt our sinful natures and manipulate our minds
by redirecting our desires and decisions away from God's will.
When we give in to temptation and allow Satan to manipulate
our minds, we may become involved in sinful and destructive prac-
tices, including sexual immorality, greed, pride, rage, addictions,
and the occult.

Because of the attacks of the enemy, and the sinful nature that
wars against the Spirit of God within us, the Scriptures tell us how
we should think and what we should be thinking about:

Let this mind be in you which was also in Christ Jesus.
                                        (Philippians 2:5)

*Finally, brethren, whatever things are true, whatever things
are noble, whatever things are just, whatever things are pure,*

> *whatever things are lovely, whatever things are of good report,*
> *if there is any virtue and if there is anything praiseworthy;*
> *meditate on these things.* (Philippians 4:8)

AUTHORITY OVER THE POWER OF THE ENEMY

Jesus understands our temptations as human beings, for He was tempted when He was on earth, though He never sinned. *"For we do not have a High Priest who cannot sympathize with our weaknesses, but was in all points tempted as we are, yet without sin"* (Hebrews 4:15). Jesus also knows what it is like to experience the direct attack of the enemy, and to overcome him. (See, for example, Matthew 4:1–11; Luke 22:39–42.)

Whether the devil uses our sinful nature against us through temptation or attacks us directly, we need to hold fast continually to the profession of our faith. When we do this, the strength and power of Jesus will save and deliver us from *all* the power of the enemy. Jesus said,

> *I saw Satan fall like lightning from heaven. Behold, I give you the authority to trample on serpents and scorpions, and* **over all the power of the enemy,** *and nothing shall by any means hurt you. Nevertheless do not rejoice in this, that the spirits are subject to you, but rather rejoice because your names are written in heaven.* (Luke 10:18–20, emphasis added)

1

ATTACKED BY THE GATES OF HELL

AN INCREASE IN DEMONIC ACTIVITY

It was the mid-1970s when Jesus first revealed to me the horrors of hell, the tactics Satan uses in his attempts to destroy humanity, and how people need to be delivered from these attacks. Jesus warned me that Satan's assaults on the earth would increase as he released more demons from hell to cause rebellion and destruction.

Today, we are seeing the effects of these increased attacks on our world. There is more sin, and there have been more disasters, than ever before. We have had hurricanes, floods, tsunamis, and wars. (See Matthew 24:6–8.) Many people are facing intense spiritual attacks in their own lives and in the lives of their family members.

FOR SUCH A TIME AS THIS

I recently read over some of the prophecies that I have been writing down over the years, and I was in awe when I realized that many of these prophecies had come to pass without my even realizing it. I thought of how, in the 1980s, the Spirit of the Lord began to lead and guide me into all truth. (See John 16:13.) As I reflected, I sought God diligently, and I began to understand the purpose of my recording all the notes I had written throughout the years. God was preparing me then for what I am doing today. He was preparing me to share divine revelations with people and to assure them that they hold the power, through Christ Jesus, to stand tall and overcome the persistent obstacles that are holding them back in life. God wants us to put mere "religious" thinking under our feet and instead to build a secure relationship with Christ Jesus based on faith and trust in God—a relationship that will enable us to overcome all the assaults of the enemy.

With this book, I begin a journey of revealing some things I have not divulged in any of my other writings. It is by faith that I am able to share these visions God has shown to me. These are facts and truths that have been held back until such a time as this because the world could not receive them many years ago. I want to share with you from my heart what God has so graciously shared with me. It's very important to understand the hour in which we are living so that the will of God can be manifested in our lives.

POWER OVER HELL'S GATES

Two weeks before Christmas 2006, the Lord told me He wanted me to go on a fast, explaining that it would be very profitable for me. I was home alone and had time to pray, study and mediate on the Word, and seek the Lord. This opportunity excited me because I love God's Word. I believed that God would do what He said He was going to do during this time. (See Psalm 1:1–3.)

Sometimes, when you are in the midst of spiritual warfare through fasting and prayer, you pray continuously. You get little sleep, and you are totally on your face before the Lord. You are travailing because God wants the Holy Spirit to move through you. You yield yourself to God completely, saying, "Here I am, God.

Use me." As you submit yourself to Him through prayer, the Lord exposes revelation to you that can only be made known through the spirit realm.

A few days before Christmas, therefore, as I was really praying and seeking the Lord, I found myself being caught up in a vision. I saw the earth, and on it was a giant hole. I knew this was a gate of hell—which I will explain to you in more detail shortly—because God had been training me in the area of spiritual warfare. Out of this hole came hundreds of huge figures that were about twelve feet tall and looked like transparent penguins. As I was praying to the Lord, He said, "Call upon Me in the day of trouble, and I will deliver you." I began to say, "God, in the name of Jesus, I don't understand this, but I will call upon You to deliver us from whatever these things are."

I saw the hand of God come down, and I noticed the enormity of its size—it was about half as large as the earth. Out of His fingers came streams of fire. The flames shot into the large hole where these hideous, penguin-like figures were coming out at the surface of the earth, and cremated them. We read in Malachi,

> "You shall trample the wicked, for they shall be ashes under the soles of your feet on the day that I do this," says the LORD of hosts.　　　　　　　　　　　　　　　　　(Malachi 4:3)

The ashes of these figures began to blow away in the wind, and the Lord said, "I am destroying these evil powers." I watched as He burned millions of them. I concluded that this was God stopping some kind of attack of the enemy on us in regard to outbreaks of disease and other demonic activities. This is not to say that these figures always symbolize sickness, but that is what I discerned from this particular vision.

Later that day, I received a phone call from a prophet. As I began sharing with her what I had seen in the vision, she informed me that there had been a warning about bird flu. I began to praise the Lord for His deliverance because I knew that God had answered my request and given me my heart's desire. I have learned to obey God and to shut a gate of hell whenever He reveals it to me in a vision.

As I continued praying, I asked the Lord to bind this gate. I saw the earth shake, and I witnessed the hand of the Lord place a large cover, which looked as if it was made of iron, on the hole. Then I saw large angels swoop down with keys and chains and lock that gateway to hell. I began rejoicing in the Lord, saying, "Thank You, Jesus! You love us so much. Honor and majesty belong unto You, Lord. I put my trust in You!"

JESUS IS OUR DELIVERER

This incident illustrates just one of Satan's attacks against humanity in the last days. The gates of hell are assailing us, but Jesus can deliver you and your loved ones. We must know what we are battling and who is our Deliverer, so that we can fight effectively against these forces of evil. Many people on earth are being deceived and may fall into the schemes of Satan, or the devil, if we do not tell them of salvation and deliverance through Christ. We must return to the truth of Christ's death for us on the cross and our need for redemption through His sacrifice.

Satan desires to destroy every person on earth in whatever way he can. Yet the mercy of the Most High God has provided deliverance for you and me from the spiritual forces that attack us. Although we live in a day of great trouble and spiritual deception, we also have a great Deliverer, who has promised, *"Call upon Me in the day of trouble; I will deliver you, and you shall glorify Me"* (Psalm 50:15).

The devil uses a variety of schemes and methods to keep people from coming to know and love God, and to prevent those who do know and love Him from living productively for Him. He may attack us directly, or he may try to provoke our sinful human nature to do the work for him. I am very concerned because I see people falling into the enemy's traps, out of ignorance, and failing to find salvation through Christ. I also see Christians becoming discouraged, losing hope, and forsaking their faith because of the tests, temptations, and trials they experience. This alarms me because I have seen the cruel hatred the enemy has for humanity, and I have seen the fate of those who die without the Lord. I therefore urge you to learn and apply the deliverance God has provided for you. Jesus said,

> I am He who lives, and was dead, and behold, I am alive forevermore. Amen. And I have the keys of Hades and of Death.   (Revelation 1:18)

Everything I am sharing with the body of Christ and with people at large through this book concerning the gates of hell is what God wants revealed to the world. Now is the time for these truths to be exposed to both Christians and non-Christians, to anyone who can grasp them and understand their significance.

A MESSAGE OF DELIVERANCE

God has a message of deliverance for us, and He has called me to give this message to the world. During my travels, I was once in a foreign country to preach the gospel and an invitation came for me to have dinner with the wife of the president of that nation. I had set up a booking weeks prior to my arrival for another place about two hours away to preach a message on hell. After receiving this dinner invitation, however, I had to make a decision: either cancel my previously scheduled engagement or forgo the dinner invitation from the president's wife and send her a copy of the book instead. I decided to send the first lady an autographed copy of my book and continue with the previously scheduled engagement.

I went and preached to the people with love, and several souls were saved. I then returned to my room to retire for the night. Where I was staying, everyone always locked their doors, and dogs were let out at night to protect the property and people's belongings due to the high rate of theft in the area. They had dogs that guarded everything. I was really troubled because I had heard rumors approximately two weeks prior to my arrival about people carrying bombs into the city. About midnight, I heard guns going off and I thought, *Oh, my God! War has broken out! I'm going to die over here where nobody knows me, and without my family.* "Lord, You have to help me!" I pleaded.

As I continued praying, I had peace in my heart that surpassed all human understanding. (See Philippians 4:6–7.) I could hear thousands of guns going off and still did not have a clue as to what was taking place. The dogs were out and were barking. I thought that if I stepped outside, they would bite me, so I remained shut up within the safety of my quarters. As I sat huddled inside my room, I kept thinking about all the rumors that had been brewing—that war was about to break out and bombs were going to go off—so I prepared to die. I placed towels over the windows so that no one could see inside. I turned off all the lights, and when I peeked out the window I could see the flashes of guns being fired in the dark of the night. As I sat there and said my prayers, I looked at the clock, and it was close to one in the morning. *At any minute, they're going to break in and kill me,* I kept thinking. Then, I had peace in my heart.

All at once, in one corner of the room, a bright light appeared on the wall. It circled around and then stopped. *They shot a missile in here!* I thought.

The more frightened I became, the more the light seemed to burst into a big flame, and then I saw what looked like a bush on fire. I realized, *This is what Moses saw—the burning bush!*

This bush was about five feet high and full of flames. I went over to it, put my hand in the fire, and felt a leaf. It looked like an oak leaf, and it was approximately half an inch thick of solid gold. I thought, *How beautiful.* I was in such shock that I forgot about the guns while looking at this tree. I began to worship and praise the Lord. Looking down at my feet, I said, "God, I've got my shoes off. You told Moses to take his shoes off because he was on holy ground, and Lord, I'm right here to listen to You." (See Exodus 3:2–5.)

I continued looking at this bush and telling God all my problems. All at once, everything became very quiet, and suddenly power came from the tree straight at me, and I fell backward. I remember crawling and forcing myself up so I could get into the bed. I looked back at the bush and prayed in my heart, *Dear God, what can I do for You?* I got back out of bed, pushed myself against this force, and stood in front of the bush again and tried to talk to God with all my heart, mind, and voice. The effect of this whole experience scared me so badly that I jumped into bed, pulled the covers over my head, and fainted!

The next morning, the birds were chirping, the dogs were still barking, the guns were still going off, and I realized, *I'm still alive.* I heard the men come to get the dogs and lock them up. Jumping out of bed, I screamed, "What is going on...and why all the guns? Has war broken out?"

A gentleman burst into laughter.

"Why are you laughing?" I asked.

"It's Mother's Day," he explained, "and here in this country we shoot the guns from midnight until noon to celebrate the mothers for the birth of the children."

I thought, *Why didn't someone tell me!*

As the people tried to comfort me, the guns were still going off, and I remained very upset. A few minutes later, I heard a truck pull up out front, and the person who had been my interpreter came in and said that she had a message for me from the Lord. "As I was doing my dishes, the Lord spoke to me," she began to share. "He told me to give you a message, and here it is. He told me to first ask you, 'Did He appear to you last night?'"

I was still so scared that I answered, "Maybe...sort of...kind of...yes, He did."

Then she said, "You fainted, right?"

"Yes...I did."

"The message is this: God has given unto you the keys to the kingdom, and as He was with Moses, He shall be with you. You are His deliverer in this hour to deliver people from the devil's hand, as Moses delivered the people of his day from the hands of Pharaoh. You are His deliverer, and you are to take these messages all over the earth to set the people free from the devil's hand. You are to do what the Lord has called you to do and to fear no man. He wants you to be encouraged and go tell these stories in other lands and countries."

Although my concern about the guns had been a misunderstanding, God used this circumstance to give me guidance about my life and ministry. He showed me that He would be with me and that I was not to be afraid of what others might say or do. I began to cry and praise the Lord. I thanked the interpreter for the message, and she was so glad that she had obeyed the voice of the Lord and told me these things. I continued to praise God and to hang on to His promise.

I have experienced many things, such as this one, that I have never before told anyone. Yet now is the time for me to share even more of my miraculous and supernatural experiences. I tell these stories in obedience and according to the leading of the Holy Spirit. We must truly know that God is more than able to deliver, according to His Word.

AN ARMY STRONG AND UNAFRAID

We are living in a time when many more demons have come out of the gates of hell and into the earth's atmosphere to cause widespread deception. Yet, in the midst of it all, God has an army of His people that is fighting for the truth—an army that is standing tall and preaching holiness and righteousness to rescue individuals and families.

With this book, I hope to add to this army of believers that is not afraid of the devil but understands Satan is fighting a losing battle. Jesus holds the keys to death and hell. He knows every trick the devil tries to use for our demise, and He gives us instructions on how to counteract these evil attacks. As we learn Satan's tactics, we must always remember that Jesus has the power to overcome anything that may come against us and anything that we may face, and that we can have complete victory over the enemy.

There are great tribulations in the earth, but God Almighty wants to lock the gates of hell, and He wants you to join in the battle against the enemy.

2

DEMONIC DECEPTION

In this chapter, I will describe in more detail some of the assaults that are coming against us in our nation and around the world, as well as the depth of the deception and torment Satan seeks to inflict upon us. We will see how much we need our Deliverer, who gives us the authority to overcome all the power of the enemy.

THE WORLD IS BEING DECEIVED

DESENSITIZED TO THE DANGERS OF THE DEMONIC

There are three main ways in which the enemy is deceiving the world today. First, among people who are seeking a "higher power" for answers to life's crises, there is a growing curiosity about mysticism, Eastern religions, and the occult. Through these avenues, many are unknowingly being lured into the demonic realm of Satan's domain. Television and other media have romanticized magic and the demonic to the point that it is no longer considered taboo for a person to dabble in the world of the occult; it has become a fad. People do not realize these things are detrimental to their spiritual well-being. Society has become desensitized to the dangers of embracing the demonic realm, and people are increasingly opening their homes and hearts to satanic and ungodly influences.

The devil takes advantage of any opportunity that presents itself to inject false doctrines into the minds of those who are in spiritual pursuit of a higher power and peace. This is how people often wind up in cults and occult worship, for example, or engulfed in demoralizing behavior. Many of their relatives and friends are bewildered about how their loved ones could ever have become deceived by such obvious religious fallacies. The person being deceived has no idea that what he or she considers spiritual "completion" is actually a ploy from the devil to promote false doctrine and spiritual deception in his or her life, leading to destruction.

The apostle Paul warned against the dangers of worshipping false gods or anything that exalts itself above the knowledge of the true and living God. (See 2 Corinthians 10:4–5.) Yet the worship of false gods and idols continues to run rampant in our world. Those who know God and His Son Jesus Christ must take a stand against the manipulation of the true gospel of salvation through Christ. False gospels are luring people away from God instead of bringing them into His presence.

We must take the initiative to help people understand what is happening to them as they are influenced by the unseen forces of evil principalities and powers that seek to destroy them. We must proclaim the liberty they can have in the Lord Jesus Christ. If we don't, not only will they remain captives of the enemy on this earth, but they will also experience a horrible hell in eternity. We must warn people of God's judgment before it is too late.

We cannot take lightly the significance of what Jesus accomplished on the cross in order to save the world from this destruction. The gospel of the Lord Jesus Christ must be proclaimed in order to set people free.

LACKING A REVERENCE FOR GOD

Second, multitudes of people are dying and going to hell because they have no reverence for God or don't acknowledge His existence. More and more, the devil is attempting to portray God as a fictional character rather than allowing people to see Him for who He really is—the Creator and Sustainer of our lives. The Scriptures tell us, *"For in* [God] *we live and move and have our being"* (Acts 17:28). At the same time, Satan is trying to hide the reality of hell so that it appears as science fiction concocted in the imagination of creative storytellers, rather than the hideous place it truly is.

I really believe that if people had a reverence for God, they would become much more cognizant of their actions and realize the priceless gift of eternal life offered through Jesus Christ. No longer would they continue to bow to the beckoning of demonic voices.

CONFUSED AND LIVING IN IMMORALITY

Third, Satan is camouflaging and watering down the gospel of Jesus Christ in order to seduce people through sensuality and addictions. The youth of our day have especially seen much corruption. Their minds have been so polluted by ungodliness disguised as morality that they find it difficult to discern God's truth from deception. The devil preys upon their vulnerabilities, luring them into a world of idolatry and deceit that undermines their spiritual well-being and can lead to complete self-destruction. He manipulates youthful naiveté to promote his false doctrine through peer pressure and by romanticizing toxic behavior. More and more, the depraved content of many television programs reveals the work of demons that have been released to influence those who have lost their fear of God. Nothing seems off-limits, and people are more prone to act upon whatever lust or perversion appeases the fleshly nature.

This cultural attitude has opened our homes to moral turpitude beyond comprehension, with wickedness being viewed as a normal lifestyle rather than as a pathway to degradation and destruction. For example, a young Christian man met a beautiful girl in college. As the relationship began to flourish, she asked him, "Will you come to my home and meet my parents?" He agreed to do so, but when he arrived at her home, he became very dismayed. He saw two women, and inquired of his companion, "Where is your father?" to which she replied, "This woman is my father, and my mother's husband." The young man was so upset that he went home and wept before the Lord, "What can I do, God? What can I say to help people?"

The challenges that our youth face today are even more demanding and overt than those of previous generations; these challenges cling to them like a glove, and they need the freedom that can only come through Christ.

GATEWAYS OR PORTALS TO HELL

We must truly understand the underlying demonic causes that are behind many of the personal and societal troubles we are currently facing. At the same time, we must be assured that there is complete victory in Jesus Christ. In some of my previous books, I have described how Christ appeared to me and showed me, through visions and revelations, the depths of hell and the peace and joy of heaven. He took me on a journey for three hours each night for thirty nights to the very bowels of the earth to show me the judgment of His Father upon rebellion and sin.

He also showed me visions of the "gateways to hell," which are the sources of many of our demonic attacks today. These experiences were so incredibly real that I could reach out and touch the images as He revealed them to me. He led me to what first appeared to be a whirlwind of powders mixed with different lights and colors of brown and white. Upon further investigation, however, I noticed that this tornado-like image was not moving. It was still, and it was hooked onto the earth. There were several of these circular figures; some of them were transparent, while the others were opaque, and they swung back and forth very slowly. These gates of hell came out of the earth and extended high into the galaxy.

Jesus explained, "These are the gates of hell. I'm going to take you down one of these gates and into hell." As we descended into this gate, Christ reminded me that in His hand was a ring of keys. The keys were the keys of death and hell that He took from the devil. In Revelation 1:17–18, Jesus said, "*I am the First and the Last. I am He who lives, and was dead, and behold, I am alive forevermore. Amen. And I have the keys of Hades and of Death.*" We do not have to fear Satan because Jesus has already gained the victory over him.

Around the inside of this gate of hell, which looked like a tunnel, there was a transparent gray mesh. Behind the mesh were many demons or devils. Some of them were clinging to the wall, while others were climbing about and screaming at me. Doors were at the top of the tunnel.

Among the demons I encountered in this gate, some were about twelve feet tall and appeared as silhouettes of cockroach-like figures. There were also demonic figures in the form of enormous spiders that crawled around and looked extraordinarily sinister. Other creatures had faces that were about two feet wide, with very long, pointed noses, and fangs; they had tails with a fork at the end, and wings that allowed them to fly. They had hooves, with sharp, razor-like claws that could tear you to shreds. Worms crawled about in their wings, and they were some of the most gruesomely demonic figures I have ever seen. In this gate of hell there was also a horrendous odor of demonic sulfur mixed with the smell of mud and the worst odor of burning flesh.

As we went down this gateway, Christ told me the day would come when all these evil beings would be released upon the earth to do the devil's bidding. It has been a long time since Jesus showed me hell, but as I wrote earlier, in the past few years, more sin has abounded. These hideous spirits have now come out of hell and attacked the masses.

THE REALITY OF HELL

The reality of Satan, demons, and hell is written about in the Scriptures. Jesus said there is an *"everlasting fire prepared for the devil and his angels"* (Matthew 25:41). Hell was prepared for the devil and the angels who followed him in his rebellion against God. Yet, since Satan also enticed human beings to rebel and follow him, people who do not love and serve God—who continue to be self-indulgent, following their own ways and rejecting God's commandments and forgiveness through Christ—will end up there, too. (See Matthew 25:14–46.)

The Scriptures refer to following our own way, rather than God's, as doing the *"works of the flesh."*

> *Now the works of the flesh are evident, which are: adultery, fornication, uncleanness, lewdness, idolatry, sorcery, hatred, contentions, jealousies, outbursts of wrath, selfish ambitions, dissensions, heresies, envy, murders, drunkenness, revelries, and the like; of which I tell you beforehand, just as I also told you in time past, that those who practice such things will not inherit the kingdom of God.* (Galatians 5:19–21)

Again, hell was not made for people, especially God's people. (Please be assured that babies do not go to hell, nor do young children. Jesus is merciful, and God continues to protect the innocent.) Yet because of humanity's rebellion and sin against the Creator, hell has enlarged itself and made room to hold people's souls. (See Isaiah 5:11–15.) Many who mocked the Lord Jesus Christ instead of embracing Him while they were alive on the earth now reside in hell. Others are there who committed hideous offenses and never repented.

Jesus made these statements, among others, about the reality of hell:

> *Do not fear those who kill the body but cannot kill the soul. But rather fear Him who is able to destroy both soul and body in hell.*   (Matthew 10:28)

> *And you, Capernaum, who are exalted to heaven, will be brought down to Hades; for if the mighty works which were done in you had been done in Sodom, it would have remained until this day. But I say to you that it shall be more tolerable for the land of Sodom in the day of judgment than for you.*
>   (Matthew 11:23–24)

Hell's reality is inexplicable. When I witnessed it in my visions, all I could feel was fear and death all around me. Thank God that Jesus was with me and consoled me to "fear not." He reminded me that I would share these visions with people throughout the world, and because of it, many souls would be saved.

THE COST OF REJECTING JESUS

NO MORE OPPORTUNITIES TO REPENT

I have spoken to others who have encountered gateways to hell, and I remember their descriptions of how it felt as they descended into the tunnel. They actually felt as if the evil spirits were trying to reach out and grab them. These same spirits would boldly articulate threats, such as "We've got you now," "It's too late," "We deceived you," "You could've had Jesus!"

When you reject Jesus, you invite into your life the toxicity of ungodliness and a future of torment. It's the most hideous thing to walk among the dead in hell. The souls there are very cognizant of the fact that life is continuing on the earth and that they had every chance to repent before they were doomed to this awful, eternal place. I can still remember the screams of the dead echoing in the darkness, along with their cries of repentance—their regret and the realization that they were burning in hell. My heart broke for them, and I cried out, "Lord, how can I help them? What can I tell them?" I thought of the people's ignorance concerning the judgment of God, and I began to think clearly of this journey through hell and of the need to be very specific and precise in what God was showing me so that I could better relay this truth to the world.

PUNISHMENT OF FIRE

When people on the earth have rejected the gospel and die without Jesus, demons seize them, put a chain around them, and drag them down a gateway into hell. There, they are thrown off a cliff into a valley of fire and are held in a holding place. Many souls are thrown into this valley of fire before being thrust into their places of judgment within the different compartments of hell.

The compartments of hell have varying degrees of fire—some hotter than others. Each compartment represents certain laws of God that have been broken. If you are a murderer, you are placed in a compartment with all the murderers; if you are a liar, you are put with all the liars, and so forth. The souls in these compartments had served their fleshly nature rather than God, and had not chosen to repent.

FEAR AND LOSS

As I traveled with Jesus down the gateway to hell, fear came upon me, and I felt as if everything within me and everything precious to me had departed—my love, my home, my family. It was the most horrible feeling you can ever imagine.

THE NEED FOR HOLINESS

As we progressed down the gateway, great snakes, large rats, and many evil spirits ran from the presence of the Lord. When we entered one place, the snakes hissed at us, and the rats squeaked; they made evil sounds. Large vipers and dark shadows were all about us. Jesus was the only light, and I stayed close to Him. Imps and devils were all along the side of this tunnel. I knew these evil beings had the ability to become invisible to the natural eye because I had seen them going upon the earth to do Satan's bidding. Feeling my fear of this dark, dirty place, Jesus said, "Fear not. We will be at the end of this soon. I must show you many things. Come, follow Me."

Snakes slid past us, and dirty smells were everywhere. The snakes there were very fat and round—about four feet around and twenty-five feet long. I saw black muck, and it seemed to billow up and down. An odor of dung was in the air and evil spirits were everywhere. Fear filled the air, and I knew there was still much ahead that I had to see, but Jesus gave me peace. He told me, "We'll soon be at the center of hell."

The center of hell appeared to be more than fifteen miles high, and the belly of hell looked approximately three miles in circumference. I remembered Jesus' words—that He was showing me all these things to tell the world that they are real.

There is a section in hell for the souls who have done great wickedness against the Lord and His people. Sorcerers, evil women and men who would not repent, are in jail cells. Evil and sin are their gods. I heard the Lord say to me, "Be ye holy, for I am holy. Do good and repent in My name. I am the Door. If you are faithful and true, come and follow Me." (See 1 Peter 1:16; John 10:7–9; Matthew 19:21.) I made up my mind to walk clean before the Lord. I knew that even if I failed, He would be right there to pick me up if I repented, because I belonged to Him.

DEMONIC FORCES RELEASED FROM HELL

While hell is a place of punishment for those who reject God, it is also a place from which evil spirits come to attack us. When Jesus took me into hell, He explained that, at certain times, Satan gives orders, and demonic spirits are released into the atmosphere to go into the earth and other places. Today, many gates of hell emerge from the middle of the earth. Demonic powers are sent upon the earth to do bidding for the devil.

These things, you can be assured, are very real. We are fighting spiritual battles, just as we read about in the book of Daniel. (See Daniel 10.) I remember so well seeing the warfare that takes place in the heavenly realm against seducing spirits that come against us. I pleaded, "Oh, God, please help us not to fall into the hands of these seducing powers and into these evil ways." It broke my heart to see this evil leader sending demonic forces upon the earth to spread his deception.

ENGAGED IN A FIERCE SPIRITUAL WAR

Although demonic power is hideous and strong, Jesus is stronger, and He is our Deliverer. Jesus told me that the gates of hell will *not* prevail against the church. (See Matthew 16:18.) That is why it is so important that I relay this message of deliverance to everyone. We must learn to trust Jesus fully as Deliverer and to bind demonic forces while loosing the blessings of God in the name of Jesus.

We are engaged in a spiritual battle that must be fought with the supernatural armament of God, through His power. God alone can give us victory over Satan, the *"prince of the power of the air"* (Ephesians 2:2), and the rulers of demon darkness and spiritual wickedness in the heavenly places. Ephesians 6:11–12 admonishes us,

Put on the whole armor of God, that you may be able to stand against the wiles of the devil. For we do not wrestle against flesh and blood, but against principalities, against powers, against the rulers of the darkness of this age, against spiritual hosts of wickedness in the heavenly places.

We are to engage in spiritual warfare not only for our own sakes, but also for the sake of multitudes of people who are being ensnared by the devil. In Matthew 18:21, Peter asked how many times he should forgive the offense of his brother, and Jesus replied, *"I do not say to you, up to seven times, but up to seventy times seven"* (v. 22). Forgiveness is the nature of God. He is a God of mercy and grace. He admonishes us to offer the same love to others as He bestows upon us. We must restore those who have fallen away from God and bring into His kingdom those who do not yet know Him. We must help to free people from the attacks and control of Satan.

It bothers me greatly to think of the many people who are going to hell because they do not have a healthy fear of God and are not saved. As we have seen, people today openly invite hell into their lives by embracing ungodly, demonic behavior. The demons oppress or possess them and use them as vessels to carry out their evil acts. When I was with Jesus in hell, I thought, *These gates of hell need to be bound shut because the enemy is spewing all kinds of evil forces into the earth, such as pornography and the destruction of marriages, homes, and children.*

I wrote this book as a tool to expose the deeds of darkness, reveal their origin, and give those who are bound the hope of knowing they can be set free by the power of God. Hideous things come out of hell when Satan gives orders for them to go upon the earth. Evil spirits are walking about, seeking whom they may devour (see 1 Peter 5:8), and people are yielding themselves to these ungodly powers. Yet God is warning people to stop the evil they are doing and to turn to the Lord Jesus Christ before it is too late.

You may use whatever philosophy you like to tone down the reality and danger of ungodly acts, but the truth remains the same. We must take hold of reality, giving no more loyalty to groups of people who want to make excuses for living a life of demoralization and ungodliness. In the Bible, the Lord rained down fire on Sodom and Gomorrah because of their utter rejection of His ways, and the Scriptures tell us that a final judgment day will come upon all people of the earth. (See, for example, 1 Peter 4:5; Revelation 20:11–15.) Jesus promised, "*The sign of the Son of Man will appear in the sky, and all the nations of the earth will mourn. They will see the Son of Man coming on the clouds of the sky, with power and great glory*" (Matthew 24:30). We have to watch for Jesus, believing that He's coming back and will judge the world. "*The Lord Jesus Christ…will judge the living and the dead at His appearing and His kingdom*" (2 Timothy 4:1).

DESTRUCTIVE DOCTRINES OF DEMONS

Make no mistake about it: We are in a war of good versus evil. This is a crucial war for multitudes of souls. We are battling doctrines of demons that have come into our land to deceive the people.

> *Now the Spirit expressly says that in latter times some will depart from the faith, giving heed to deceiving spirits and doctrines of demons, speaking lies in hypocrisy, having their own conscience seared with a hot iron.*   (1 Timothy 4:1–2)

These doctrines teach lies and hypocrisy. They tell us not to believe the Word of the Lord and try to belittle the truth and power that reign from heaven. They tell you that you can behave anyway you want because God lives in you and He "understands." These false doctrines imply that God will simply look the other way and accept teachings that contradict His Word. Some even say there is no God at all.

For false christs and false prophets will rise and show great
signs and wonders to deceive, if possible, even the elect.

(Matthew 24:24)

Those who promote false doctrines sometimes back up their claims with counterfeit signs and wonders, which do not come from God. These are seducing spirits that are manifesting in order to promote their demonic propaganda.

There is a time and a place where you need to hear the truth and be set free. That time and place is now. Learn the truth of the gospel, not only for your own sake, but also for the sake of others who are suffering under doctrines of demons and need God's deliverance. Fight the devil and know that you have power over him in the name of Jesus. We have to believe that Jesus is Lord and that His mercy will reach out to those who are being deceived. While Satan comes to kill, steal, and destroy, Jesus comes to give us life, and to give it more abundantly. (See John 10:10.)

EXTINGUISHING DOUBT AND UNBELIEF

Throughout the Word of God, the Lord extinguishes doubt and unbelief while showing forth His great power. He will do the same for us today. In 1 Kings 18, we read how God sent His prophet Elijah to expose the powerless god Baal. Elijah said to the people of Israel, who were worshipping this false god,

> *"Then you call on the name of your gods, and I will call on the*
> *name of the LORD; and the God who answers by fire, He is*
> *God." So all the people answered and said, "It is well spoken."*
> *Now Elijah said to the prophets of Baal, "Choose one bull for*
> *yourselves and prepare it first, for you are many; and call on*
> *the name of your god, but put no fire under it."*

(1 Kings 18:24–25)

In vain, the followers of Baal called upon their god. Yet, when Elijah called upon the name of the Lord over His sacrifice, there was no question as to who was and remains the true and living God: *"Then the fire of the LORD fell and consumed the burnt sacrifice, and the wood and the stones and the dust, and it licked up the water that was in the trench"* (v. 38).

Just as God defeated Baal, He continues to defeat false gods and doctrines of demons today. The Word of God and His power are extraordinary and too remarkable for our natural minds to comprehend. You can accept this truth or reject it, but I admonish you to hear and receive the Word of the Lord. God's Word means what it says and performs what it promises. We must remove our doubt and unbelief, stand in the office of God's Word, speak His Word, and remind the devil that he is defeated by the blood of the Lamb.

God's Word is greater than any attack the enemy tries to conjure up for our demise. This is why we must let go of moaning and complaining and being fearful—our frequent reaction to trouble—and arm ourselves with the weaponry God has given us as we fight the good fight of faith!

> *Those who desire to be rich* [including any of the world's false riches and promises] *fall into temptation and a snare, and into many foolish and harmful lusts which drown men in destruction and perdition. For the love of money is a root of all kinds of evil, for which some have strayed from the faith in their greediness, and pierced themselves through with many sorrows. But you, O man of God, flee these things and pursue righteousness, godliness, faith, love, patience, gentleness. **Fight the good fight of faith**, lay hold on eternal life, to which you were also called and have confessed the good confession in the presence of many witnesses.*
>
> (1 Timothy 6:9–12, emphasis added)

3

WHOM WILL YOU SERVE?

In these times of increased spiritual warfare, we are being called to make a decision. Just as the people of Israel had to make a clear decision between the living God and the false god Baal, each of us has to make a clear decision between God's kingdom of light and the devil's kingdom of darkness. Will we serve God, or will we serve Satan—either through outright allegiance to the enemy, or through succumbing to his lies and the enticements of the flesh and forfeiting our relationship with God?

The Lord often reveals to me His desire to see spiritual captives set free. God does not want anyone to go to hell. This is why He has commissioned me to share the deep revelations He has shown me in the Spirit and why I am so candid about urging people to turn back to God.

We must comprehend the nature and implications of our choice: we are choosing between the ferociousness of hell and its opposite—the love of God. God desires to keep us close in His care. He is not a vicious dictator, hovering over us and waiting for us to sin so He can cast us into the lake of fire. He tells us in His Word that He did not send Jesus to condemn the world but to redeem it. *"God did not send His Son into the world to condemn the world, but that the world through Him might be saved"* (John 3:17). His desire is that we will embrace the gift of eternal life by repentance through Christ, and that we will continue to follow Him all the days of our lives.

To whom will *you* give your allegiance—a loving God or a hateful devil? Where will you spend eternity—living an abundant life with your loving Creator or suffering terrible punishment along with His enemy? God loves and respects us so much that He does not force Himself or His gifts upon us. He allows us to make the decision.

In the book of Joshua, the second generation of Israelites was also admonished to make this significant decision. By the same decree that He spoke through Joshua to the Israelites, the Lord poses to us our option: *"choose for yourselves this day whom you will serve"* (Joshua 24:15). The Word of God is clear:

> *No man can serve two masters: for either he will hate the one, and love the other; or else he will hold to the one, and despise the other.* (Matthew 6:24)

Whom are you currently serving? What is your "god"? Is it money, sex, addiction, your job, or even your family? Whatever is capable of occupying your attention and loyalty more than God ultimately becomes your god. Satan then uses these things to keep you from hearing the Word of the Lord and to steer you further into the depths of darkness. The devil knows that if he can clog your mind with the cares of this world, then you are less able to discern spiritual matters and more inclined to give in to the constant tug of the fleshly nature. This is why the Word of the Lord instructs us concerning what to keep our minds focused on at all times:

> *Finally, brethren, whatever things are true, whatever things are noble, whatever things are just, whatever things are pure, whatever things are lovely, whatever things are of good report,*

*if there is any virtue and if there is anything praiseworthy;
meditate on these things.*   (Philippians 4:8)

CONSEQUENCES OF THE FALL OF HUMANITY

Imagine, for a moment, that you are living in complete utopia
in the garden of Eden, just as the first man and woman on earth
experienced. Your thirst is quenched by pure water drawn from
Eden's river. Your hunger is satisfied by food grown in the garden
of God as you picnic beneath shade trees strategically placed as
nature's shield from the sun. Meanwhile, you are serenaded by the
melodious tunes of the heavenly host. This band scripts its lyrics
from God's Word, and its tunes throb directly from God's heart.
You have a sense of complete purpose and fulfillment as you carry
out God's work in the world He created especially for human
beings, who are made in His image.

When we compare this scenario with the strife of the world
today, we see that humanity's rebellion and fall caused a tremendous loss to human beings. Yet God still paved a way to reconcile
humanity to Himself. Consider the following Scriptures:

*For God so loved the world that He gave His only begotten
Son, that whoever believes in Him should not perish but have
everlasting life.*   (John 3:16)

*God was in Christ reconciling the world to Himself, not
imputing their trespasses to them.*   (2 Corinthians 5:19)

While the devil deceived the first human beings, promoting
their downfall (see Genesis 3), and continues to deceive the human
race, the Lord has provided a way of escape for us. It was never
God's intention that we suffer by becoming disconnected from His
presence. Although sin separated us from Him, our repentance
and submission through Christ's sacrifice reconnect us. When

God becomes our Father through Jesus Christ, we are the heirs of God, and He grants us access to Himself and His kingdom.

> *For as many as are led by the Spirit of God, these are sons of God. For you did not receive the spirit of bondage again to fear, but you received the Spirit of adoption by whom we cry out, "Abba, Father." The Spirit Himself bears witness with our spirit that we are children of God, and if children, then heirs; heirs of God and joint heirs with Christ, if indeed we suffer with Him, that we may also be glorified together.... For the earnest expectation of the creation eagerly waits for the revealing of the sons of God.*   (Romans 8:14–17, 19)

GOD'S NATURE VERSUS THE DEVIL'S NATURE

The love, forgiveness, and grace of God are in complete contrast to the utter evil of Satan. The enemy desires to deceive and torment people. When I was taken to hell and saw the many demons with their distorted faces, they were always mocking and speaking to the doomed souls, "You could have had Jesus, but we deceived you." Then they would laugh at the screams of the dead. Over and over, I would see these foul spirits tormenting souls. Some would put fire on them, while others would come to the edge of where they were locked in their various compartments and burn them even more. In one part of hell, I watched as, over and over, gigantic snakes slithered while fire protruded from their mouths in a frightening way.

I would also see the devil. Sometimes, he would make the demons look like humans and send them upon the earth. He would give them certain jobs to perform, and if they did not carry out their tasks, he would expose them to the people. This is the nature of the devil. He is true to nothing and no one, not even his vehicles of deception.

Though the truth concerning the hideousness of hell must be revealed, we must fully realize that this horrible place does not have to be our destination. Because of Christ's love for us, He died on the cross—taking the punishment we deserved. He took the keys of hell and the grave; He saved us and gave us the gift of eternal life with Him, so we would not have to experience torment.

WHOSE VOICE WILL YOU LISTEN TO?

In the garden of Eden, the ears of human beings were originally attuned to the voice of God. At the fall of man, however, Adam and Eve sought the knowledge of good and evil, presuming they could be equal with God; they became wise in their own sight, choosing to ignore the wisdom and omniscience of God. It was then that humanity's ears became attuned to the seductive enticements of the devil.

From the point of humanity's rejection of God, every human being has been born in sin and *"shaped in iniquity"* (Psalm 51:5 kjv). Have you ever wondered, for instance, why you never have to tell an infant or toddler how to misbehave? He automatically knows what to do to get into trouble. He has to be taught the proper actions in order to do what is pleasing to his father or mother. Likewise, we have to be taught that we have a Father who loves us and has our best interests at heart. At first, we may not always want to take the advice of our Father, but in the end we must realize that He knows what is right and that His intention is to lead us out of harm's way. God knows how to take care of those who belong to Him.

All human beings are sinners by nature, and sin births condemnation. The feelings of unworthiness that are associated with condemnation often prevent people from coming back to God for restoration. This sense of being condemned comes to people who are not Christians, but it can also come to Christians who fall, feel guilty, and don't believe they can be restored to God. Yet, again, God is merciful and does not stand by waiting for us to sin so He can toss us away. His grace, poured out through His Spirit, gives us the opportunity to come to Him for forgiveness, wisdom, and strength.

We must listen to what God offers us and not be deceived by the lies of the enemy, who tells us we can never be forgiven and return to God. People who constantly operate according to their own wills, without ever consulting God about anything and without coming to Him in repentance, are some of the most dangerous people in the world.

WHAT ARE YOUR INWARD INTENTIONS?

God does not look on the outward appearance but judges us based upon the intentions of the heart. (See 1 Samuel 16:7.) We can hide our sins from other people, but we cannot hide them from God; neither can we hide from Him the true intentions of our hearts. He cannot be fooled.

There was a Buddhist monk in China who died and witnessed the treachery of hell. He testified how, although his body was dead for three days, his spirit was very much alert. In hell, the truth concerning the plight of those who worship idols and false gods, and who reject Jesus, was revealed to him. He was astonished to see many of the great teachers of old there, who had been condemned to hell because of their unbelief and false doctrines. The monk was allowed to come back to life, and when he awoke in his coffin— much to the astonishment of those attending his funeral—and gave his testimony, many still did not believe.

The gospel has been preached over and over again, but thousands continue to love their own personal lifestyles more than they love and reverence God. If they were to turn back to God and trust Him to protect them, they would see significant changes take place in their lives and in the lives of their loved ones.

God has given me a burden to reveal the love of Christ so that you may escape the snare of the enemy and be filled with the fullness of God. Today, you can possess the power of God in your life while experiencing peace, love, and joy in the Holy Spirit.

YOU MUST MAKE A CHOICE

As I was crying out for souls one day and praying with a prophet, a vision of a valley appeared to me. There were mounds of dirt in certain places with hands emerging from them, and I heard screaming. As the hands appeared from out of the dirt, I saw blackness rolling off them and also from the hearts of these people. The Lord was speaking, "I want souls to be saved."

When I had the vision of hell, Jesus showed me the significance of repenting and turning back to Him. Now, more than ever, God is calling people back to Him to repent of their sins. His grace, through the blood of His Son, will wash you clean. His mercy is everlasting, and His love is reaching out to you today.

These are evil times when we especially need Jesus. I must do everything that I can to make this generation aware of the options concerning its eternal fate. The Lord told the Israelites, "*I call heaven and earth as witnesses today against you, that I have set before you life and death, blessing and cursing; therefore choose life, that both you and your descendants may live*" (Deuteronomy 30:19). Again, God does not force His love on us, but He sets before us two options: life or death, blessing or cursing. He allows us to make the choice for ourselves and does not force His will upon us. "*He who believes in Him is not condemned; but he who does not believe is condemned already, because he has not believed in the name of the only begotten Son of God*" (John 3:18). I admonish you to choose life so that the blessings of God will not only be upon you, but also upon your descendants.

Jesus shed His blood on the cross because He knew His destiny. He knew He would have the joy of saving multitudes of lost souls and providing eternal life for them. He knew He would rise from the dead and return to the Father in heaven to intercede for His people.

> *Looking unto Jesus, the author and finisher of our faith, who for the joy that was set before Him endured the cross, despising the shame, and has sat down at the right hand of the throne of God.* (Hebrews 12:2)

> *Therefore He is also able to save to the uttermost those who come to God through Him, since He always lives to make intercession for them.* (Hebrews 7:25)

God loves you so much that He gave His only Son to save you from eternal damnation. Please do not take this lightly. This is the time that we must turn back to God. We must learn of His eternal grace and mercy and how He wants us to be clean and pure through the blood of His Son and His righteousness. Yes, you may fall at times; however, if you continue to seek the Lord earnestly with a sincere heart to be led by Him in paths of righteousness, you can get up again. If you continue to reach out to Jesus, you will begin to see His perfect will, authority, and power manifested in your life as never before.

> *For a righteous man may **fall** seven times **and rise again**, but the wicked shall fall by calamity.*
> (Proverbs 24:16, emphasis added)

YOU CAN BE SAVED

How do you receive salvation and remain in the power and protection of Christ? First, the Scriptures tell us,

> *If you **confess** with your mouth the Lord Jesus **and believe** in your heart that God has raised Him from the dead, you will be saved.* (Romans 10:9, emphasis added)

Salvation begins with a confession. Ultimately, what you believe in your heart will to come out of your mouth; therefore, what you confess reveals what is in your heart. What are you currently confessing over your life that is contrary to a confession of faith in Christ and is causing you to remain in a bad predicament? What beliefs do you have in your heart that keep you disconnected from God? Whatever these things are, get rid of them and believe the Word of God. Confess with your mouth that God raised Jesus from the dead; believe this in your heart, and you will be saved.

> *For with the heart one believes unto righteousness, and with the mouth confession is made unto salvation.*
> (Romans 10:10)

You cannot confess with your mouth until you first believe in the Lord Jesus Christ in your heart. This is why salvation can never be forced on anyone. It is an act of *voluntarily, willingly* surrendering your will to the will and purpose of God.

Whatever lies in your heart shapes your beliefs. This means that the more you receive the Word of God into your heart, the more your faith can be built. *"Faith comes by hearing, and hearing by the word of God"* (Romans 10:17). If you continue to confess the Word of God, as an outgrowth of your desire to serve Him, you will eventually begin to see the manifestation of the fruits of your lips. Therefore, whenever you are tempted to speak a negative outcome concerning various matters in your life, confess the Word of God instead and hold fast to the confession of your faith.

> *For the Scripture says, "Whoever believes on Him will not be put to shame."*
> (Romans 10:11)

Thousands of souls in hell are experiencing the shame of their actions, which have led to their eternal demise. As a believer, however, regardless of what threatens to expose your vulnerabilities and struggles, as long as you continue to believe and to seek the face of God, you will not be ashamed.

One time, after I had been praying for several days about many people whom I knew and loved who were in spiritual bondage, I had a vision. I saw heaven open and chariots charge out of it. A big, powerful angel was in each of the chariots. They all came down to the earth to help people who were in bondage and to deliver them. They went to the families that I had been praying for to set them free. My prayer is that if you are in spiritual bondage, you will reject Satan's demonic devices. You, too, have power over them in the name of Jesus. Demons tremble at Jesus' name and flee from His presence.

I often liken our relationship with God to many ships that make up the spiritual sea of our existence. He is the Captain of them all, and we are the passengers who embrace the ride with joy and gladness. One ship represents our fellowship with God, which He allows us to experience as we come to know our Lord and Savior Jesus Christ. Another ship represents our worship, where we are allowed to enter into the most sacred compartments of our Captain's quarters. Again, God does not cut Himself off from us when we commit wrongful acts. Rather, as we repent, He opens His doors and allows us access to His presence because of the sacrifice of His Son Jesus Christ on our behalf. In this way, we can reestablish our spiritual stand with Him.

It is imperative that I convey a clear message of the love of God and His desire to see you saved. When you repent from your heart before God Almighty and admit to Him your struggles and that you need deliverance in Jesus' name, He will hear you—wherever you are—and will deliver you and set you free.

The mistake many people make is thinking they have to overcome the wrong things in their lives before submitting to God and serving Him. The best thing to do is to give your heart to Jesus

Christ now, repent of your sins, and allow Him to wash you clean. He went to the cross to save you from eternal damnation.

RECEIVE GOD'S OFFER OF MERCY

Many souls who are now in hell heard the gospel yet rejected its truth. They essentially chose hell by not believing in Jesus Christ and giving Him their whole heart and mind.

Do we really understand what eternal damnation is? In my visions, I saw that hell is a place of unrest and torment where the souls of people are doomed to live forever. The souls in hell long for a final death to eliminate their pain and torture, but it never comes. They scream for water and mercy, but nobody cares. Demons come up and stab at them while cursing obscenities, saying, "If you don't shut up, we will burn you more." I saw rats biting souls, and they screamed, "Help us! Get us out!" The cries of the dead are beyond belief, and the filthy odors are overwhelming.

Jesus came to earth to save us from this. That is why I am calling on you to repent of your sins and ask Christ to come into your heart, save your soul, and make you clean. We have no promise of life on earth tomorrow because no person knows the day he will die or the day when Christ will return.

The extent of God's love surpasses all human understanding. His mercy and grace still reach out to those who are committing terrible offenses, but it is up to each individual to receive His offer of repentance and to completely surrender his life over to God through Christ.

God wants you to know He has great mercy and that He is still reaching out to you today. If you are not yet a Christian, or if you are a Christian who is struggling with unbelief and the things of this world, there is deliverance for you in Jesus Christ. Turn to Him, trust in Him, and surrender your life to Him completely.

[Jesus said,] *All that the Father gives Me will come to Me, and the one who comes to Me I will by no means cast out.*

(John 6:37)

If we confess our sins, He is faithful and just to forgive us our sins and to cleanse us from all unrighteousness. (1 John 1:9)

Now may the God of peace Himself sanctify you completely; and may your whole spirit, soul, and body be preserved blameless at the coming of our Lord Jesus Christ. **He who calls you is faithful, who also will do it.**

(1 Thessalonians 5:23–24, emphasis added)

4

GUARDING YOUR CONFESSION OF FAITH

Scripture teaches that it is the Lord's will for us to remain blameless and to shine as lights in the world—revealing the love, grace, and power of God.

> *That you may become blameless and harmless, children of God without fault in the midst of a crooked and perverse generation, among whom you shine as lights in the world, holding fast the word of life.* (Philippians 2:15–16)

There are several truths and principles we need to follow in order to guard the confession of our faith and to shine as lights in the midst of this dark world.

BE AWARE OF YOUR ENEMY

When you receive Christ as Lord and Savior, you must become aware of the fact that there is an unseen evil realm whose purpose is to deceive you into returning to your old way of life. You may not want to deal with this reality, but ignoring it will not make it less real or cause it to go away. If you want more of God, and if you want to remain in Him, you have to continue your walk of faith and not give up when challenges arise. Everything I have is from being on my knees in prayer and pressing into God.

I remember a particularly difficult time. I was attempting to get my first book published on the topic of hell, and for various reasons, I was extremely discouraged. I had no money left to complete the project and I was very upset, so I said to myself, "I'm going to take this book down to the river and throw it in. There is no way I can get it published."

On the day I had decided to throw the manuscript into the river and forget about it, I was in bed dreaming when I felt a smack on my ankle. I looked around, but no one was there. All of a sudden, I was translated from the room and found myself standing in the galaxies, overlooking the earth.

Oh, my God! What have I done? I said to myself. I began to repent, saying, "Lord, this book is the work of the Holy Spirit! Please forgive me." Then I heard a voice say, "Who are you to be afraid of man? Child, I gave you the divine revelation of hell, and you shall go forth to share with others the reality of what I have shown. You shall also make a movie at the time appointed."

As I was listening to the voice of God and trembling, I looked over to my left and saw a huge ball of fire. Inside the flame I saw the outline of a face; it looked like molded iron. Fire came out of its eyes and shot up to the universe. Its jaws were like iron. Its mouth opened, fire came rushing out, and I screamed. Again, God said to me, "Who are you to be afraid of man, whom I created? They are like grasshoppers in My sight." He then said, "I'm going to put you back into the earth and you are going to do My will. You are not going to throw what I have given you into the river, and I will get the book published." And with that, I was back in my home, shouting and praising the Lord. I was terrified of what I had seen, yet I knew it was the Lord.

I thought to myself, *Who are we that we can manipulate God?* You have to be real and honest with Him. If you are sinning, tell Him you are a sinner. If you are doing things in the wrong way, then tell Him you are wrong and ask Him for instructions on how to change. God is concerned about the decisions that you make and is committed to assisting you in making the right choices when you seek Him for the proper guidance.

BECOME ESTABLISHED IN YOUR FAITH

Second, you must become established in your faith. God may send others to pray with you and to stand in the gap for you, but you must also pray for yourself. In addition, you must find a good church that believes in deliverance and the power of the Holy Spirit. I cannot stress enough the importance of staying in a church with a pastor who really cares about your soul and preaches the gospel without watering it down with what the carnal, or fleshly, mind wants to hear.

You also have to read the Bible for yourself. The Bible is your main weapon for destroying the devil's kingdom. It is a tool you can use to mature in your faith and become wise concerning both the devices of Satan and the blessings of God. When you are confronted by the demonic warfare of Satan's kingdom, you will be better equipped to maintain your deliverance if you are receiving a continuous impartation of the truth concerning the power of God.

A person who has the righteousness of Christ has the right to reign with God forever. The devil knows this, which is why he attempts to get you to speak everything except the Word of God over your life. The devil knows that in the confession of your faith lies life-giving sustenance and power. To maintain your confession, therefore, counteract the devil's ploy by speaking the Word of God. This is what Jesus did when He was tempted by the devil after fasting and praying for forty days. When the devil came to tempt him, He answered him only with Scripture.

The biggest mistakes people make when confronted with Satan's temptations are (1) giving up and indulging in the temptation the devil is offering, and (2) wasting time going back and forth arguing with the devil when they should be taking authority over him. There is no use trying to convince the devil of your spiritual strength. He already knows the power of Christ that lies within you. This is why he attempts to use deceitful tactics of distraction to prevent you from using that power over him. Instead, *"submit to God. Resist the devil and he will flee from you"* (James 4:7). Counteract his deception with the truth of God's Word.

KEEP SPIRITUALLY AWARE AND STRONG

Scripture also admonishes us to work out our own salvation with *"fear and trembling"*:

> *Therefore, my beloved, as you have always obeyed, not as in my presence only, but now much more in my absence, work out your own salvation with fear and trembling; for it is God who works in you both to will and to do for His good pleasure.* (Philippians 2:12–13)

Why does verse 12 include the phrase *"with fear and trembling"*? I believe God wants us to realize there is a price to pay for living a lawless and careless lifestyle and dying without repentance. With all the love, joy, and peace that God offers us, there is no justifiable reason to reject Him.

People who have strayed from God often say things like, "I'm done with the church! I'm going to do what I want and whenever I want to do it." We should never love an institution so much that we turn away from God when it hurts us. Bitterness is a demonic attack that is strategically designed by the enemy to trick you into resenting God. Nothing or no one should be so important to you that it becomes powerful enough to threaten the stability of your spiritual stand with God. Hatred and unforgiveness are deceitful forces that come from the gates of hell to annihilate your confession of faith and to keep you as far away as possible from the will of God.

Think about it. What better breeding ground for contention among Christians is there than the church? The local church is the place where the believers of God spend much of their time. We improve our lives and raise our children in the church. We gather there for support in the midst of crises. So much of our lives is invested there. Is it any great surprise, then, that the enemy is using this place, which is meant to bring us strength, to expose our weaknesses and use them against us?

The devil wants the world to look at the church and see divisiveness in order to give people more ammunition to stay as far away from God as possible. This is a trick of the enemy that, unfortunately, many churchgoers and even church leaders often fail to see. Just as there is a very real heaven that God would like us to see, there is also a very real place called hell that the devil would like us to be condemned to forever. As the devil continues to use everyday aspects of our lives to distract us from the will of God, demons in hell are laughing at the souls who are being exported into the gates of hell. These invisible portals are hungry for souls and will stop at nothing to carry out their plans of deceit.

REMAIN FOCUSED ON THE ESSENTIALS

In keeping spiritually aware and strong, we also must focus on these three aspects of our walk with Christ, because God's judgment of us will be based on them:

1. The *truth* of God's Word.

2. The *belief* and *confession* of our hearts.

3. The *actions* that follow from our confession.

KEEP TO THE TRUTH OF GOD'S WORD

First, keep to the truth of God's Word because regardless of how much the world changes, the Word of God remains the same:

For I am the LORD, *I do not change.* (Malachi 3:6)

The grass withers, the flower fades, but the word of our God stands forever. (Isaiah 40:8)

The entirety of Your word is truth, and every one of Your righteous judgments endures forever. (Psalm 119:160)

But the word of the LORD *endures forever.* (1 Peter 1:25)

What truth should you believe about salvation? It is revealed in Romans 10:9: *"If you confess with your mouth the Lord Jesus and believe in your heart that God has raised Him from the dead, you will be saved"* (emphasis added). We must know that salvation comes only through Christ. Today, more than ever, we must maintain a firm stand against demonic strongholds and know, without a doubt, in whom we believe and in what we believe.

See to it that no one takes you captive through hollow and deceptive philosophy, which depends on human tradition and the basic principles of this world rather than on Christ.
(Colossians 2:8 NIV)

Likewise, whenever you are in doubt about how to respond to something in your life, you can always refer to the Word of God to measure the appropriateness of your actions. The ordinances in God's Word serve as a road map, not only to lead us to salvation, but also to guide us in our everyday lives so that we live according to His will. They teach us how to be good wives or husbands, how to treat our children and parents, and how to avoid being deceived by the devices of Satan.

In our own strength, many of the things that we go through in life seem absolutely unconquerable. Yet nothing is impossible to those who believe in God and His love and power. (See Mark 9:23.) When we sincerely turn to Him in prayer, God hears us and sends help. Therefore, we should do our best to obey God in everything He tells us to do.

HAVE A HEART OF TRUE BELIEF

Second, make sure you have a heart of true belief. Regardless of how much we claim to be in right standing with God, ultimately, it is the condition of our hearts that will determine the veracity of our confessions.

As we have seen, both belief and confession are vital for salvation:

> *If you confess with your mouth the Lord Jesus and believe in your heart that God has raised Him from the dead, you will be saved. For with the heart one believes unto righteousness, and with the mouth confession is made unto salvation.*
>
> (Romans 10:9–10)

We can confess faith in Christ with our mouths all we want. Yet if the Word of God has not also dwelled in our hearts, so that our confession is genuine, we will be made aware of the error of our ways during God's judgment.

> *For the LORD does not see as man sees; for man looks at the outward appearance, but the LORD looks at the heart.*
>
> (1 Samuel 16:7)

All too often, we judge a person's spiritual stand based upon what we see outwardly. Nevertheless, God looks past the physical façade and peers directly into the heart. The prophet Samuel almost made the mistake of looking at outward appearance in choosing a king for Israel from the household of Jesse based upon the physical stature of Jesse's sons. Yet the Lord was quick to correct him. He caused Samuel to look past the physicality of each of the older sons and instead to see through the eyes of God to recognize the youngest son, David, as the upcoming king of Israel.

When God judges, He looks at the heart.

LET YOUR ACTIONS MATCH YOUR CONFESSION

Third, make sure your actions match your confession. We are justified by faith, but we are also to do good works as an outgrowth and evidence of our faith. Remember that your works don't save you. However, you cannot say you truly have a relationship with Jesus if you continue to disobey Him and aren't doing the works He calls you to do.

> *For we are His workmanship, created in Christ Jesus for good works, which God prepared beforehand that we should walk in them.* (Ephesians 2:10)

> *Those who have believed in God should be careful to maintain good works.* (Titus 3:8)

> *As the body without the spirit is dead, so faith without works is dead also.* (James 2:26)

It's not enough just to confess Jesus as Lord; we must also make a conscious effort to adhere to His commands and do good works. We are to seek the things that are above, not the things of the earth. (See Colossians 3:1–2.) Our life is to be *"hidden with Christ in God"* (v. 3). We are to *"put on the new man who is renewed in knowledge according to the image of [Christ]"* (v. 10).

God gives us faith (see Romans 12:3) in order to carry out His good will. Let us put God before all else; let us treat others with godly love and show mercy, grace, and forgiveness, just as our Lord and Savior administers these gifts to us.

LIVING BY FAITH

Finally, it is imperative to remember that Christ is the one and only, true and living Judge. We are never to assess someone's salvation (including our own) based only on his or her struggles. Each of us has a unique relationship with Christ through which He determines His final judgment. Paul wrote in Romans 14:4, "*Who are you to judge another's servant? To his own master he stands or falls. Indeed, he will be made to stand, for God is able to make him stand.*"

This is not to say that the Lord casually tolerates a sinful lifestyle. If you are in the midst of wrongdoing, God's grace is available to you so that you can turn away from it. However, if you persist in it, you are breaking the commandment of God. Do not be deceived into thinking you are born again and are going to heaven if you continue to sin without repentance.

> We know [absolutely] that anyone born of God does not [deliberately and knowingly] practice committing sin, but the One Who was begotten of God carefully watches over and protects him [Christ's divine presence within him preserves him against the evil], and the wicked one does not lay hold (get a grip) on him or touch [him]. (1 John 5:18 AMP)

> If we say that we have fellowship with Him, and walk in darkness, we lie and do not practice the truth. But if we walk in the light as He is in the light, we have fellowship with one another, and the blood of Jesus Christ His Son cleanses us from all sin. If we say that we have no sin, we deceive ourselves, and the truth is not in us. (1 John 1:6–8)

God's grace is available to us. "*If we confess our sins, He is faithful and just to forgive us our sins and to cleanse us from all unrighteousness*" (1 John 1:9). Furthermore, God has given each of us a measure of faith; we are to strengthen our faith according to His Word and activate that faith, in order to remain in righteousness.

For I say, through the grace given to me, to everyone who is among you, not to think of himself more highly than he ought to think, but to think soberly, as God has dealt to each one a measure of faith.   (Romans 12:3)

So then faith comes by hearing, and hearing by the word of God.   (Romans 10:17)

The just ["righteous" NIV] shall live by faith. (Romans 1:17)

5

RECOGNIZING AND COUNTERACTING DEMONIC TACTICS

God does not want us to be in bondage to the enemy and his schemes. We have a God who loves us so much He provided a way of freedom in the name of Jesus Christ and by His blood. He truly wants to deliver you from the hand of Satan. Therefore, He wants you to understand the reality of the demonic deception and the tactics associated with the gates of hell—and how to counteract them.

The Lord is an awesome God, and He can carry you through whatever dilemma presents itself in your life. When you know who you are in Christ Jesus, nothing can stop you—not even the deceptive devices of Satan's kingdom that come to kill, steal, and destroy. (See John 10:10.) Again, this is why it is vitally important for you to be under the leadership of a church that presents biblical teaching, since much of the world today rejects the teachings of Jesus Christ. There are truths concerning the kingdom of darkness and spiritual warfare that you must learn in order to recognize and thwart the attacks of Satan.

SATANIC INFLUENCES

From the average citizen to the most prominent figure in society, no one—without the power of God—is impervious to the influences of Satan's manipulative forces. Hell has much deception, seduction, and evil. Even the demons do not trust each other. They cannot believe each other because they are all liars.

The devil is not going to do anything that will be beneficial to your existence, but will wage spiritual warfare against you in order to destroy you. The difficulties you are currently experiencing in your life may not be human battles at all. Rather, they may be spiritual strongholds caused by demonic powers in order to beguile or discourage you into relinquishing your royal inheritance as a king and priest in God's kingdom. Jesus provided this inheritance for us, and we are to guard it. In the book of Revelation, we read,

> [Jesus] *has made us kings and priests to His God and Father.* (Revelation 1:6)

> [Jesus has] *made us kings and priests to our God; and we shall reign on the earth.* (Revelation 5:10)

Do not allow the enemy to steal what God has given you.

SPIRITUAL WICKEDNESS IN HIGH PLACES

The unseen truth we all must understand is that spiritual wickedness rules over various territories. If the rulers of darkness are not cast down, they will govern whatever yields to their demonic influences within those territories.

In one vision, I saw demonic powers hovering over a certain state. They were huge creatures—perhaps fifty feet tall—and they were resting upon seven large cement thrones. They were all in a circle, mumbling to each other. They tried to imitate the authoritative voice of God, which is like the sound of many waters. (See

Revelation 1:15; 14:2.) Because God had already allowed me to hear His voice when He took me into heaven, I recognized that although this contrary voice was very similar to the one I had heard, it was not the same.

The true and living God said to me, "It sounds similar to My voice, child, doesn't it?" He explained, "This is the prince of the power of the air, the rulers of demon darkness, the spiritual wickedness in high places that sit in the heavens above the earth. They cause chaos in the lives of people and brainwash those who acquiesce to their ungodly influences. I want you to see this, understand it, and tell the world about it. Explain to them that in the name of Jesus they have the authority and the power to pull this evil kingdom down."

I soon began to understand the reality and necessity of the spiritual armor Paul wrote about in Ephesians 6. Paul exhorted us to always be spiritually dressed for battle in order to counteract demonic attacks and strongholds.

> *Put on the whole armor of God, that you may be able to stand against the wiles of the devil. For we do not wrestle against flesh and blood, but against principalities, against powers, against the rulers of the darkness of this age, against spiritual hosts of wickedness in the heavenly places.*
>
> (Ephesians 6:11–12)

As I prepared to pray, the Lord reminded me, "Whatever you bind on earth is bound in heaven, and whatever you loose on earth is loosed in heaven. [See Matthew 16:19; 18:18.] Take dominion over these things and bind them. Command them to fall off their thrones, in the name of Jesus, and by the blood of Jesus Christ."

Jesus said that if we believe in Him, we can accomplish even greater works on earth than He did, through the power of the Holy Spirit: "*Most assuredly, I say to you, he who believes in Me, the works that I do he will do also; and greater works than these he will do, because I go to My Father"* (John 14:12). As God reveals the kingdom of darkness to us, we can truly exercise our power to prevail over every demonic attack. I think it is wonderful that God has endowed us with His power—not that we are exalted, but that we exalt the Lord Jesus Christ.

As I watched these evil forms manifest upon their cement thrones, I knew that many people were going to be deceived on the earth. So I began to pray to God and praise Him for deliverance. Then I saw a group of angels descending from heaven. I saw them circle these demons, put chains around them, and yank them from their thrones. One by one, they began to fall off their thrones as the angels of God dragged them away. The angels were shouting and praising the Lord in the name of Jesus Christ.

Through the blood of Jesus and in His name, we can defeat every demon. In the sport of bowling, the object is to knock down the bowling pins that are lined up at the end of the lane. As you throw the ball toward the pins, the ball may sometimes roll into the gutter. But your goal is to hit the front pin so that it will fall and knock over all the other pins as well. This is the way I look at spiritual warfare against demons. If we deal with evil spirits directly, by striking them with the name of Jesus Christ, they will respond by falling over in defeat. They will flee because they cannot stand against the name of Jesus and the blood He shed on our behalf.

Let us now look at some key elements to recognizing spiritual attacks.

OPERATIONS OF DEMONS

DECEPTION THROUGH FALSE TEACHING

As I wrote in chapter 1, the devil uses the strategy of deception to entrap people and destroy them, and one of the ways he deceives is through false teaching. It is no coincidence that there are so many books and other materials available today on how to "realize your full potential." We are being taught to hear from our "inner voice" while ignoring the voice of God. This is not to say that we shouldn't continually seek to learn more about ourselves and the world around us, and to improve our lives. Yet many teachings in the popular culture negate the reality of God and His Word while promoting the supposed superiority of humanity and human beings' own intellectual and "spiritual" abilities. We must be cautious that we do not buy into these ideas, which are based upon the flawed opinions of fallen humanity rather than on the truth of God's Word.

Anytime we fail to recognize God's voice or mistake the devil's voice for God's voice, demons rejoice at our ignorance. When we lend our ears to the devil's voice, we can risk our inheritance, just as Adam and Eve lost their inheritance to the devil when they listened to his lies in the garden of Eden.

Satan wants to trick you into giving away your spiritual standing by using tactics of manipulation and intimidation. He uses the fact that people are searching for God as an opportunity to present them with a form of godliness that actually has no power. (See 2 Timothy 3:5.) In the last days, many teachings will be made available to us disguised as godly and pure counsel. We will be presented with all types of doctrines that seek to open our minds to receive erroneous gospels. This is why the truth and wisdom of God's Word is such a vital source to those who already believe, as well as for those who are searching for God.

We must be able to discern erroneous teaching from the true gospel of Jesus Christ. Our inheritance is not hell's gates but eternal life.

> *The Spirit Himself bears witness with our spirit that we are children of God, and if children, then heirs; heirs of God and joint heirs with Christ, if indeed we suffer with Him, that we may also be glorified together.*   (Romans 8:16–17)

The following are some guidelines that will help us to distinguish the difference between biblical truth and error.

1. *Does the teaching say that salvation is found only in Jesus Christ?* Today we are inundated with teachings about all types of "gods" and "prophets" through whom we are supposed to find truth and salvation. Some of these teachings even promote the idea that we ourselves are "gods" or "goddesses." If the teaching encourages the deification or worship of anyone other than God the Father, His Son Jesus Christ, and the Holy Spirit, then it is not the true gospel. Moreover, if another man or woman claims to be the Christ, he or she is presenting an erroneous gospel. (See, for example, Acts 4:10–12; Jeremiah 10:11–12; Matthew 24:4–5.)

2. *Does the teaching affirm that Jesus was born of a virgin, led a sinless life, died for our sins, and was physically resurrected?* Any teaching that contradicts even one of these biblical doctrines is an erroneous gospel. (See, for example, Isaiah 7:14; Hebrews 4:15; 1 Corinthians 15:3–4.)

3. *Does the teaching deny the reality of the physical body of man or the eternal spirit of man?* Humanity consists of body, soul, and spirit, and the human spirit is eternal. *"It is appointed for men to die once, but after this the judgment"* (Hebrews 9:27). After we die, we are not reincarnated as another human being or as an animal. Our eternal destination is determined forever by the decisions we make while upon the earth. (See, for example, 1 Thessalonians 5:23; 2 Corinthians 5:1; Matthew 25:31–46; Mark 16:16.)

4. *Does the teaching claim to know the date the world will end?* If the teaching makes such a claim, it is not the authentic gospel of Christ, because Jesus said no one

knows the day or the hour at which He will return. (See, for example, Matthew 24:36; 25:13.)

PREYING ON PEOPLE'S VULNERABILITY

Another operation of demons is to prey on the vulnerability of both Christians and non-Christians. When I was taken into hell, I saw groups of demons speaking. They were huddled together in groups consisting of twelve to twenty demons, and the largest demon of each group was giving the others orders to carry out on the earth. I saw a group of ten smaller demons whose job was to go upon the earth to a certain state in America and wreak havoc in the lives of the family members of powerful men and women of God.

There was one minister, in particular, whom I saw the demons discussing. They had been assigned the job of attacking this minister's cousin in order to distract the minister from doing the will of God. The order went out to cause accidents in the cousin's life. "We want you to cause accidents and problems because this minister is not watching and praying, nor is he reading his Bible. He is not covered with the Word of God, so I want you to expose an issue that he has in his life." The demons were giggling and laughing, and they couldn't wait to do this. They offered rewards to other demons for accomplishing even more turmoil.

As I was listening to this, I heard the largest demon say to a group of demons that were about ten feet tall, "Your job is to go and cause total chaos and hardships in their finances. You are the 'strong man,' and you are going to cause a lot of divisions in the marriages of this family, and this, too, will distract the minister." (See, for example, Matthew 12:29.) They warned each other that the minister would eventually become concerned about his cousin and begin to pray. "He has the power in the name of…the name we don't like to say…he has power in that name to cast you out, but if you go and do these things quickly before he has time to discern or pray, we can invoke damaging crises to prevail over this family."

This minister did not know that all this chattering and scheming was going on in order to tear down his family. He did not know he should pray and begin seeking the Lord diligently. Nevertheless, the angels of God heard this plan, and protective angels were sent. While these demonic schemes were being planned, God already had a plan in place to send a group of angels to protect both this individual and his family. God is brilliant. He knows everything the devil is doing, and He knows how to send help from His sanctuary. (See Psalm 20:1–2.) If you read the book of Psalms, you will notice that He has done this many times.

Much as they tried to do in the minister's life, the operation of demons is to wreak havoc and cause annoyances in your life that are so overwhelming you will focus your attention solely on what is going on around you. They try to keep you from remaining diligent in prayer and maintaining a state of faithfulness and obedience to God. For example, they may cause your automobile to break down and your electric bill to be increased beyond comprehension right when you are trying to come up with enough money to pay the mortgage on your home. These evil presences try to attack anything that we deal with in the natural world in order to destroy our spirits.

Demons will attack vulnerable children as well as vulnerable adults. For instance, if a child is being raped or otherwise abused, she usually has so much fear and torment in her heart and mind that demonic spirits come to keep her in a state of bewilderment and low self-esteem throughout her entire life. She can often break free only by deliverance through the grace of God and in the name of Jesus. That is what deliverance is all about—setting the captives free.

Another vulnerable area is many people's lack of understanding of the true nature of spiritual warfare. They think it is always rare or dramatic, and so they shy away from it. Or they argue about what spiritual warfare really involves. Instead, we must realize that we all confront spiritual warfare practically every day. The devil's attacks against both believers and nonbelievers are relentless because he desires to keep us from our heavenly Father.

There is unseen warfare going on in the heavenly realm that we actively take part in, often without even realizing it. For instance, have you ever said to yourself, "Tomorrow, I am going on a fast"? Even if you normally skip breakfast, when you wake up the morning of your fast, you are so hungry that you find yourself holding a doughnut in your hand before you even remember that this is the day you had promised to sacrifice to God. This type of circumstance is usually not coincidental. The devil will use whatever vulnerability he can find to tempt you to breach your faithfulness to God. During a fast, he may tempt you with food; in times of financial lack, he may bombard your mind with the fear of unpaid bills; in illness, he may intensify the pain; and in grief, he may cause oppression.

TEMPTING PEOPLE TO MAKE BAD DECISIONS

Another trick of the enemy is to use your appetite for earthly things to get you to compromise or neglect your spiritual stand with God through foolish decisions. Making a bad decision based on earthly desires, therefore, not only can potentially have an adverse effect on your family, job, or economic status, but it can also sometimes devastate your relationship with the Lord.

When you are tempted to make a decision based on unbiblical motivations, recognize that your spiritual health is at stake. Seek God's guidance in prayer and look to His Word when making decisions. Do not think through only the material consequences of your decision, but also the spiritual consequences.

Sometimes, we make negative, life-altering decisions simply because we do not heed the voice of God. When God speaks, it is for a specific purpose, so always take time listen to what He has to say. Never become so busy in life that you no longer have time to hear God's voice.

Hell's gates are not to be the reigning force behind the believer's decision-making process. When you take the time to get to know God, you are also able to experience the dominion that He has given you over the earth through the Holy Spirit and the name of Jesus, and the gates of hell are incapable of prevailing against you.

ENCOURAGING PEOPLE TO REACT BADLY TO LIFE'S CRISES

The enemy would also like us to nurture uncontrolled emotions so that we will react to life's crises according to our feelings rather than according to God's Word. For example, in the midst of a crisis, the worst thing you can do is to respond or to make a life-altering decision while enraged. Rage is the devil's playground, and he will use it to his full advantage. Many who become intoxicated with anger have great remorse after sobering from their indulgence in this potentially poisonous emotion. They say things like, "I don't know what came over me."

Always take time to walk away from a situation that is out of control instead of resorting to handling it without the assistance of God. Remember what the Scripture says: *"Be angry, and do not sin": do not let the sun go down on your wrath, nor give place to the devil"* (Ephesians 4:26–27). We may find ourselves angry in certain situations, but we are not to sin by becoming enraged, seeking vengeance, or harboring unforgiveness. We are not to give the devil any opening to work in our lives.

TRAPPING PEOPLE THROUGH SPIRITUAL STRONGHOLDS

Another job of demonic forces is to affect our behavior through "strongholds." Generally defined, a stronghold is a supporting beam or a fortress that people build to keep their enemies out. Our enemy is the devil. Yet the devil's enemy is anything that pertains to godliness and truth, and he tries to create strongholds in your life that will block godliness and truth from reigning there.

Satanic strongholds may be manifested in the form of "generational curses." These are strongholds that often take hold under a certain name or a particular problem or ailment, such as abuse or addiction. These strongholds are passed along in families and may date back to your great-grandparents or even earlier.

Again, demonic forces may try to bind you in a certain area in order to prevent the Spirit of God and His blessings from fully manifesting in your life. To bind means to firmly tie up. If strongholds are never confronted by a spiritually mature person who knows how to take authority over them, they may become resident forces of evil that stubbornly refuse to give up their domain. For example, when a person binds himself or herself to the wrong person in marriage and becomes one with that person, he or she sometimes begins to inherit many of the negative traits of the spouse.

Territorial demons may have the "right" to bind you in certain areas due to the generational curses that have been allowed to fester in the family throughout the years—unless you overcome them through the name and blood of Christ, who took the punishment for them on the cross to set you free. You therefore have to take authority over these strongholds through Christ in order to experience liberty. Unless you cast them down, they will likely continue to fester in your life and in succeeding generations.

COUNTERACTING DEMONIC ATTACKS AND STRONGHOLDS

Satan refuses to give up his rule over this world without a strategic fight. We can counteract him and his cohorts by the name and blood of Christ, by the power of the Word of God, and by living according to God's ways. Here are some ways to protect yourself from strongholds, as well as to wage spiritual warfare.

LIVE UNDER GOD'S PROTECTION

In order to be protected from Satan's strongholds and other devices, you must live in a place of safety built by the Master

Architect—the Lord Jesus Christ. The shelter He provides is (1) capable of sustaining you, and (2) strong enough to keep the enemy from penetrating your confession of faith. This place of safety has a foundation built on the true gospel of salvation through Jesus Christ, the living Word of God.

> *According to the grace of God which was given to me, as a wise master builder I have laid the foundation, and another builds on it. But let each one take heed how he builds on it. For no other foundation can anyone lay than that which is laid, which is Jesus Christ.*   (1 Corinthians 3:10–11)

> *Since you have purified your souls in obeying the truth through the Spirit in sincere love of the brethren, love one another fervently with a pure heart, having been born again, not of corruptible seed but incorruptible, through the word of God which lives and abides forever.*   (1 Peter 1:22–23)

Anytime your spiritual foundation becomes shaky, it is because you are mixing it with something that does not belong. Check out whatever is contaminating your foundation. Are you listening to the wrong voices, taking bad advice, or doubting the strength of God's Word?

Your Master Architect understands the necessity of having a structure that can protect you from turbulent winds and rains—the tests and trials of life. Within your strong fortress are supporting beams built by the Master Architect to help sustain it. The lessons of life teach us to stay put under the protection of the fortress during tumultuous seasons!

These beams of protection can be removed only by the delicate hands of God. He may do so temporarily, as He did with the patriarch Job, to fulfill His purposes, after which He will restore them. However, if you remove these beams of protection on your own, through spiritual neglect or pride, this can cause the entire structure to collapse—with you inside.

Again, these beams have been strategically placed in the dwelling to sustain the structure of your existence and to keep you close to God. He wants to talk to you and dwell with you in the innermost places of your personal existence. He uses these times to impart divine wisdom to you before releasing you into the world to face demonic elements that desire to sift you like wheat. (See Luke 22:31–32.) This is why Psalm 91:1–2 is such a powerful revelation:

> *He who dwells in the secret place of the Most High shall abide under the shadow of the Almighty. I will say of the Lord, "He is my refuge and my fortress; My God, in Him I will trust."*

In this passage, the psalmist revealed the omnipotence of God. It does not matter where we are or what type of demonic strongholds come against us, God is always right there with us to give us the victory. There is no place too dark for the light of God to shine and reveal His marvelous power of deliverance. (See Psalm 139:7–12.) We do not have to be afraid of the attacks of the enemy, for they are no match for the power of God residing within us through His Spirit.

> *Beloved, do not believe every spirit, but test the spirits, whether they are of God; because many false prophets have gone out into the world. By this you know the Spirit of God: Every spirit that confesses that Jesus Christ has come in the flesh is of God, and every spirit that does not confess that Jesus Christ has come in the flesh is not of God. And this is the spirit of the Antichrist, which you have heard was coming, and is now already in the world. You are of God, little children, and have overcome them, because He who is in you is greater than he who is in the world.*   (1 John 4:1–4, emphasis added)

Remember the confident and comforting words of King David:

> *Yea, though I walk through the valley of the shadow of death, I will fear no evil; for You are with me; Your rod and Your staff, they comfort me.* (Psalm 23:4)

David did not fear death because he knew it was no match for God. When his opponent Goliath showed up, even though Goliath's large, shadowy figure eclipsed the sun, not even this would prevent David from taking off his enemy's head. He understood that anything looks larger in the shadows. He was so bold that he even warned Goliath of his impending death. Because David had spent time in the secret places with God Almighty, he was not intimidated by this public display of demonic intimidation. (See 1 Samuel 17.)

KNOW THAT CHRIST HAS ALREADY WON THE VICTORY

"For we do not wrestle against flesh and blood, but against...the rulers of the darkness of this age, against spiritual hosts of wickedness in the heavenly places" (Ephesians 6:12). Today, most "professional" wrestling matches are predetermined. The one who is favored drives the outcome of the match. In a similar way, the spiritual wrestling matches that we deal with have already been predetermined by God. Whether you know it or not, the battle that you are presently in is "fixed"; in God's eyes, you have already won the fight because of Christ's complete victory over the devil—as long as you remain spiritually strong and rely on Him. We must recognize that we are favored to win because we belong to the one who is the Victor.

> *For this purpose the Son of God was manifested, that He might destroy the works of the devil.* (1 John 3:8)

> *When [Jesus] ascended on high, He led captivity captive.* (Ephesians 4:8)

To be effective in spiritual warfare, therefore, you must know who you are in Christ. If you have been born again, you are His child, you belong to Him, and Christ has already won the victory for you. When you belong to God, even though it seems as if you are getting knocked around and are losing, you can know that you are already wearing the winner's belt because Christ has destroyed the works of the devil.

MAINTAIN FELLOWSHIP WITH THE HEAVENLY FATHER

We gain knowledge about defeating the devil by fellowshipping with God in the Spirit. Fellowshipping with God means acknowledging Him in all our ways. God will sometimes allow us to encounter difficulties that He knows can be overcome only by His Spirit so that we will learn to rely on Him.

I have also found that God sometimes allows us to be caught up in smaller storms and to experience bumps and bruises in order to protect us from larger storms that have the potential of actually "killing" us. Moreover, the storms in our lives may have been allowed by God for a season in order to build us up for what lies ahead. The "hell" that you are going through right now may be for the purpose of strengthening you with wisdom to endure future crises.

In Acts 27, the apostle Paul was on a boat heading for Rome, where he was to testify before Caesar. The Holy Spirit told him a storm was coming that would destroy the boat, but that everyone on board would be rescued. Likewise, in your life, before the "storm," God prepares you, and if you can hold on to His Word, you can make it through. God has called you and prepared you so that regardless of how turbulently the winds of life may blow, you can live and mature rather than be destroyed.

By worshipping our faithful Father in the midst of life's storms, we can float through adversities. He is the Lord of the storm as well as the Lord of the harvest. (See Mark 4:35–41.) He is the strength of our lives. (See Psalm 27:1.)

SEEK GOD'S KINGDOM FIRST

To avoid being ensnared by the cares of the world and becoming spiritually weak, do not worry about the material goods you do or do not have. Take your eyes off what you see in the physical and trust in God to provide for you as you seek His kingdom first in your life. Jesus said,

> *Do not worry, saying, "What shall we eat?" or "What shall we drink?" or "What shall we wear?" For after all these things the Gentiles seek. For your heavenly Father knows that you need all these things. But seek first the kingdom of God and His righteousness, and all these things shall be added to you.*
>
> (Matthew 6:31–33)

As you trust in your heavenly Father, His presence will come upon your life and rest on you. If you have been relying on yourself or others more than on Him, He may first rebuke you and then remind you, "I have already spoken the rest of your life into existence. I have given you your marching orders. If you want to know what you should do, ask Me."

Develop a lifestyle of seeking first the kingdom, and all your needs will be supplied. Activate the words of Romans 4:17 and believe God, who *"calls those things which do not exist as though they did."* Speak what you want according to His Word, write it down, and declare it to be so.

MAINTAIN YOUR FAITH IN GOD

When the devil sets his mind to destroy you, he may constantly remind you of failures or setbacks from your past in order to discourage you and get you to give up on your future. Always remember that your spiritual health depends upon your holding on to your faith in God, even if that faith seems small to you. As you do this, realize that it is difficult to stay close to God if you are continually around people who are not committed to God themselves.

TRUST IN GOD'S COMMITMENT TO YOU

> *Finally, my brethren, be strong in the Lord and in the power of His might.*   (Ephesians 6:10)

When you are under demonic assault, people may call you a failure or say you do not have enough faith because they do not realize why you are under such an attack. Yet you belong to God, and He remains committed to setting you free and purifying your mind. The apostle Paul wrote,

> *Now may the God of peace Himself sanctify you completely; and may your whole spirit, soul, and body be preserved blameless at the coming of our Lord Jesus Christ. He who calls you is faithful, who also will do it.*   (1 Thessalonians 5:23–24)

Everything you will be able to achieve and to conquer spiritually will be due to the strength of God that dwells within you. No matter what the crisis is, you can know that *"all things work together for good to those who love God, to those who are the called according to His purpose"* (Romans 8:28).

God is truly revealed in the midst of crises. When you come through to the other side of a dilemma, you may contemplate all that you have gone through and ask, "How did I ever get through that?" The strength of God was made perfect during your weakest moments. (See 2 Corinthians 12:9.)

ALLOW THE WORD OF GOD TO SUSTAIN YOU

You must be prepared with the truth and power of God's Word in order to stand boldly in His righteousness and to war against the demonic strongholds of Satan's kingdom. If you speak His Word over your life, He is committed to seeing you through to the other side of the storms in your life. Utilize the power of confessing God's Word, and watch as His miraculous power begins to be revealed in your life. Confess…

- "I am the righteousness of God." (See 2 Corinthians 5:21.)

- "Jesus' blood covers my household." (See Exodus 12:13; Acts 16:31.)

- "No weapon formed against me will prosper." (See Isaiah 54:17.)

- "I can do all things through Christ." (See Philippians 4:13.)

Immediately after you make these confessions, demons may try to keep the blessings of God and the positive words of faith that you have spoken from manifesting in your life. Even so, you must continue to *"stand against the wiles of the devil"* (Ephesians 6:11) and remind yourself that God has spoken words over your life that cannot fail.

Not only can you have heaven when you die, but you can also experience heaven on earth by allowing His will to be done in your life here, as it is already done in heaven. (See Matthew 6:10; Luke 11:2.) Though you eat the bread of adversity and drink the water of affliction, His divine Word will sustain you. God says He is going to bring you out on top. (See Isaiah 30:20–21.) Do not ever believe that God has turned you over to the devil.

WAGE SPIRITUAL WARFARE THROUGH GOD'S POWER

We must always remember that there is nothing we can do by our own human means to counteract the satanic attacks in our lives. Only God can do this. God sometimes pulls down strongholds before we even recognize that they need to be pulled down. Other times, He wants us to recognize and pull them down in His power.

For the weapons of our warfare are not carnal but mighty in God for pulling down strongholds, casting down arguments and every high thing that exalts itself against the knowledge of God, bringing every thought into captivity to the obedience of Christ.   (2 Corinthians 10:4–5)

The key to spiritual warfare in this verse is the phrase *"mighty in God."* For example, I never advise casting out demons without being sure of who you are in Christ. If demons do not recognize your authority in the heavenly realm, and you attempt to cast them out of someone, they will try to destroy both you and the person who is possessed. (See, for example, Acts 19:13–17.) You should never put another person's life in danger by playing the hero in a situation over which you have no control.

Jesus never fought with demons. He simply spoke a word and cast them out. (See, for example, Matthew 8:16.) He could do this because He walked in the authority of the Father. You cannot be intimidated by the hideousness of the gates of hell. Mathew reminds us that all power in heaven and in the earth was given to Jesus. (See Matthew 28:18 KJV.) If the Spirit of God resides in you, then you hold the power through Christ Jesus to come against the principalities, the powers, and the rulers of the darkness of this age, and to cast out demons in His name.

In the book of Jude, we read that when Moses died, God told the archangel Michael to bury the patriarch. Yet the devil went searching for Moses' body, apparently so that he could try to rule the children of Israel. Michael did not waste time with a *"reviling* [*"railing"* KJV] *accusation"* against the devil, but simply announced to him, *"The Lord rebuke you!"* (Jude v. 9).

It is never a good idea to argue with the devil. If you do, you will likely allow him to win the fight. You cannot defeat him with the weapons of human speech and reasoning. We should follow Michael's example when waging spiritual warfare, rebuking Satan in the name of Jesus in order to cast down every stronghold that the enemy uses as an attempt to keep us bound.

As you mature in your faith, you must also learn to put on the full armor of God to counteract the enemy's schemes. In Ephesians 6:11, we read, *"Put on the whole armor of God, that you may be able to stand against the wiles of the devil."* Then the Lord teaches us how to dress for battle:

> *Therefore take up the whole armor of God, that you may be able to withstand in the evil day, and having done all, to stand. Stand therefore, having girded your waist with* **truth**, *having put on the breastplate of* **righteousness**, *and having shod your feet with the* **preparation of the gospel of peace;** *above all, taking the shield of* **faith** *with which you will be able to quench all the fiery darts of the wicked one. And take the helmet of* **salvation**, *and the sword of the Spirit, which is the word of God.* (Ephesians 6:13–17, emphasis added)

The armor of God includes…

+ Truth
+ Righteousness
+ Preparation
+ Faith
+ Salvation

Your spiritual armor will protect you, and your training in spiritual warfare will guide you as you battle the enemy's tactics.

RELY ON GOD'S GRACE

When we are weak, the grace of God steps in to give us the strength that we need to make it.

> *My grace is sufficient for you, for My strength is made perfect in weakness.* (2 Corinthians 12:9)

God is well aware of the devices of the enemy. He understands the spiritual warfare in which we must often engage in order to secure our spiritual stand. Therefore, throughout the Word of God, He gives us the proper instructions on what to do when we are weak and how to lean on Him to become strong.

God is always listening when you speak. The devil tries to trick you into believing that because you have sinned, God does not want to hear anything you have to say. Countless numbers of people have put off serving God for years with the excuse, "I'll serve Him once I get myself together." If you wait until you feel worthy enough to serve God, then you will probably never serve Him.

What makes God so spectacular is that, despite His sovereignty, He reminds us,

> *For we do not have a High Priest who cannot sympathize with our weaknesses, but was in all points tempted as we are, yet without sin. Let us therefore come boldly to the throne of grace, that we may obtain mercy and find grace to help in time of need.*   (Hebrews 4:15–16)

Several significant truths are revealed in these verses that extinguish the enemy's lies of condemnation. We should never feel there is anything we are experiencing that God does not understand or cannot give us a resolution for. Hebrews 4 tells us the following:

1. Christ Jesus was tempted *"in all points,"* just as we are tempted.

2. Although Jesus was tempted, He remained *"without sin."* Therefore, in Him, we hold the power to conquer our sinful nature and the things that have been keeping us bound. *"For if we have been united together in the likeness of His death, certainly we also shall be in the likeness of His resurrection, knowing this, that our old man was crucified*

with Him, that the body of sin might be done away with, that we should no longer be slaves of sin. For he who has died has been freed from sin" (Romans 6:5–7).

3. If we do sin, the Lord does not cut off communication with us. Instead, He invites us to embrace His grace to find *"help in time of need."* First John 2:1 says, *"If anyone sins, we have an Advocate with the Father, Jesus Christ the righteous."*

Again, anytime you feel the need to stay away from God because of sin, it is because you have succumbed to the condemning lies of the devil. In the garden of Eden, the first thing Adam and Eve did after they had eaten the forbidden fruit was to hide from God. (See Genesis 3:6–10.) Today, people stay at home on Sunday mornings and refuse to come to church because they, also, are hiding from Him. Yet God knows everything. He knew that Adam and Eve had been conversing with the devil in the garden of Eden, and He knows when we "converse" with the devil, as well— by listening to his lies, allowing ourselves to be deceived by him, and following his suggestions.

Rather than casting us down when we fall, God restores us to Himself through the grace of salvation and forgiveness in Christ when we come to Him. God's grace not only restores us, but it also keeps us from sinning. Despite what you may be going through, if you run *to* God instead of *away* from Him, the burden of keeping from sinning will become less of a weight as you take upon yourself the yoke of Christ. Jesus said,

Come to Me, all you who labor and are heavy laden, and I will give you rest. Take My yoke upon you and learn from Me, for I am gentle and lowly in heart, and you will find rest for your souls. For My yoke is easy and My burden is light.

(Matthew 11:28–30)

Don't ever become so obsessed with what you cannot do that you forget to celebrate all that God has done for you. God is well aware of the enemy's hatred toward you, especially when you decide to serve Him with all your heart. The devil's hatred, however, is of no consequence compared to God's love for you. Those who are in a relationship with the Lord do not live their lives based upon fear and doubt. They understand that as they keep their commitment to remain faithful to Him, He will supply all their need *"according to His riches in glory by Christ Jesus"* (Philippians 4:19).

YOU CAN PREVAIL OVER THE GATES OF HELL

Though the gates of hell are very real, you do not have to succumb to them. Hell's attacks do not prevail over those who know their God. Often, the hesitancy we feel about taking steps toward building a relationship with God comes from our awareness of the responsibility that accompanies it—the responsibility of living for Him and counteracting the work of the devil through spiritual warfare. Consequently, we unknowingly stagnate our own growth by shying away from the only One who holds the power to set us free from what has been holding us captive and limiting us.

The devil uses intimidation to keep you from activating the power that God has given you. He tells you that you cannot do certain things when God has said you can do all things through Christ Jesus. (See Philippians 4:13.) He tries to convince you that you are weak and are no match for him and his attacks, when God has said, *"Therefore submit to God. Resist the devil and he will flee from you"* (James 4:7). He uses scare tactics and bullies you into thinking you are going to hell because of your hidden struggles, when God has said, *"My grace is sufficient for you, for My strength is made perfect in weakness"* (2 Corinthians 12:9). He pulls many people away from the church and defuses their potential spiritual power through Christ by deceiving them into believing in other gods, when God has said, *"You shall worship no other god"* (Exodus 34:14).

We must be aware of all the devil's tactics and subtle insinuations while remaining grounded in our relationship with God and the truth of His Word. In this way, we can counteract Satan's schemes and gain full victory over him.

6

DELIVERANCE FROM OUR FLESHLY NATURE

We have seen that there are literal gates of hell through which the unbelieving and unrepentant are led to an eternity of doom. Yet there are also other "gateways" that conduct people to hell. These are avenues of selfish, fleshly living that lead people to lifestyles of spiritual and physical destruction and ultimately to eternal punishment. Satan uses the *"lusts of our flesh ["sinful nature"* NIV]" (Ephesians 2:3) as a means of manipulating us, so that his voice becomes the prevailing influence in our lives, instead of God's voice. You cannot hear God when fleshly or carnal appetites control you.

The Scriptures outline many of the works of the flesh, born out of sinful desires:

> *Now the works of the flesh are evident, which are: adultery, fornication, uncleanness, lewdness, idolatry, sorcery, hatred, contentions, jealousies, outbursts of wrath, selfish ambitions, dissensions, heresies, envy, murders, drunkenness, revelries, and the like; of which I tell you beforehand, just as I also told you in time past, that those who practice such things will not inherit the kingdom of God.* (Galatians 5:19–21)

The sinful nature controls those who do not know Christ. It can also be a snare for Christians. It is at war with the new nature of the Spirit, which believers receive at salvation. Paul wrote in Romans,

> *For I delight in the law of God according to the inward man. But I see another law in my members, warring against the law of my mind, and bringing me into captivity to the law of sin which is in my members. O wretched man that I am! Who will deliver me from this body of death? I thank God; through Jesus Christ our Lord! So then, with the mind I myself serve the law of God, but with the flesh the law of sin. There is therefore now no condemnation to those who are in Christ Jesus, who do not walk according to the flesh, but according to the Spirit. For the law of the Spirit of life in Christ Jesus has made me free from the law of sin and death.*   (Romans 7:22–8:2)

The remedy for living according to the sinful nature is this: *"Walk in the Spirit, and you shall not fulfill the lust of the flesh"* (Galatians 5:16). If we live and walk in the Spirit, we can overcome our sinful desires, shut these "gateways" that lead to destruction, and inherit the kingdom of God.

> *Those who live according to the flesh set their minds on the things of the flesh, but those who live according to the Spirit, the things of the Spirit. For to be carnally minded is death, but to be spiritually minded is life and peace. Because the carnal mind is enmity against God; for it is not subject to the law of God, nor indeed can be. So then, those who are in the flesh cannot please God…. For if you live according to the flesh you will die; but if by the Spirit you put to death the deeds of the body, you will live. For as many as are led by the Spirit of God, these are sons of God.*   (Romans 8:5–8, 13–14)

The sinful nature wants to fulfill fleshly desires, so we must do everything we can to overcome our sinful nature. Jesus said, *"If anyone desires to come after Me, let him deny himself, and take up his cross daily, and follow Me. For whoever desires to save his life will lose it, but whoever loses his life for My sake will save it"* (Luke 9:23–24). We must lay down earthly, ungodly desires and take up the cross of Christ daily. We must die daily to the works of the flesh in order to reign with Christ for eternity.

To *die daily* means that we must continually allow the will of God to become more prevalent in our lives than the desires of the flesh. This doesn't mean we won't have struggles and challenges. It simply means that because Christ has put all things under His feet, we have the power through Him to defeat every foe that attempts to annihilate us—including our sinful nature and the demonic forces that try to incite us to yield to it. Again, the gates of hell cannot prevail against you when you know who you are in Christ Jesus.

THE DEVIL'S THREE TEMPTATIONS

In order to learn how to overcome the fleshly nature, let us begin by seeing how Jesus defeated temptation.

Then Jesus was led up by the Spirit into the wilderness to be tempted by the devil. And when He had fasted forty days and forty nights, afterward He was hungry. Now when the tempter came to Him, he said, "If You are the Son of God, command that these stones become bread." But He answered and said, "It is written, 'Man shall not live by bread alone, but by every word that proceeds from the mouth of God.'" Then the devil took Him up into the holy city, set Him on the pinnacle of the temple, and said to Him, "If You are the Son of God, throw Yourself down. For it is written: 'He shall give His angels charge over you,' and, 'In their hands they shall bear you up, lest you dash your foot against a stone.'" Jesus said to him, "It is written again, 'You shall not tempt the LORD your God.'"

Again, the devil took Him up on an exceedingly high moun-
tain, and showed Him all the kingdoms of the world and their
glory. And he said to Him, "All these things I will give You if
You will fall down and worship me." Then Jesus said to him,
"Away with you, Satan! For it is written, 'You shall worship
the LORD *your God, and Him only you shall serve.'" Then*
the devil left Him, and behold, angels came and ministered to
Him.   (Matthew 4:1–11)

The devil used three main temptations against Jesus, and these are the same poisonous ingredients he uses to deceive us into ruining our lives today: (1) appetite, (2) recklessness or self-destruction, and (3) materialism or ill-gotten gain. Let us look generally at these three areas and then see how they play out more specifically in our lives.

THE TEMPTATION OF THE APPETITE

The devil knew that after fasting for forty days, Jesus would be hungry. He used this opportunity to play on Jesus' basic physical needs to try to get Him to stop relying on His heavenly Father and to satisfy his hunger the devil's way. He tried to control Jesus by attempting to trick Him into taking matters into His own hands before the Father's angels could minister to Him.

You never want the devil to be the one you take advice from or obey, especially right after coming off a fast. At that time, your spirit is especially open to receive from the spiritual realm, and you do not want it to be contaminated by evil forces that seek its destruction. Instead of responding to your needs according to your fleshly appetites, live according to Jesus' example of self-control and trust in God. Jesus told Satan, *"It is written, 'Man shall not live by bread alone, but by every word that proceeds from the mouth of God'"* (Matthew 4:4).

THE TEMPTATION OF RECKLESSNESS OR SELF-DESTRUCTION

Satan next tried trickery in an attempt to get Jesus to leap from a high pinnacle, saying that God would protect Him. Today, the devil continues to try to entice us to destroy ourselves, either by encouraging us to live reckless and lawless lifestyles, or by oppressing us to the point that we willingly take our own lives. Jesus thwarted this temptation by telling the devil, *"It is written again, 'You shall not tempt the* LORD *your God'"* (Matthew 4:7). We are not to live recklessly or dangerously, with the false belief that God will protect us no matter what we might do. Moreover, if we are oppressed and are tempted to be despondent or suicidal, we must hold on to our trust in God and His love.

> *Blessed be the God and Father of our Lord Jesus Christ, the Father of mercies and God of all comfort, who comforts us in all our tribulation, that we may be able to comfort those who are in any trouble, with the comfort with which we ourselves are comforted by God.*   (2 Corinthians 1:3–4)

THE TEMPTATION OF MATERIALISM OR ILL-GOTTEN GAIN

Finally, the devil tried to bargain with Jesus over things that already belonged to Him through the Father. Satan said, in effect, "I will give you the whole world on one condition: fall down and worship me." Jesus made it clear to the devil that this was not a bargain He was willing to accept: *"Then Jesus said to him, 'Away with you, Satan! For it is written, "You shall worship the* LORD *your God, and Him only you shall serve"'"* (Matthew 4:10). Anytime you are offered power, influence, or wealth in exchange for your soul, realize that it is much too high a price to pay, and walk away.

We must also remember that, in making decisions and choices about our behavior, what we do today has the potential to affect someone else for a lifetime. If you are telling someone about the love of God, you do not want this same person to see you acting out a sinful lifestyle. Often, the only picture of God an individual is able to see is the one you reflect through your actions. It is therefore not only for your own sake, but also for the sake of others, that you must keep yourself in a strong relationship with God and resist yielding to the desires of the sinful nature.

SNARES OF THE SINFUL NATURE

The temptations of fulfilling the desires of the appetites, living recklessly, and having worldly success at the cost of eternal life with God can be seen in many of the snares and destructive behavior people fall into today. Among these snares are sensualism, materialism, pride, and seeking escape and relief through ungodly indulgences. Why do people become ensnared by the sinful nature? Let us look at several "gateways" to hell we need to be watchful over.

THE GATEWAY OF SENSUALISM

One gateway to hell that pulls people away from their moral base is the lure of sensualism. Our senses are one of the most vulnerable areas of our lives, so the devil intrudes on them and tries to entice us into all types of ungodly behaviors. Satan knows what buttons to push to cause his desired reaction. In my visions of hell, I saw that demons laugh at those whom they have been able to entice. They laugh because they know that hell will be waiting for them, and it is a place of unrest; there is no love, joy, peace, or compassion there—only torment.

With the sexual revolution of the 1960s, the gateway to sexual degradation was clearly revealed, even though it has been in existence since the beginning of history. In the Bible, we see examples of sexual immorality in the people of Sodom and Gomorrah, whose misplaced passions cost them their existence, and in Amnon, David's son, who raped his own sister. (See Genesis 18:20–19:26; 2 Samuel 13:1–19.) Today, sexual immorality has increasingly become a way of life in our culture, rather than being recognized as an opposing force that we are to resist.

The deception of Satan is like a canker that begins its infestation with individuals, then spreads to annihilate entire communities. Jude, referencing Sodom and Gomorrah, wrote,

> Sodom and Gomorrah, and the cities around them in a similar manner to these, having given themselves over to sexual immorality and gone after strange flesh, are set forth as an example, suffering the vengeance of eternal fire. (Jude v. 7)

The people of these cities gave themselves over to self-indulgence. As Satan walked about seeking whom he could devour, they proved the perfect targets. They showed him no resistance and gave him no reason to flee. They were the perfect breeding ground for contention, vile acts, and lawlessness—attributes that he used to his benefit until, ultimately, they were all destroyed for their insolence.

The devil will use any means necessary to entrap nonbelievers and to distract believers from doing the work of the Lord. He presents what is appealing to the eyes, says things that tickle the ears, and entices us to satisfy the flesh with what God has forbidden us to touch.

What happened after the serpent beguiled Eve in the garden of Eden through her senses and her pride? *"When the woman saw that the tree was good for food, that it was **pleasant to the eyes**, and a tree **desirable to make one wise**, she took of its fruit and ate"* (Genesis 3:6, emphasis added). The devil played upon her senses to get her to indulge the appetites of her soul and body with something God had forbidden. Satan knows that if he can get you to see through his eyes and distract you long enough, he can eventually entice you into partaking of the very thing God has warned you to reject. Consider the following account from Bishop Bloomer:

Sometime ago, when I was away preaching, I was suddenly faced with a very unfamiliar temptation. I have never been one to watch pornography, even before I knew God and accepted Him as Lord and Savior. Nevertheless, during one of my speaking engagements to preach, I found myself in my hotel room clicking through the television channels when I heard my inner voice suggest to me to watch a "flick." I pressed the menu button and began scanning down the menu options. It was as if I was being overtaken by some force; at the same time, I was embarrassed, so I closed the curtains and locked the door. No one else was in the room with me, yet I still knew in my heart that this was wrong. To ensure that what I was about to do would remain "my secret," I called the room of my attendants to make sure that they would not be returning to my room. By then, the gate was wide open. I was moments away from entering the world of pornography and had no idea what was drawing me there. The channel menu came up with thirty different pornographic titles from which to choose: *Naughty House Wives, Girls Just Want to Have Fun, Lesbian Lovers, Two Guys and a Girl.* Still, none of these titles struck my interest. Just when I was about to give up, I saw it—*Sexual Chocolate*—and I thought, *I like chocolate.* The preview popped up…$39.99. When I saw this price, the gate immediately closed. Maybe it's because I'm frugal, but I could not see myself paying forty dollars for something such as this.

As I began to snap out of this daze, I decided to find out what was going on in the hotel. I called down to the front desk and asked, "What type of convention did you have in the hotel recently?" The front desk clerk answered, "Yesterday was the last day of the Gay Convention." Finally, it dawned on me! The residue was still in that room. Had

I not been a person disciplined with my money, I most certainly would have opened the door to a series of pitfalls by pressing that button on the menu and entering into the damaging world of pornography.

God knows how to get our attention long enough to show us a way of escape. Curses do not come without a cause. There is a reason for what we go through. It is not always our fault that the curse exists. Sometimes it is a generational ailment that has been permitted to fester for years without anyone taking authority over it and ceasing its existence. Still, there is definitely something that we can do to destroy it and keep it from taking over our lives. (See, for example, Psalm 50:15; James 4:7.)

Sensualism can create a false sense of reality. For instance, two people of the same sex who decide to come together in an intimate relationship still must resort to God's original plan in order to have a child. The egg of a woman must be fertilized by the sperm of a man in order to replenish the earth with children. Unfortunately, many people tend to use God's plans only when it is convenient for them. Afterward, they usually resort to their own way of doing things, even when it goes against the commandments of God and perverts God's truth. We read in Romans,

Although they knew God, they did not glorify Him as God, nor were thankful, but became futile in their thoughts, and their foolish hearts were darkened. (Romans 1:21)

When the heart is darkened, it engages in its own truth, regardless of who it hurts or damages along the way.

Professing to be wise, they became fools, and changed the glory of the incorruptible God into an image made like corruptible man; and birds and four-footed animals and creeping things. (Romans 1:22–23)

When you begin creating your own truth, you ultimately create your own idols. You no longer rely on God for your provision but instead create prefabricated illusions as a means of fulfillment.

> *Therefore God also gave them up to uncleanness, in the lusts of their hearts, to dishonor their bodies among themselves.*
> (Romans 1:24)

God created the senses, and when they are used in the proper way, they are wonderful gifts that enable us to enjoy the world God has created and to exercise dominion over it. Yet we must be on guard against sensualistic desires and pitfalls. Temptation is real, and it is a trick of the enemy. When you feel tempted to engage in ungodly and immoral acts, take time to call upon the strength of God to pull you through it. You may need to ask a strong believer to agree with you in prayer to stand against the temptation. Rebuke the devil in the name of Jesus, pray the blood of Jesus over your life, seek God diligently, and fill the atmosphere of your life with a spirit of praise.

THE GATEWAY OF MATERIALISM

Another gateway to hell is materialism. While material goods, in themselves, are not evil or wrong, an overemphasis on them can be spiritually deadly:

> *For we brought nothing into this world, and it is certain we can carry nothing out. And having food and clothing, with these we shall be content. But those who desire to be rich fall into temptation and a snare, and into many foolish and harmful lusts which drown men in destruction and perdition. For the love of money is a root of all kinds of evil, for which some have strayed from the faith in their greediness, and pierced themselves through with many sorrows. But you, O man of God, flee these things and pursue righteousness, godliness, faith, love, patience, gentleness. Fight the good fight of faith,*

lay hold on eternal life, to which you were also called and have confessed the good confession in the presence of many witnesses.   (1 Timothy 6:7–12)

God often provides for us through material goods, and our dominion over the world includes the stewardship of physical resources. There are practical, everyday activities and pursuits involving material goods we must engage in to support our families and maintain our homes. We deal with the material world in order bring about certain dreams and aspirations, which involve jobs, careers, businesses, and so forth. God wants us to enjoy His gifts to us, and we may be blessed materially. Yet Satan wants to take away our God-given dominion by enticing us with materialism and other lusts. We must therefore never lose sight of the fact that God is the Giver of all good things, and we must follow His leading in all we do.

And whatever you do in word or deed, do all in the name of the Lord Jesus, giving thanks to God the Father through Him.   (Colossians 3:17)

Do not be deceived, my beloved brethren. Every good gift and every perfect gift is from above, and comes down from the Father of lights, with whom there is no variation or shadow of turning. Of His own will He brought us forth by the word of truth, that we might be a kind of firstfruits of His creatures.
                                    (James 1:16–18)

Unfortunately, we often work tirelessly to obtain our desires, and then we ask God to bless them, instead of consulting Him first. Your number one priority as you seek to fulfill your goals and aspirations under God's guidance should be to inspire others by your actions so that they can clearly see the Spirit of God resonating from your character.

Moreover, even though we may acquire earthly riches and material gain, we still need God's divine wisdom and guidance to attain all the things He has supplied for us according to His good pleasure.

> *And my God shall supply all your need according to **His***
> ***riches in glory** by Christ Jesus.*
> (Philippians 4:19, emphasis added)

The book of Luke gives a very descriptive parable regarding the fate of a certain rich man who was more concerned with his riches than with heeding the Word of the Lord.

> *There was a certain rich man who was clothed in purple and*
> *fine linen and fared sumptuously every day. But there was a*
> *certain beggar named Lazarus, full of sores, who was laid at*
> *his gate....*   (Luke 16:19–20)

Again, you cannot judge the true nature of a person's spiritual level and godly authority by his or her outward appearance.

> *...desiring to be fed with the crumbs which fell from the rich*
> *man's table. Moreover the dogs came and licked his sores. So*
> *it was that the beggar died, and was carried by the angels to*
> *Abraham's bosom. The rich man also died and was buried.*
> *And being in torments in Hades, he lifted up his eyes and saw*
> *Abraham afar off, and Lazarus in his bosom.*   (vv. 21–23)

Unfortunately, many on earth are consumed by a lust for material goods. It is not until they get to hell that they awaken to see the full scope of their spiritual deception.

> *Then [the rich man] cried and said, "Father Abraham, have*
> *mercy on me, and send Lazarus that he may dip the tip of*
> *his finger in water and cool my tongue; for I am tormented in*
> *this flame." But Abraham said, "Son, remember that in your*

*lifetime you received your good things, and likewise Lazarus
evil things; but now he is comforted and you are tormented."*
(Luke 16:24–25)

When the rich man realized there was no way out, he begged
Abraham to send Lazarus back to the earth to warn his brothers
to heed the Word of the Lord so they would not succumb to the
same fate. Abraham reminded the rich man that if his brothers
would not listen to Moses and the prophets of God, neither would
they listen to one who rose from the dead. (See verses 27–31.) God
has sent people throughout the earth to spread the good news of
the gospel of Jesus Christ. It is up to those who hear the Word to
take heed as God speaks through those whom He has strategically
placed in their paths.

We are never to become so obsessed with material gain that
we trade our eternal souls for it! *"For what will it profit a man if he
gains the whole world, and loses his own soul?"* (Mark 8:36). Never
think that you have so much in life that you no longer need God.
As we saw in the previous chapter, we are to seek God first, and
everything else we need will be supplied. *"But seek first the kingdom
of God and His righteousness, and all these things shall be added to
you"* (Matthew 6:33).

You can become so consumed with the cares of this world
that you no longer desire to hear what God has to say about the
world and its false promises. This is a very dangerous mind-set
to embrace. The devil's trick is to cause your mind to become so
inundated by the pursuit of wealth and materialism that the fear
of *not* having these things takes precedence over your pursuit of
the kingdom of God. The rich man in the parable from Luke 16
had become so intoxicated with securing his wealth that he had no
time to give to God. By the time he realized the consequences of
his error, it was too late.

Material riches mean nothing without God. I am sure that the rich man would gladly have traded all his riches for one more chance to repent, serve God, and help the poor. This does not mean that God expects us to live a life of poverty, but that we are to acknowledge Him in all our ways. Even if we are prosperous, we are not to turn our backs on God and refuse to hear what He has to say. We are instead to reflect His abundantly generous and giving nature. When you receive Jesus as Lord of your life and obey His commands, you will prosper in a way that causes God to remember you in both life and death.

You do not have to be wealthy to become caught up in materialism, relying on earthly resources rather than God's provision. If you do not trust God to provide for you, you can fall into the devil's trap. We read in Numbers 13 that God had already promised the children of Israel the land of Canaan before He commanded Moses to send men to spy out the land. When the spies reported to the people, instead of rejoicing over the abundance in the promised land, the majority of them gave a negative assessment of it and, as a result, planted fear and doubt in the minds of the Israelites.

It is vital to trust in God's provision, in His way. You do not have to live in misery and strife, seeking after things of the earth, when God has already promised that if you trust in His provision, you will have all you need. Apply your faith, and simply receive.

> Bring all the tithes into the storehouse, that there may be food in My house, and try Me now in this," says the LORD of hosts, "If I will not open for you the windows of heaven and pour out for you such blessing that there will not be room enough to receive it."   (Malachi 3:10)

> Do not worry, saying, "What shall we eat?" or "What shall we drink?" or "What shall we wear?" For after all these things the Gentiles seek. For your heavenly Father knows that you need all these things. But seek first the kingdom of God and His

righteousness, and all these things shall be added to you.
                                                    (Matthew 6:31–33)

All the spies except Joshua and Caleb said,

*We went to the land where you sent us. It truly flows with milk and honey, and this is its fruit. **Nevertheless**....*
                                    (Numbers 13:27–28, emphasis added)

When God makes a promise to you, never use the word *nevertheless* to sum up His blessings. The spies became overwhelmed by the thought of the walled cities and the strength of the people: "*Nevertheless the people who dwell in the land are strong; the cities are fortified and very large*" (v. 28). They forgot about the fact that God had *already* given them the land. All they needed to do was to follow the Lord's instructions and walk into what He had already promised was theirs. Instead, they felt they had to rely on their own resources, which weren't sufficient.

You have to be able to distinguish between the voice of God and the lies and enticements of the devil. Hear as God hears, and see as He sees. When God says that eternal life is yours, believe Him. Likewise, when He says He has given you dominion over the earth and that He will supply all your needs, believe Him and do not allow contrary voices from Satan's kingdom to persuade you to be filled with doubt and unbelief.

THE GATEWAY OF PRIDE AND SELF-SUFFICIENCY

A third gateway is one of intellectual pride and religious self-sufficiency. As we discussed earlier, many people today are buying into all types of false ideologies and philosophies. These subtle demonic doctrines teach us to live without God and to look only to ourselves for absolutely everything we need. Satan's pride and desire to rise above the One who created him, in order to live for himself according to his own standards, caused him to fall from glory. He entices us to give in to the same temptations, as he did with Adam and Eve.

Satan has been upon the earth for many years promoting his product called "Create Your Own Truth" or "There Is No Absolute Truth." This doctrine says, "Reject the life God has designed for you to fulfill and instead create your own *cosmos*." The more we accept this doctrine, the more we allow ourselves to become engulfed in deception that leads to ungodliness, immorality, and more falsehood. Satan always sprinkles enough truth on his poison to get you to swallow it. He says what you want to hear and what makes you feel good for the moment. Yet rest assured that beneath the surface, there is an unstable foundation just waiting to crumble under his lie, burying you with it.

A very clear account of the depths of Satan's deception is outlined in the book of Jude:

> *And the angels which kept not their first estate [*"proper domain*" NKJV], but left their own habitation, he hath reserved in everlasting chains under darkness unto the judgment of the great day.*   (Jude v. 6 KJV)

These angels had everything they needed in their *"first estate"*—until Satan came along and deceived them. Their original estate consisted of the presence of God and His miraculous works and craftsmanship. It was an estate handed to them by the King Himself—worth more than silver or gold. Yet they left this habitation in exchange for deceitfulness and death.

How were they so easily deceived by the devices of Satan? They simply took time to listen to what the devil had to say. They voluntarily allowed Satan's lies to enter into their ear-gates and then into their wills. So they also succumbed to the same fate as the devil—becoming bankrupt in the things of God, evicted from His habitation, and under His condemnation. It is the devil's agenda to spread his ungodly doctrine so that we fall prey to the same fate as he and the fallen angels.

A passage from Isaiah 14 allows us to see how Satan boasted of his rebellious and ill-fated agenda:

> For you have said in your heart: "I will ascend into heaven, I will exalt my throne above the stars of God; I will also sit on the mount of the congregation on the farthest sides of the north; I will ascend above the heights of the clouds, I will be like the Most High." Yet you shall be brought down to Sheol, to the lowest depths of the Pit. (Isaiah 14:13–15)

Instead of accomplishing the impossible and unimaginable feat of becoming like the Most High, Satan was defeated by God. He was made a public disgrace and was brought down to hell.

Never allow the devil into your ear-gates; do not let him estrange you from the place that God has established for your existence. Your inheritance is an estate from the Father filled with everything that you will ever need in life: *"And my God shall supply all your need according to His riches in glory by Christ Jesus"* (Philippians 4:19). There is no need to go searching anywhere else. Everything that you need has already been supplied to you in Christ. You should never allow anything that you hear to dissuade you from God's truth.

If you subscribe to the false doctrine of "create your own truth" that is currently circulating in our culture, then this will be a very dangerous place for your existence. Truth can be discovered only by seeking God's Word. It is through the Word of God that you will learn His ways and will for your life.

Paul wrote to the Galatians,

> There are some who trouble you and want to pervert the gospel of Christ. But even if we, or an angel from heaven, preach any

other gospel to you than what we have preached to you, let him
be accursed.   (Galatians 1:7–8)

Our eternal salvation depends on knowing and following the true gospel of Christ. We must be very clear concerning in whom we believe and what we believe.

The gospel of Jesus Christ does not come to tickle the ears of people; it is given in order to reveal God's truth. *"You shall know the truth, and the truth shall make you free"* (John 8:32). The truth makes you free by exposing the lies of Satan. There is no truth in the devil (see verse 44), and he would like to create a false image of truth in your mind that you spend the rest of your life needlessly trying to fulfill.

Yet the gates of hell will not prevail against the principles of God's Word. Seek God's ways and learn His Word in order to discover and put these principles into practice. We have a firm promise from Jesus Christ that if we remain grounded on the foundation He has set forth for us to follow, the enemy will not gain the victory over us.

THE GATEWAY OF UNGODLY INDULGENCES

Another gateway to hell is that of seeking escape and relief in life through ungodly indulgences. We have seen that when we go through very difficult times, the enemy often uses our vulnerabilities against us. Instead of turning to God during these times, we can be tempted to seek comfort through such things as unhealthy relationships and substance abuse. Sometimes, we seek these things as a means of self-medication when the problem can only be truly resolved through divine intervention and a change in lifestyle.

The danger of alcohol and drugs is that they can be life-altering substances. Drinking to excess, for instance, clouds people's minds and can cause them to make bad decisions or to unveil secrets that should remain confidential. Because its effect is impaired judgment, it uproots self-control, rendering its victims susceptible to even further humiliation and danger due to a lack of awareness. Countless stories are told of individuals who compromised their principles and were lured into sexual immorality while under the influence of alcohol.

The influence of alcohol has no consideration for the well-being of loved ones, friends, or other innocent victims. Once it activates its effects on the one who is drinking, it can spill over into the lives of everyone who is associated with the person.

How can so many people overlook the danger of such a mind-altering and debilitating gateway such as alcohol? The statistics regarding its devastating effects on humanity are staggering, yet alcohol abuse is still not perceived as a serious threat to society. Consider this data for the United States:

+ Alcohol abuse wastes an estimated $184.6 billion per year in health care, business, and criminal justice costs.

+ Alcohol abuse causes about 75,000 deaths per year.

+ In 1997, 40 percent of convicted rape and sexual assault offenders said they were drinking at the time of their crime.

+ In 2002, more than 70,000 students between the ages of 18 and 24 were victims of alcohol-related sexual assault or date rape.

+ Alcohol played a role in 28 percent of suicides in children ages 9 to 15.

+ An estimated 480,000 children are mistreated each year by a caretaker with alcohol problems.[1]

Satan would love to keep your mind impaired rather than soberly watching for his attacks (see Titus 2:11–13), and alcohol is one of his "portals" to unhappiness upon the earth. Unfortunately, even in the church, people use certain Scriptures to justify engaging in excessive consumption of alcohol, such as *"No longer drink* only water, but use a little wine for your stomach's sake and your frequent infirmities" (1 Timothy 5:23). Yet anything done in recreation that has the potency to alter a person's behavior in a way that causes him to lose control of his senses should be something from which a person should consider disciplining himself.

The real danger of indulging in substance abuse is that people may forsake their relationship with the living God. There are backsliders in hell who once served the Lord, but then returned to the bondage of their old lifestyles. I know many people, for instance, who had a drinking problem. They were saved and delivered for a while, but the day came when the tempter enticed them to go with their buddies to get drunk. At that moment of enticement, when they were lured into temptation, many of them were involved in accidents. They wound up being arrested, losing their jobs, or even being sent to prison.

In such situations, people are tempted to feel like failures and to give up their faith. Meanwhile, the devil sits back and laughs because he feels that his mission toward them has been accomplished.

There is a lying spirit in the land, telling you that you cannot overcome bondages such as substance abuse. The spirit of religion tells you that once you have committed an offence, you are doomed for hell. This is not true. You can overcome, and God is still reaching out to you. The Man called Jesus, who shed His blood on your behalf, has more power to deliver you from drinking, adultery, fornication, lying, and all the sins of your flesh than you could ever imagine. "[Jesus] *is also able to save to the uttermost those who come to God through Him, since He always lives to make intercession for them*" (Hebrews 7:25).

Regardless of what we go through in life, we can still be saved through Jesus Christ. He did not come to condemn you—a fact that He so eloquently confirmed in John 3:17: "*God did not send His Son into the world to condemn the world, but that the world through Him might be saved."* He did not come to destroy you; He came to give you life, and to give it to you more abundantly. (See John 10:10.) That is the truth of God's Word. The Son of God did not come into the world to point out our wrongdoings or to condemn us. He came to reveal that eternal life is available to all who will receive it, all who will repent and embrace Jesus Christ as Lord and Savior.

We must recognize that when we are faced with adversity, the devil will tempt us to resort to ungodly means of having our needs met. Instead of inclining our ears to God for understanding and knowledge, we are often quick to listen to the advice of those who lack divine revelation about our lives and circumstances. We must stop focusing so much upon what we see with our natural eyes and allow the Spirit of God to reveal what is truly going on behind the scenes spiritually.

God counteracts what we see in the natural with the comforting words of 2 Corinthians 5:7: *"For we walk by faith, not by sight."* Often, it's the complexity of our lives and our lack of understanding about it that land us in trouble. Our confusion can be unraveled in an instant by replacing it with the voice and wisdom of God. If we give our ears to the wisdom of God, He promises to give us understanding.

Be still, and know that I am God. (Psalm 46:10)

Incline your ear to wisdom, and apply your heart to understanding. (Proverbs 2:2)

If any of you lacks wisdom, let him ask of God, who gives to all liberally and without reproach, and it will be given to him.
(James 1:5)

There is absolutely no struggle that you are experiencing that God does not understand. And there is nothing that affects you in life, whether physically, mentally, or emotionally, that God cannot give you divine revelation about how to overcome. He is very familiar with our plight, and He reminds us of this in Hebrews 4:15: *"For we do not have a High Priest who cannot sympathize with our weaknesses, but was in all points tempted as we are, yet without sin."*

We do not need to turn to ungodly indulgences to relieve our fear and pain. Whether we are affected by what we see, hear, smell, taste, or touch, God has already provided a way of escape for us. (See 1 Corinthians 10:13.) He knows what to do to resolve any conflict that attempts to hinder us from developing a proper relationship with Him. "[God] *is able to do exceedingly abundantly above all that we ask or think, according to the power that works in us"* (Ephesians 3:20). Anything you can think or imagine, God is able to exceed.

OVERCOMING TEMPTATION AND THE SINFUL NATURE

The devil not only wants to destroy your confession of faith, but he also wants to destroy *you*—both in life and in death. As we have seen, he uses people's uncontrolled fleshly nature as one of his avenues of destruction.

Giving in to the sins of the flesh can destroy us physically and spiritually. Yet, regardless of how strong a grip the enemy seems to have on you, you can be released from it in the name of Jesus. In my walk with Christ, I have learned that if we are honest and true with God regarding our struggles, His mercy reigns in us. *"God is Spirit, and those who worship Him must worship in spirit and truth"* (John 4:24).

The apostle Peter wrote, *"Be sober, be vigilant; because your adversary the devil walks about like a roaring lion, seeking whom he may devour"* (1 Peter 5:8). Never allow yourself to be an easy target for the devil. This means that you should never become so intoxicated by your natural environment that you begin to neglect the spiritual warfare that is needed to secure your spiritual stand with God. Satan knows that he cannot just destroy you at will. Rather, he must walk about and seek the perfect opportunity in which to devour you. If you remain vigilant in your spiritual stand with God, however, when the devil walks about seeking this opportunity, it will not be found in you. Instead, he will walk past you time and time again, wanting to possess you, oppress you, and even kill you, but the power of God that resides within you will present him with a sign that reads OFF LIMITS!

Sometimes, it takes time to grow up spiritually and learn to live and walk by the Spirit rather than by the sinful nature. Temptation is real and demonic powers are real. This is why God often brings people into our lives to pray for us and help us overcome situations that are holding us in captivity. We need to support one another in order to thwart the attacks of the enemy and overcome the lusts of the sinful nature.

What is currently standing between you and God? Is it a vicious or all-consuming pursuit of wealth, idolizing your job, bad relationships, sensualism, feelings of condemnation, addiction, a negative mind-set, pride, or self-sufficiency? Whatever it is, you should not postpone being reconciled with God because of it. Remember that when Jesus ended His forty-day fast, the devil did everything within his power to try to pull Him away from His relationship with the Father, and this is the same tactic the devil uses today. He presents everything that he can possibly think of to feed our fleshly appetites and keep us distracted from God and His ways. He will promise you the world—in exchange for your soul.

People who live to please their sinful nature cannot inherit the kingdom of God and face eternal punishment. Individuals in hell see the results of their earthly indulgences. The lies they believed begin to unravel and reveal the depths of their deception.

Seducing lies, such as "There is no hell...don't fear God...do what makes you feel good....God understands" are straight from the pit of hell. These lies undermine your reverence for God, convincing you to reject Him and ignore His coming judgment. The devil makes sure that those who are vulnerable to his voice enjoy the lusts of their flesh more than the commandments of God. This is why I weep and cry for souls—and pray they will heed the Word of the Lord:

> *Reckon yourselves to be dead indeed to sin, but alive to God in Christ Jesus our Lord. Therefore do not let sin reign in your mortal body, that you should obey it in its lusts. And do not present your members as instruments of unrighteousness to sin, but present yourselves to God as being alive from the dead, and your members as instruments of righteousness to God. For sin shall not have dominion over you, for you are not under law but under grace.* (Romans 6:11–14)

Why should you serve the temporal and corrupt desires of the flesh while you are on the earth and then die and go to hell forever? Think about what you're doing. Change your mind and way of life now by turning to the living God, who is begging you to stop living according to your sinful nature. Believe what the Spirit is saying to the churches: "Repent, My people, and turn to the living God. He will wash you clean."

GOD WILL NEVER FORSAKE US

There are many pitfalls in regard to the sinful nature. Each of us has issues, but God has given us the power to overcome them. This is what the gospel is all about. You must understand that if you fall, God is more than able to pick you up and to show you His love, just as a parent shows love toward a baby. When you have a newborn baby, you love, protect, and watch over her, and as that baby grows, you are attentive as she learns to crawl and walk.

When she stumbles, bumps her head, and begins to cry, you bring her close and comfort her.

Likewise, God will never leave you or forsake you. (See Hebrews 13:5.) Regardless of the circumstances, He is committed to your well-being when you earnestly seek Him for deliverance. The many visions I have had are a true testament to His power and determination to see us through whatever challenges we face.

NOTES

1. Alcohol statistics were derived from the following sources: "Updating Estimates of the Economic Costs of Alcohol Abuse in the United States: Estimates, Update Methods, and Data," U.S. Department of Health and Human Services, December 2000 <http://pubs.niaaa.nih.gov/publications/economic-2000/alcoholcost.PDF> July 10, 2007; <http://www.msnbc.msn.com/id/6089353> July 10, 2007; "Alcohol, Crime, and the Criminal Justice System," L. Greenfield and M. Henneberg, "Alcohol and Crime: Research and Practice for Prevention," Alcohol Policy XII Conference: Washington, DC, 11–14 June 2000; <http://www.niaaa.nih.gov/AboutNIAAA/AdvisoryCouncil/CouncilMinutes/min4-02.htm> July 10, 2007; Tegan A. Culler, "The Poison Within," *Children's Voice*, a publication of Child Welfare League of America, November/December 2003 <http://www.cwla.org/articles/cv0311poison.htm> July 10, 2007; *Collaboration, Coordination and Cooperation: Helping Children Affected by Parental Addiction and Family Violence* (New York: Children of Alcoholics Foundation, Inc.,) 1996.

7

DELIVERANCE THROUGH SPIRITUAL WARFARE

In the last chapter, we saw how important it is to live by the Spirit and not to let the sinful nature take control of our lives. Keeping a rein on the sinful nature not only preserves our stand with God, but it also enables us to be spiritually alert and prepared for spiritual warfare.

As we have seen in previous chapters, we are fighting against demonic forces whose assignment is to destroy us. In my visions, I have seen armies of demons in hell. Just as armed forces upon the earth have different levels and ranks, there are also ranks among these demonic militant forces. They have lieutenants, corporals, and privates. I saw many of them standing at attention, awaiting their orders. They had fangs and broken wings, and a horrendous odor came from them. They also had the power to change their forms.

I also saw many demons and evil forces in an arena-like area in hell. Some of them had teeth. Some of them had hair. Some of them had tails like monkeys, and others were as large as bears. A few of the demons were about twelve feet tall and were shaped like vipers with large fangs protruding from their mouths. They would scream at each other. In front of them would stand an even bigger, more powerful demon holding a slate. He would be giving the smaller demons orders. There were also demons that would take orders from Satan himself and cause chaos in the lives of people and in places upon the earth.

When I saw these things, I heard the voice of the Lord remind me, "Whatever you bind on earth is bound in heaven. Whatever you loose on earth is loosed in heaven." (See Matthew 16:19; 18:18.) I thought, *We need to bind these demons to keep them from coming upon the earth, and to cancel their assignments.*

In order to bind evil forces through spiritual warfare, we must keep the following essential guidelines in mind.

LIVE IN THE AUTHORITY CHRIST GAVE YOU

First, we must live in the authority that Christ has given us. Jesus allowed Himself to be tortured and to die on the cross in order to gain victory over the devil and to give us access to His authority on earth. Mark 16 reveals the power and authority of the believer in Jesus' name, including the believer's authority over the forces of darkness.

> *He who believes and is baptized will be saved; but he who does not believe will be condemned. And these signs will follow those who believe: In My name they will cast out demons; they will speak with new tongues; they will take up serpents; and if they drink anything deadly, it will by no means hurt them; they will lay hands on the sick, and they will recover.*
>
> (Mark 16:16–18)

Those who believe in the Lord Jesus Christ…

+ receive eternal salvation.

+ have Jesus' authority to cast out demons.

+ become filled with the Holy Spirit and can speak in heavenly languages (*"new tongues"*) in order to communicate with God and intercede for others.

+ are endowed with the ability to overcome attacks that cause others to succumb to sickness or death.

+ are the instruments of healing.

Jesus instructed His disciples, *"Heal the sick, cleanse the lepers, raise the dead, cast out demons. Freely you have received, freely give"* (Matthew 10:8). With the authority we have been given in the name of Jesus, we are to freely give the gift of deliverance to those who are bound by Satan. The devil hates the name of Jesus Christ, and he hates it when we call upon Jesus' name for deliverance because he knows he will be defeated. We must be submitted to God and believe without a doubt that Jesus is real and has all authority in heaven and on earth if we are to effectively wage spiritual warfare.

DEVELOP COMPASSION FOR THOSE BOUND BY SATAN

Second, we must have God's heart of compassion for those who are oppressed by the enemy. We read in the Scriptures,

> *The LORD is gracious and full of compassion, slow to anger and great in mercy. The LORD is good to all, and His tender mercies are over all His works.* (Psalm 145:8–9)

> *When evening had come, they brought to [Jesus] many who were demon-possessed. And He cast out the spirits with a word, and healed all who were sick, that it might be fulfilled which was spoken by Isaiah the prophet, saying: "He Himself took our infirmities and bore our sicknesses."* (Matthew 8:16–17)

> *When [Jesus] got into the boat, he who had been demon-possessed begged Him that he might be with Him. However,*

Jesus did not permit him, but said to him, "Go home to your friends, and tell them what great things the Lord has done for you, and how He has had compassion on you."

(Mark 5:18–19)

The Lord is deeply concerned for those who are bound, and we need to have the same compassion for them to set them free in His power. If we have no compassion and do nothing to help others, what are we going to do when we stand before the Lord and He asks, "Where are the souls you helped bring to salvation? Where are those you set free from Satan's oppression in My name? Where are those who were afflicted by sickness, and for whom you prayed to be healed?" You cannot say, "Lord, I was afraid to talk to people about you" or "I didn't have time" or "I didn't really care about the welfare of others." God gives us gifts and fills us with His holy power to draw others to Him and to set them free from what binds them.

As ambassadors of Christ, we must carry the bloodstained cross and reveal Christ's sacrifice on behalf of the world and His desire to set people free. The church is to spread the Word of God and to reveal the love of Christ. Moreover, we should never allow the warfare that we face to prevent us from spreading the good news of the gospel. For example, one of the enemy's targets is our finances. A demonic stronghold may come against our financial stability in order to hinder us from spreading the Word to those who are destitute. We must stand against this stronghold and continue to reach out to those who are in need.

God wants you to be aware of demonic, seducing powers from hell that are working on the earth and how they try to control people to get them to succumb to their suggestions. As I mentioned in the previous chapter, demons will prey on people's vulnerability. Demonic deception causes people to do things they would not ordinarily do under clarity of mind. Two areas of attack I have encountered are depression and suicidal thoughts. We must know how to address these attacks in order to minister to others, as well as ourselves.

COMPASSION FOR THOSE SUFFERING FROM DEPRESSION

People often develop depression as a result of hurts, rejection, sorrow, and grief. Jesus knows the pain of these emotions and the impairment it can have upon people's minds. He Himself suffered the pain of rejection and grief, but He overcame any temptation to succumb to depression. He took our griefs and sorrows, bearing them for us on the cross.

> *He is despised and rejected by men, a Man of sorrows and acquainted with grief. And we hid, as it were, our faces from Him; He was despised, and we did not esteem Him. Surely He has borne our griefs and carried our sorrows.*
>
> (Isaiah 53:3–4)

You have to rebuke depression in Jesus' name and believe that God will deliver you. Sometimes, you may need to call upon the faith of another strong believer to stand with you in prayer to defeat this demonic hold upon the mind. Don't allow the enemy to bring depression upon you. Over the years, I have prayed to the Lord to set people free, and I have actually witnessed the power of God shake them like a leaf as they were freed. Then I have asked God to rebuild and restore their minds.

COMPASSION FOR THOSE WITH SUICIDAL THOUGHTS

Suicide demons come out of hell and crouch on the shoulders of people whispering lies: "Kill yourself...nobody loves you... nobody cares about you." I will never forget one day when I was ministering in a service in Chicago, and the Holy Spirit showed me the manic-depressive demon. A young man came up to me and said, "I've blasphemed the Holy Spirit."

I looked at him and thought to myself, *He can't even be thirty years old yet. I wonder how long he's been saved and what he's talking about.* I had already preached the Word of God, and I had begun praying for people. So the Lord told me, "Listen to him again."

The young man spoke again and said, "Will you pray for me that I don't go to hell? I'm really headed there because I blasphemed the Holy Spirit." Immediately, the Holy Spirit gave me wisdom to ask him how old he was when he was born again. He answered, "Just a couple of years ago."

"Well, how old were you when you blasphemed the Holy Spirit?"

He responded, "I was twelve years old."

I asked, "Honey, how could you have blasphemed the Holy Spirit if you didn't know Him?" I went on to explain, "In our earth today, many people curse and swear and do all types of wicked things before they become born again. After they accept Christ, sometimes they need help in being delivered and sometimes the Lord will just deliver them from these foul powers. The Lord really loves you, and I don't understand how you could have blasphemed Him at twelve years of age when you have only been saved for two years."

The young man began to talk to me and explain some circumstances in his life, when all at once my eyes were opened to the spiritual realm, and I saw something green sitting on his head. It was shaped like a round object with four arms on one side and four arms on the other side. I remember noticing that it had eyes that were peering back at me. I just shook my head and prayed in my heart, "Jesus, what is that?"

The Lord answered, "It's a manic-depression demon. This thing has been on him since he was twelve years old. It has lied to him, seduced him, and told him all kinds of things that aren't true."

I looked again and saw four angels standing around him. One had a chain, one had a sword, one had the Bible, and one had a scroll. The Lord then revealed to me, "I'm going to deliver this man tonight. You're going to see Me deliver him to encourage the people."

I have learned that nearly everything that happens to me is to encourage God's people. So I asked this young man to pray the "Sinner's Prayer" with me for repentance and for recommitting himself to God. I prayed for him, and again I saw this evil being sitting on top of his head. It had a mouth and it was snarling at me. Its hands were extremely skinny, and it had one finger around the man's forehead, one around his eyes, one around his mouth, and one around his neck.

The Lord told me to loose this man from this manic-depression spirit in Jesus' name. I began to pray, "In the name of Jesus, you foul power of manic depression, I command you to loose this young man in the name of Jesus!" As I commanded this evil force to loose him, the young man began to shake up and down. One of the angels pried loose those four hands of the manic depression demon. As he pulled them off, another angel wrapped a chain around the demon, and I saw a Scripture written out:

> Whatsoever thou shalt bind on earth shall be bound in heaven: and whatsoever thou shalt loose on earth shall be loosed in heaven.   (Matthew 16:19 KJV)

As I continued commanding that evil demon to loose the man and to be cast into the "dry places" in the name of Jesus (see Matthew 12:43; Luke 11:24), the angels began to take it away. The man then fell down on the floor, shaking and trembling. The Lord told me to pray for his restoration, due to the damage the demon had done to him. I prayed in the name of Jesus, as the Lord led me. Moments later, the man got up from the floor shaking his head.

His eyes were so clear and beautiful when he finally said, "I feel good. I feel like something has lifted from my head."

"Son, it sure did," I responded. "God delivered you from that manic-depression demon." I began to pray for the restoration of his brain and his soul, in the name of Jesus, and I exercised faith that God would make him whole.

STAND STRONG DURING DEMONIC ATTACKS

Finally, we need to stay strong during demonic attacks and show others how they can do this, as well. There are many people in the world who are distressed and do not know what to do or how to be set free from the devil's assaults. In his play, *A Demon in My Bedroom*, Bishop Bloomer dramatically reveals the real-life encounter with evil spirits that numerous people experience. Likewise, many people call me and write me letters, pleading, "Mary, please tell me what this is. I hear these voices at night and I feel them pulling at my body. What do I do?"

If you are experiencing something like this, do not succumb to these evil spirits but know that God's strength is made perfect in your weakness. (See 2 Corinthians 12:9.) It's time for us to hear how much grace God has for us. It's time to know that only the name of Jesus causes demons to flee and that the blood of the Lamb protects us. Just as the Lord was a wall of fire surrounding Jerusalem, He will also surround you with His glory and power, so that no weapon the enemy forms against you will prosper. (See Zechariah 2:4–5; Isaiah 54:17.)

Remember the following truths during difficult times in order to keep from succumbing to the deceptive voices of seducing spirits.

KNOW THAT GOD IS WITH YOU

Even when you feel as if you are alone, God is always there.

For He Himself has said, "I will never leave you nor forsake you."   (Hebrews 13:5)

If I take the wings of the morning, and dwell in the uttermost parts of the sea, even there Your hand shall lead me, and Your right hand shall hold me. If I say, "Surely the darkness shall fall on me," even the night shall be light about me; indeed, the darkness shall not hide from You, but the night shines as the day.   (Psalm 139:9–12)

KNOW THAT GOD LOVES YOU

The love of God is unconditional. He loves you in spite of the challenges you are currently facing, and He is waiting and willing to receive you to Himself when you call upon His name.

Yes, I have loved you with an everlasting love; therefore with lovingkindness I have drawn you.   (Jeremiah 31:3)

For God so loved the world that He gave His only begotten Son, that whoever believes in Him should not perish but have everlasting life.   (John 3:16)

But God demonstrates His own love toward us, in that while we were still sinners, Christ died for us.   (Romans 5:8)

Who shall separate us from the love of Christ? Shall tribulation, or distress, or persecution, or famine, or nakedness, or peril, or sword? As it is written: "For Your sake we are killed all day long; We are accounted as sheep for the slaughter." Yet in all these things we are more than conquerors through Him who loved us. For I am persuaded that neither death nor life, nor angels nor principalities nor powers, nor things present nor things to come, nor height nor depth, nor any other created

> *thing, shall be able to separate us from the love of God which is in Christ Jesus our Lord.* (Romans 8:35–39)

> *Call upon Me in the day of trouble; I will deliver you, and you shall glorify Me.* (Psalm 50:15)

RECOGNIZE THAT GOD'S WORD IS TRUE

It is impossible for God to lie. If He made you a promise, He will fulfill it.

> *God is not a man, that He should lie, nor a son of man, that He should repent. Has He said, and will He not do? Or has He spoken, and will He not make it good?* (Numbers 23:19)

> *The entirety of Your word is truth, and every one of Your righteous judgments endures forever.* (Psalm 119:160)

> *Your word is truth.* (John 17:17)

You do not have to be intimidated by the taunting of satanic threats against you. When you learn the truth in God's Word, you will become less susceptible to the devil's vicious assaults against you. Read and memorize God's promises of protection and deliverance and apply them to your life. Whenever I encounter those who are fearful of the enemy's attacks, I instruct them, "Just tell the devil that you are already dead in Christ Jesus and that you continue to die daily to the things of the world in order to worship and serve the living God." (See Romans 6:4; Galatians 2:20.)

You have to study the Word of God to show yourself approved to God and to remind the devil of who you are in Christ Jesus. (See 2 Timothy 2:15 KJV.) Even in death, victory belongs to those who know their God and are called according to His divine purpose. (See Romans 8:28.)

DON'T GIVE UP!

God said that troubled times would come in the last days (see, for example, Matthew 24:6–7; 2 Timothy 3:1–5), and it breaks my heart when we tell God we are going to serve Him yet give up and return to our old ways because of apathy, guilt, or fear. Our troubled times should not prevent us from serving God and waging warfare against the enemy. If you are struggling, don't quit! Repent and come back to God, and He will help you.

When we call on Jesus in times of trouble, He dispatches very powerful angels on our behalf to deliver us from the hand of the enemy. Sometimes they stand around us, watching over us. They also go into warfare and fight battles for us. They put chains around demons and drag them away. They send fire from their swords, after which God's Word is written in the air. These angels are truly powerful, and God has sent them to minister to us as heirs of salvation. *"Are [angels] not all ministering spirits sent forth to minister for those who will inherit salvation?"* (Hebrews 1:14).

In visions, I have seen chariots charge out of heaven, guided by angels who continually come to our rescue when we earnestly seek God in prayer. These war angels are very fierce-looking and are focused on their purpose of fulfilling the will of God. They have jaws of iron and eyes of fire. Their garments are made out of metal and iron, as well as other material I could not identify. They wear helmets, are adorned with the garments of warfare, and fight fiercely with demons on our behalf. These angels of the Lord go all over the earth. With their huge swords of fire, they cut the evil presence and powers of darkness.

The more we believe God, the more the heavenly hosts fight against the devil on our behalf. The more we study and apply the Word of God, the more they deliver. Be encouraged, because *"joy comes in the morning"* (Psalm 30:5).

What I have learned and am still learning about angels is how real and powerful they are, and how God sometimes allows us to see them. Many years ago, my child had a very high fever, and I had been praying for days for his fever to break. I had his bed by mine, and as I was praying one day, strange things began to happen. A bright light appeared in the bedroom. In this circle of light was the face of an angel with the most beautiful hair. The only way I can describe its color is to compare it to a bright carrot. He also held a sword. I looked at my son and God opened my eyes to see the spirit of fever on him. It was wrapped around him like a caterpillar and it was black. Yet there was a prominent look of determination upon the angel's face. He pointed the sword at my son's body, and when he did, he commanded the spirit of fever to come off. It fled and wrapped around the sword of the angel. The angel then lifted the sword and exited with it through the window. Immediately, my son was delivered from the fever.

I have seen angels work to bring God's Word to pass, and believe me, His Word cannot fail. God wants you to know that you hold the power to change your circumstances through the name of Jesus and by invoking His power upon every circumstance that threatens to bring about your demise.

> *Fight the good fight of faith, lay hold on eternal life, to which you were also called and have confessed the good confession in the presence of many witnesses.*   (1 Timothy 6:12)

You will never receive the benefits of the warfare going on in the heavenly realm by constantly giving up on the things of God. You have to fight and remain faithful to God in order to lay hold of eternal life because the enemy will do everything possible to keep you from obtaining it. It is a fight of faith, but remember that God has already won it on your behalf. Wherever you go, and regardless of what you go through in life, continue seeking the Lord, and He will reveal an answer to your needs.

8

DELIVERANCE
THROUGH PRAYER

I now want to discuss intercessory prayer, which is a powerful weapon in deliverance. Paul admonished us, *"Praying always with all prayer and supplication in the Spirit, being watchful to this end with all perseverance and supplication for all the saints"* (Ephesians 6:18).

When God allows me to see supernatural manifestations, I sometimes see demons on the shoulders or legs of people, or whispering in their ears. The demons do not always possess the people, but they *oppress* them. Because many people have not been taught how to pray and reject demonic influences, they don't always know how to fight against them. In this chapter, I want to help you understand how to pray for yourself and others to be set free.

WALK IN YOUR CALLING

One of the gifts God has given me is the gift of mercy and love. After I saw the visions of hell, I was never the same again. Beforehand, I did not understand the driving force behind the depth of horrible sins people commit. Now, when I pray for someone, I can earnestly travail for him to be set free by the power of God because I possess the revelation that's necessary to connect with his need to be delivered. I have the calling of God upon me to act on what He has anointed me to do. I earnestly admonish others to do the same—to walk in the calling of God upon their lives.

Thousands in our land are dying as a result of people's bondages and sin. I know that God wants a change in the earth. We must let the Father know we love Him by the way we love others. When you were in need—spiritually lost, struggling with addiction, sick, or helpless—who prayed for you? Who stood in the gap for you? Who wanted you to overcome? The Spirit of the Lord was persuading people to intercede on your behalf. You need to intercede for others in the same way.

When you have been called by God, you can't follow the crowd. God does not want copycats. He wants you to be led and taught by His Spirit. Some people would rather turn a deaf ear to the Word of the Lord, close their eyes to His spiritual foresight, and harden their hearts because to receive truth and take responsibility also means we have to *change* and do things God's way. Change can be very inconvenient to our lifestyle and ways of doing things; nonetheless, God commands it. We must repent of our selfishness and return to the foot of the cross.

Perhaps you don't feel worthy or able to intercede for others. Again, though you may sometimes stumble and fall in your journey of faith, this does not mean you should turn from God and give up. You might get bumps and bruises on your way down, but if you reach up to Him, the Lord will alleviate the pain with His healing balm from heaven. Regardless of what you are going through, God has an answer to relieve every affliction; He has all knowledge and can provide you with a peaceful solution. Reach out to God, and He will make you an overcomer, able to rise above everything that is trying to take you under. Then you can minister to others in turn.

We must believe God and let go of our doubt and fear. We have to believe that God is a dwelling place, and that if we do sin, we can still go to Him in repentance and receive forgiveness through Christ. (See 1 John 1:7–9.) If He has to prune us again, so be it. The Lord chastens us because of His undying love for us and His commitment to saving our souls and the souls of others. Therefore, repent, have communion with God, and allow Him to cleanse your heart. Seek Him in earnest prayer, such as this one:

> Lord, I believe I have victory through Christ over every area of my life. I repent of my sins. [Name them.] I ask You to cover my entire household with Your blood and Your Word so that no weapons formed against it shall prosper. Hold me close to You; teach me and guide me today. In Jesus' name, amen.

This type of prayer, along with the Lord's Prayer, is what I ask people to pray when they seek me for advice concerning spiritual attacks. Pray these prayers every day so that they will become a part of your daily walk with God.

THE POWER OF PRAYER

When you pray, remember that Jesus has all power and authority. (See Matthew 28:18.) We must put these demonic influences under His feet, in His name. (See Psalm 8:6; 110:1; 1 Corinthians 15:25–27.) I have seen visions of people praying, and their prayers go up like beams of light. As they approach the throne, the prayers appear as written words, and God commands them to return to the earth in the form of an answer.

As we are in this prayerful state, the enemy will be held back. It becomes impossible for him to penetrate the protection of prayer. Demons flee and report to the devil, "We could not attack them because of this hedge of prayer." I have seen visions of this actually happening. I have seen people pray and have witnessed a circular hedge of fire coming up to protect entire families.

Let me give you another example of the power of prayer. There was a little boy whom I used to minister to and encourage in the Lord. I told him, "Honey, if you ever get into trouble, call upon the name of Jesus Christ." Little did I know that just two weeks later, this little boy would be in a car accident. He was a passenger in the backseat, and the car tumbled over an embankment and landed in the river. The car sank, and it took about fifteen minutes to get him and the other passengers out of the car. Unfortunately, two of the young men died, but this young boy miraculously survived. In the hospital, after the medics had pumped his stomach, he told the medical staff, "I remembered what Mrs. Baxter said—to call upon the name of Jesus. And when we were in that car, I kept praying, 'Jesus, save me!' and it's like an air bubble formed around my head and I could breathe. I remember breathing until they pulled me out, and I know it was because of the name of Jesus." I hear many stories about the power of prayer in Jesus' name.

PRAYER AGAINST THE GATES OF HELL

Years ago, I had a vision of one of the gates of hell while I was on a preaching trip in Pennsylvania. There was a place in the woods there where satanic worshippers practiced rituals with symbols on the ground and all kinds of demonic activity. A group of us, all of whom were Christians, went there to anoint the ground because one man was terrified by the demonic activity that was taking place in this area. We had anointing oil, and we opened the Bible and asked God to send His army of angels to shut this gate of hell. As we prayed, the earth shook and the ground began to sink. Then I saw the angels of God come and put a chain and a lock upon the door that led to that gate of hell.

We experienced a demonic attack after we performed this prayer, so that the car we were riding in got stuck on a broken sewer line. It was very cold at the time and, as the sewer line broke, sewage spilled all over the car. I kept reminding the people that it was only the response of the enemy, who was trying to harass us after we had fulfilled the will of the Lord.

After you do the work of the Lord, the enemy tries to bombard you with aggravation to make you question whether or not you were in the will of God. But the Bible assures us that whatever we bind on earth will be bound in heaven, and whatever is loosed on earth will be loosed in heaven.

None of us was injured in this incident, and after we freed the car from the broken sewer line, we were able to see that it was just another satanic distraction that was attempting to take away from the miracle that had occurred after our intercession. I believe the living Word of God. We stood on the Word of God and rejoiced at the fact that the gates of hell could not use even this foul situation to prevail against us. "The gates of hell shall not prevail" is not a cliché; it is the living Word of God, which I have witnessed on a number of occasions throughout my ministerial travels.

Another time, when I was preaching in a different state, I received a call from a lady who asked, "Since you're preaching about the gates of hell, can you please come to my house and anoint my yard and pray with me because my husband has lost his mind?"

"How did he lose his mind?" I asked.

"He believes that there are aliens that transport him out of the home and into this spaceship to do awful things to him."

"Really?" I responded curiously. So I asked some people to go with me to pray for this lady. As I entered her house, I smelled a foul odor and immediately turned to her and asked, "What in the world is that?"

She responded, "Come on; I'll show you." She opened a screen door at the back of the house, and there in her backyard were at least two inches of dog dung spread out in a big circle.

"Every dog in this subdivision comes to my house to relieve himself in my backyard," she explained.

I told her to give me a bottle of olive oil, and I immediately began to pray. I walked around the edge of this huge circle of dog dung and began to call upon the Lord to shut this gate of hell and stop the attack of the enemy on her family. As I prayed, the ground sank about eight inches. Suddenly, I saw a vision of angels coming and sealing that gate. They bound it with a chain, locked it up, and began singing the victory. "Dear God," I said, "these gates are truly real!" I began to fully understand all the times that God had anointed me to pray over the land while visiting other cities, where I would see the fire of God come down and destroy the evil forces of Satan. So I began to pay close attention to cities and towns throughout my travels. I had visions of God reaching His arm down and burning up the darkness, and I was so happy. I prayed, "God, we need a revival. We need to revive the people, and they need to get their minds clear of the devil's mentality and be renewed by the mind of Christ."

PRAYER FOR DELIVERANCE FROM BONDAGE

Recently, some intercessors and I went into deep prayer and travail that the spirit of drug addiction would be bound in the name of Jesus in the life of a certain person. We prayed for him continually. We had known this dear individual for quite a while and his tragic situation just broke our hearts. This was a very precious person who had had a reputation for working hard and making a good salary. Yet, one day, I heard that he was on drugs and living on the streets. This touched my heart so deeply that I would travail and cry for him because he appeared to have no more control over his life. He had lost all self-respect. At one point, we almost gave up praying for him, but we could not. I knew I had to continue in travail—not only for him, but also for many others in the earth who were battling this same demonic force.

My heart was seriously broken because of the massive drug use and the number of children who were dying or getting arrested and going to jail. So many people need to know that there is a way of escape, that God Almighty can deliver them from the demon of drugs. I know many parents who have had family members on drugs, and it is very heartbreaking. It hurts people so deeply that we need a mass healing from the deep wounds of drug abuse.

One evening, at six o'clock, I was greatly travailing in the Spirit for this man and others on drugs. As I was praying, a heaviness suddenly seemed to drop on me, accompanied by grief for these young people. The Spirit of God came upon me, and I just shut my eyes and continued to travail. Later, I remember going to get a drink of water, and as I looked at the clock I noticed that it was midnight, but I still did not have a release regarding this burden for souls to be saved. When the Lord has placed a burden upon you to stand in the gap and pray for certain things, He gives you the gift of the power of the Holy Spirit to see into the spirit realm and to pray until there is a release.

I kept praying, and as I went to refresh myself again, I noticed that the time was now three in the morning, but the Spirit was still upon me to continue praying. I began to quote the Word of the Lord and rely on God's promises for added strength, such as, "*Call upon Me in the day of trouble; I will deliver you, and you shall glorify Me*" (Psalm 50:15). There is deliverance in the name of Jesus Christ. In faith, I applied to the situation whatever Scripture came to me by the Holy Spirit, and I decreed the victory by the power of God. (See Job 22:28.)

By six in the morning, I could see the sun peeking through the hills. My body was tired, but I felt the joy of the Lord. I prayed by the power of Christ Jesus that God would answer this prayer. All at once, I had a mighty vision. Heaven opened up, and two or three angels were standing outside the heavenly gates. They had sheets of paper on which were listed the names of people from the earth.

The angel of the Lord let me understand that these were the people for whom the intercessors and I had been praying, who were suffering from drugs and all kinds of other addictions.

I saw the gates of heaven swing open, and out of them came droves of war angels riding on horses or chariots. The angels were about thirty feet tall, and they had jaws of iron and eyes of fire. Their entire bodies were adorned with beautiful armor made out of brass, copper, and gold. On their sides were swords as large as men. The swords glowed with flames that shot from both ends. These warring angels were given orders to come to the earth and deliver the people.

When I saw the beauty of this army, I began shouting and praising God. The way they looked, they could penetrate any darkness. I knew that the world needed to know about God's army—the army that is called to deliver us in the day of trouble.

I put my trust in the Lord, and then I had a vision of different parts of the earth; I could peer into the ghettos, parks, and houses. I saw all this in color; it was as if the scenes of a television program were unfolding right before my very eyes.

Scenes of people's plights began to flash sporadically before me: some of the people were in alleys, being beaten up; some were drunk and falling down on the ground; others were in their homes suffering in turmoil. I saw one boy near a dumpster in an alley, and someone was beating him to death with a club. He was shirtless as he lay on the ground, unconscious. I didn't want him to die, and I realized that the man who was beating him was demonically possessed.

When witnessing a situation this devastating, you might think to yourself, *How do I even begin to pray?* You pray for the will of God and for the Holy Spirit to speak through you to say the right words. Then you yield yourself to God and allow His Spirit to pray through you as you trust and believe Him. He's the

King of Kings and Lord of Lords, and when He speaks a word, He exercises diligence to perform it.

As this image faded away, I saw an influx of angels suddenly arrive on earth. They went into the towns and cities, into the streets, parks, and people's homes. I could see people who had black forms wrapped around them that looked like monkeys. The angels would rip the hands off these demonic creatures and cremate them. As the angels wrenched these figures from people, the people would shake and tremble while their deliverance was taking place. The angels would touch them and they would drop to their knees, praying and crying under the anointing of God.

Other demonic images appeared in the form of rats or snakes. I could see an angel move its hands down an alley, and the demons would be cremated and turned to ashes. At the sight of this, I began to rejoice because God was showing me His deliverance power. He was reminding me that if we call upon the Lord, stand in the gap, and pray for people to be free of their sins, He will send help from His sanctuary.

The Lord continued to show me instances of His power in action. For example, a man was sitting on a barstool and drinking. Angels pulled one demon from his shoulder, another demon from his side, and a third demon from his mouth. The man began shaking his head in disbelief. He asked, "What's happening to me? What's happening to me?" When he stepped outside the bar, the power of God hit him. He began to cry and fell to his knees to be saved. Demonic powers had been preventing him from giving himself completely to Jesus Christ, but now he was set free.

The Lord revealed to me, "You're seeing My deliverance power through prayer." I continued to watch as people whom the angels were delivering went into the streets. I would see dark shadows upon the people and shadowy figures on their legs. As the angels wrenched these figures off the people, the people would shake and tremble while their deliverance was taking place.

This vision went on for hours and hours, and the Lord said, "There will be a mighty deliverance in the earth. You watch and you see." It was wonderful to see the Lord setting the captives free. The Lord impressed on me to write the vision down and to talk about it. He wanted me to emphasize the fact that He is our Deliverer and we are never to give up hope in prayer, in asking Jesus to intervene.

When I saw the Word of God in action, I began to comprehend the extreme necessity of praying and commanding evil spirits to loose those who are bound. We need to understand that God can change the heart and save the soul of anyone. He cares about us that much.

In the next few months of my ministry, as I traveled and preached about hell and what God had shown me, young men and women would come up to me at the book table or at the altar of the church where I was ministering, and they would share with me their testimonies, which were similar to this:

> Just a few weeks ago we were delivered and healed by the power of God. I came out of this bar so drunk, and I sobered up, dropped to my knees, and accepted the Lord.

Over and over, testimonies were being reported. I want the world to know that there is hope in Jesus Christ. He is our Healer and Deliverer. He showed me visions of His Word setting the captives free as God's people stand in the gap and make a hedge of protection around those for whom they are praying. We have to keep praying and believing God Almighty for deliverance in Jesus' name.

> *The LORD is my rock and my fortress and my deliverer; my God, my strength, in whom I will trust; my shield and the horn of my salvation, my stronghold.*　　(Psalm 18:2)

PRAYER AGAINST INVISIBLE FORCES OF EVIL

I feel blessed to be able to see many manifestations of the spirit realm, yet this only happens when the Lord allows it. One time, I was grieved over people's sins because they seemed to have no reverence for God, and they were mocking Him. During this time, I had been seeking God for answers concerning certain matters. While I was coming out of my hotel one evening at twilight, I began to look at the people walking. I didn't have to preach that particular night, and the Lord said to me, "Look." He opened my eyes to see a demon walking two feet from someone and talking to him. He showed me another person on a bicycle who had a demon sitting on his shoulder. I would see people with demons wrapped around their legs and the individuals would be limping. Demons would be wrapped around the arms of others and their arms would be bandaged.

The Lord informed me that the enemy had done this. He had caused afflictions, heartaches, and grief. Then the Spirit of the Lord instructed me, saying, "Child, pray for these people." I went back to my room and I prayed for them. For several days, during the twilight hours, I would actually see these spirits in airports. Off and on, throughout the year, I would see these things again, and I would continue to pray. The people were not aware that evil spirits were causing their afflictions. They could not see them, and I would not have been able to see them, either, except that God allowed me to observe them in the Spirit.

In a church service where I was ministering, the Lord revealed someone to me and I called this individual up to pray for him. As I interceded on his behalf, God allowed me to witness his complete deliverance right before my eyes as he was loosed from the bondage that had ruled his life. For years, this young man had been bound by demonic strongholds, but in an instant, the Spirit of the Lord set him free.

God has given me the spirit of healing in praying for people. I have witnessed miraculous testimonies everywhere, especially in other countries. I have even seen God create brand new brain cells.

One time, I prayed for a little girl who was so sick she could not hold her head up. The Lord showed me a serpent wrapped around her neck and instructed me to pray in the Holy Spirit. As I prayed, I saw angels yank that demonic spirit from her. I then asked God to restore the muscles in her little neck so she could hold her head up again.

At other times, I have seen an evil spirit upon someone's intestines, and when I cast it out, the individual was healed. Or I have seen a dark spot on a person's lung. This was a spirit of infirmity that had attached itself, and I cast it out in Jesus' name. Only through the name of Jesus and His mercy does He reveal these things to me in order to help humanity.

Many people unknowingly suffer from sicknesses and diseases that come from the gates of hell to steal, kill, and destroy. (See John 10:10.) This is why the power of loosing and binding must be taught and acted upon with power and authority in the name of Jesus.

One of the most memorable visions I have had involved the healing of a ten-year-old boy many years ago. This boy was my son's best friend at the time. He was a diabetic, and I would sometimes take care of him. At one point, he became gravely ill and fell into a diabetic coma. As I sat in the hospital room by the bedside of this child, I continuously prayed, and I fasted. All at once, God opened my eyes to see that on the top of his head was the outline of what appeared to be a transparent scorpion. His tentacles were sticking in this child, and he had the boy's head in his mouth as he lay there. As I continued to pray and rebuke the devil, the Spirit of the Lord spoke to me and said, "I'm going to teach you how to pray against this situation. This is a diabetes demon. This is a scorpion demon spirit that is sent into the earth to destroy the people. I've given you authority over the power of this scorpion."

As I watched, I became aware of the cruelty of this demonic force. I did not know anything about this evil spirit, but I began to pray by the life, the power, and the blood of Jesus Christ. I asked God, in Jesus' name, to loosen those tentacles from that child and for that demon to let him go. As I did this, the room filled with angels. They had a scroll and the Word of God, and they began to loosen the tentacles. I watched this great deliverance taking place upon the boy, and I began to praise the Lord. As they pulled this thing off him, I saw the angels put a chain around it and drag it out the window and into the sky—far away to "dry places." (See Matthew 12:43; Luke 11:24.)

I looked back at the child, and he shook his head and came out of the coma. The Lord said, "Now pray for restoration—to restore the blood sugar, to restore the blood level, and for the pancreas to be healed." He was instructing me about what to do and how to pray for this child, and I was overjoyed that He had chosen me to pray for him and to see him out of this coma. As the nurses came in, I continued praying silently and thanking God for the miracle that had taken place.

For I am the LORD who heals you.   (Exodus 15:26)

Another vision I had concerning the kingdom of darkness happened many years ago. During a time when I had been in much prayer, the Lord took me and showed me the galaxies. He showed me the prince of the power of the air and how demons hinder answers to our prayers, as we read about in the book of Daniel. (See Daniel 10:1–14.) He began to reveal to me the necessity of our having a strategic plan to incorporate prayer into our lives. If we do not know how to pray, we should ask God to teach us. Jesus has blessed us to have dominion in His name, and we begin to see the manifestation of this dominion as we seek Him earnestly in prayer.

In one of my visions of angels fighting demonic powers, it seemed as if some of the angels were overcome and had somehow become bound by chains themselves. I began to watch this and pray, and for months I became engrossed in deep travail. While praying, I saw a vision of these angels flash before my eyes. Some were trying to fight for us and protect us. They were being attacked by the biggest demon I had ever seen, and warfare was being waged fiercely between the demonic spirits and the angels of God. I began to quote the Word of the Lord as the Holy Spirit led me.

Months later, I was in deep travail, and a pastor and I were sharing the Word of God when all at once this vision became very strong and vivid. It appeared as a large honeycomb with several compartments. It hovered high above the earth, and demons were sealing something inside each of the compartments. Puzzled, I thought, *God, what is this?* as I continued praying and quoting the Word of the Lord, beckoning God for deliverance. I then saw angels go in and break open those sealed compartments and rescue the angels who had been held up by these demonic forces. The Lord delivered these angels who had been in warfare with the devil as another group of angels came who were mightier and stronger than the first group to destroy these demonic powers by the thousands. We must realize that we are fighting against powerful forces, but we have the victory in the name of Jesus as we persevere in prayer.

THE SECRET TO ANSWERED PRAYER

God has allowed me to witness many beautiful things through the Holy Spirit. Many years before I had begun sharing my visions of hell and angels, the Lord appeared to me and I went with Him. He showed me various cities and towns, and as He would drop balls of fire over them, revival would begin to take place in each one.

Once, I was in a certain city, and I had been praying for the move of the Holy Spirit to go through that place. In a vision, I saw the city streets and the mountainous terrains. Down the mountainside came the white glory of God flowing like a river—a living river drifting over the trees and hills. It then flowed into certain homes, and in each of those homes a great revival would break out.

People would be asleep in their beds, and the angels would go and shake them awake; these people would jump up and start to pray. I would see other people, however, who remained asleep when the angels tried to awaken them. The angels would then knock on their doors, but no one would answer. Nevertheless, I saw a great revival come to the city, and I praised the Lord.

God wants us to pray so that salvation, revival, deliverance, and healing can take place across the nation and around the world. The secret to witnessing the miraculous is really not a big secret at all. It simply requires faith in God to do what you have asked of Him in your time of need.

The Scriptures tell us that after Jesus had traveled from Bethany to Jerusalem, He was very hungry. Seeing a fig tree in the distance, He went to it, but He found no fruit on its branches. Jesus immediately cursed the fig tree: *"Let no one eat fruit from you ever again"* (Mark 11:14).

The following morning, as Jesus and His disciples passed the fig tree, Peter was amazed when he noticed that the fig tree had dried up, and he brought this fact to Jesus' attention: *"Rabbi, look! The fig tree which You cursed has withered away"* (v. 21). Peter was surprised, but Jesus was not shocked at all. He knew His word was truth and that it was incapable of failing to do what He had commanded. Jesus simply replied to Peter, *"Have faith in God"* (v. 22).

He then went on to remind Peter that all believers hold this same power. (See verses 23–24.)

When we earnestly believe in God, our faith can move mountains. Whether you are praying for yourself or for others, you cannot allow anything to damage your faith in God, for if you do, you will hinder your prayers and delay the deliverance.

> *Jesus answered and said to them, "Assuredly, I say to you, if you have faith and do not doubt, you will not only do what was done to the fig tree, but also if you say to this mountain, 'Be removed and be cast into the sea,' it will be done. And whatever things you ask in prayer, believing, you will receive."*
> (Matthew 21:21–22)

WHY PRAYERS MAY NOT BE ANSWERED

Besides a lack of faith, there are other reasons for unanswered prayer, including the following.

THE WRONG TIMING

Regardless of how much you believe, if it is not in God's timing, you will not see the manifestation of your request. You will need to wait until God decrees it is time to bring the answer to fruition. It is during such a time of waiting, however, that many people become frustrated and give up, even though they are right at the brink of realizing their miracles. God does not always reveal the answer immediately, but this does not mean He hasn't answered the prayer.

When Jesus cursed the fig tree, it wasn't until the next morning that Peter noticed it had withered away; however, the tree was as good as withered the moment Jesus spoke the word. Again, even though you do not yet see the answer to your prayers, this does not mean that God's promise has not been fulfilled. Continue to believe, regardless of what you see in the natural, and you will soon witness the physical manifestation of your request. *"Faith is the substance of things hoped for, the evidence of things not seen"* (Hebrews 11:1).

UNFORGIVENESS AGAINST OTHERS

Throughout the Word of God, the Lord warns us of the hindrances that we bring upon ourselves when we hold grudges against others and do not forgive.

> *Whatever things you ask when you pray, believe that you receive them, and you will have them. And whenever you stand praying, if you have anything against anyone, forgive him, that your Father in heaven may also forgive you your trespasses.*   (Mark 11:24–25)

Before we can see the full manifestation of God's glory and power, we must *"lay aside every weight, and the sin which so easily ensnares us"* (Hebrews 12:1)—including bitterness and unforgiveness.

HALF-HEARTED PRAYER

If we do not pray at all, or if we pray in a half-hearted way, we cannot expect to receive.

> *The effective, fervent prayer of a righteous man avails much.*
>   (James 5:16)

> *Rejoicing in hope, patient in tribulation, continuing steadfastly in prayer.*   (Romans 12:12)

HOW TO PRAY

Many people want to know how they should pray. It isn't necessarily the length of the prayer that counts. Jesus said, *"And when you pray, do not use vain repetitions as the heathen do. For they think that they will be heard for their many words"* (Matthew 6:7). Rather, it is the quality of the prayer that gets God's attention. Jesus told us how to enter God's presence through five essential elements in His model prayer, which has come to be called the Lord's Prayer.

1. **Worship**: *"Our Father in heaven, hallowed be Your name"* (v. 9).

2. **Praying the will of the Father**: *"Your kingdom come. Your will be done on earth as it is in heaven"* (v. 10).

3. **Asking the Father to meet your need**: *"Give us this day our daily bread"* (v. 11).

4. **Repentance/Forgiveness**: *"And forgive us our debts, as we forgive our debtors"* (v. 12).

5. **Holiness**: *"And do not lead us into temptation, but deliver us from the evil one. For Yours is the kingdom and the power and the glory forever. Amen"* (v. 13).

It is equally important to keep these vital components in mind when conducting spiritual warfare. Spiritual warfare is taking authority over whatever is keeping you or the subject of your intercession bound. It's not excellency of speech or physical antics that invoke the anointing and power of God, but rather your ability to summon God's presence through the vigilance of effective prayer.

The anointing of God destroys every yoke. (See Isaiah 10:27.) God warns that we are not to enter into spiritual warfare haphazardly; we are to be properly prepared for battle. *"Do not lay hands on anyone hastily, nor share in other people's sins; keep yourself pure"* (1 Timothy 5:22). *"Put on the whole armor of God, that you may be able to stand against the wiles of the devil"* (Ephesians 6:11). Those who are prepared for battle are in right relationship with God. They are wearing their spiritual armor and have the Holy Spirit's anointing. These are the ones who are effective in exposing Satan's deception, closing gateways to hell, and setting captives free.

THE ROLE OF FASTING IN SPIRITUAL WARFARE

Finally, we must realize that we may need to fast as well as pray when conducting spiritual warfare for deliverance. Once, when Jesus' disciples asked Him why they could not cast out a certain demon, He answered, *"This kind does not go out except by prayer and fasting"* (Matthew 17:21).

In addition to praying and studying the Word of God, fasting is a vital part of the Christian experience. During a fast, the spirit of man avails itself to hear from the Lord in a special way through the denial of food. Denying the flesh through fasting can help us to maintain the purity and power of our relationship with God. Often, we hear more from God and learn more about Him and His ways through fasting than we ever could otherwise.

Jesus taught us the proper way to fast:

Moreover, when you fast, do not be like the hypocrites, with a sad countenance. For they disfigure their faces that they may appear to men to be fasting. Assuredly, I say to you, they have their reward. But you, when you fast, anoint your head and wash your face, so that you do not appear to men to be fasting, but to your Father who is in the secret place; and your Father who sees in secret will reward you openly.

(Matthew 6:16–18)

Without a doubt, although our physical bodies can seem weak when we are fasting, our spirits are being strengthened and drawn closer to God. Fasting intensifies the believer's faith and better equips him with the power to combat spiritual wickedness in heavenly places. Although the Lord Jesus Christ already defeated the devil on our behalf, fasting can give us the spiritual rejuvenation that we need to walk in the victory the Lord has made available to us.

Fasting not only opens our spirits to hear from God, but it is also an act of worship. Giving up food to draw closer to the Lord is an intimate sacrifice that we give to Him and which He graciously accepts.

When we fast, however, we must also be prepared for challenges. We may experience the resistance of the flesh and the enemy. Sometimes, it can seem that the more we seek God, the more the attacks begin to mount against us. For example, it can be an inner battle to maintain the sacrifice while simultaneously listening for the voice of God. Have you ever noticed, for instance, that when you go on a fast, even if you are normally a light eater, all you can think about is food? You may also experience other distractions or disruptions. We must be aware of these challenges and prepare for them.

The purpose of fasting is not to show others how spiritual we are. It is a true sacrifice only when our motives are in the right place. Yet as we sacrifice to God in secret, Jesus said the Father will reward us openly.

STANDING IN THE GAP

I really believe in the power of prayer through the Holy Spirit and in the name of Jesus. We do not always know how to pray. Yet if we earnestly seek the Lord and pray to Him in the Spirit, then the Spirit will make intercession for us according to His will, and His will for our lives cannot fail.

> *Likewise the Spirit also helps in our weaknesses. For we do not know what we should pray for as we ought, but the Spirit Himself makes intercession for us with groanings which cannot be uttered. Now He who searches the hearts knows what the mind of the Spirit is, because He makes intercession for the saints according to the will of God.*
>
> (Romans 8:26–27)

We can pray and fast for the deliverance of our loved ones and friends. In His righteousness, God desires to save whole households. That is His promise, and He has kept His promise to me in this regard: *"Believe on the Lord Jesus Christ, and you will be saved, you and your household"* (Acts 16:31).

When your heart is pure before the Lord, and when you call upon His name as you stand in the gap for others, He will destroy the demonic powers that are attacking them. You can take dominion over demonic forces and command them to flee. You can take authority over the "strong man" (see, for example, Matthew 12:29), pulling him down and putting him under your feet in Jesus' name.

> *And whatever things you ask in prayer, believing, you will receive.* (Matthew 21:22)

9

DELIVERANCE THROUGH THE WORD

Even though we live in troubled times and many people are being oppressed by the enemy, I have decided this: regardless of what the present and future generations hold, I am going to preach the truth concerning God's Word so strongly it will demand an audience—both with those who are searching for truth and those who are still living in rebellion—so all can know how to escape the devices of Satan.

The Word of God has the power to set people free:

For the word of God is living and powerful, and sharper than any two-edged sword, piercing even to the division of soul and spirit, and of joints and marrow, and is a discerner of the thoughts and intents of the heart. (Hebrews 4:12)

THE TRUTH OF THE WORD SETS YOU FREE

The more you pay attention to God's truth in the Scriptures and receive it as an applicable component of your life, the more evil spirits must flee and make way for the blessings of God to come upon your life. I have seen God's angels destroying demonic spirits as they attempted to come against the children of God. God watches over you as you plead the blood of Jesus and claim the name of Jesus over your life.

Hide the Word of God in your heart, and the peace of God that surpasses all human understanding will overtake you. Regardless of what demonic weapons form against you, when you know how to rebuke the devil in the name of Jesus, these weapons will not prosper. Let me give you an illustration of this.

A young man had been troubled since he was a little boy by a demon coming to his bedroom. In his first year of college, he encountered a group of people talking about orbs, which are translucent balls of light that tend to appear in "haunted" places. This group told him that "nice" spirits appear to people at night to give them orbs, and that in 2012 there would be a shift in the spirit realm that would take place on their behalf. I found out that this form of doctrine is being presented all over the world. This is a demonic agenda fueled by demonic powers.

Another gentleman, who is a Christian, prayed for this young college student to be set free from the influences of these demonic strongholds. After he prayed for the student, the demon that had visited this young man since his childhood manifested itself again. It went to his room to give him an orb. Yet when the orb came into his room, this time, he rebuked it according to God's Word in order to be set free. Once he knew the truth and received it, the Word of God immediately delivered him.

> And you shall know the truth, and the truth shall make you free.   (John 8:32)

Many of our young people are wrapped up in satanic rituals and doctrines. They think it's fine to dabble in demonic spirits as a fad to fit in with their peers. Yet this is a deception from the gates of hell. Whether you call yourself a white witch or a black witch, it is an abomination to God because witches and warlocks seek to summon up demons and all types of wickedness to go forth and invoke the manifestation of their will upon others. These are the things that God Almighty is exposing today because He wants you to know His Word will help you in every situation—even to break free from satanic involvement and the debilitating strongholds that have limited you for years.

REVEALING THE TRUTH

When God calls someone as a prophet of the Lord, he or she must go through various times of testing. It might be a test of obedience, or a test that will ultimately reveal the truth and power of God's Word. In every situation, the person must believe God's Word, regardless of what is happening around him or her.

After God called me and placed me in the ministry, it was quite a while before He revealed to me the unmistakable reality of hell. But after that time, I would periodically see a vision of a dragon. Every year, for sixteen years, during a period of deep prayer and travail to God, this image would appear, and I knew that there was much warfare taking place.

An account of a great fight involving a dragon with seven heads is recorded in the book of Revelation. It describes how the angels of God fought against the dragon, which was lying in wait to devour the child whom the woman was about to give birth to. The Scriptures describe the victory over this great dragon, revealing the protection of God, His many blessings, and how Jesus watches over the innocent. (See Revelation 12:1–11.)

In my visions of the dragon, the beast had fangs like a serpent, but its tail was that of a dragon. Its seven heads were connected to long necks that extended high into the galaxies. I have come to believe the dragon with seven heads represents the false teachings against our Lord and Savior and the warfare that we experience in trying to release the Word of the Lord to His people.

While in deep travail against false religions and false teachings that contradicted the Word of God, I would encounter part of this vision, and I began to understand the dragon represented seven major kingdoms that come against the Word of the Lord. I would pray in the Holy Spirit, rebuking the power of darkness, and binding and loosing. As I did this, huge angels would come from heaven and bind this beastly image with a mighty chain, and there would be tremendous warfare. Then the vision would suddenly vanish.

When I would see this dragon in the heavenlies, its neck would stretch out to attack something in my ministry. I knew it was the *"prince of the power of the air,"* the rulers of demon darkness, and the spiritual wickedness in high places. (See Ephesians 2:2; 6:12.) I understood, through the revelation of God, that this was the warfare He refers to in the Scriptures, and that we must use the name of Jesus to bind the devil and put these things under our feet.

The Holy Spirit began to teach me how to war against this attack of the enemy. The assaults against my ministry always seemed to manifest weeks prior to my having this vision of the warfare that was taking place in the heavenly realm. There would be hindrances through finances, sicknesses, and other situations. Yet, as we stood and proclaimed the Word of the Lord, I could see God's Word in action. I would actually see His angels coming and fighting for us. I could see an open book, and out of it would come the Word of the Lord, which transformed into a two-edged sword. The angels would fight the demon powers over and over, bind them with chains, and carry them to dark places.

When I sought the Lord's counsel about this vision, shortly afterward I had another vision that again included this seven-headed dragon. I saw the world and a pair of justice scales. One end of the justice scale was attacked by a huge serpent. It seemed to me that there was an unjust balance on this scale, and I did not know who was holding the arm of the scale. As I watched this vision, the one who held the scale turned into the devil himself.

As I sought the face of the Lord, I understood that the enemy was bringing false balances and deception into our lives because his mission is to spread lies and hypocrisy. The devil is bringing many things into our lives to tip the scales of justice against us, and I knew I had to pray to bind him and bring release.

UNCOVERING DECEPTION

As we saw in chapter 1, many people, especially in the younger generation, are being engulfed by the ungodly influences of false religions. These false teachings disguise themselves as self-help, self-awareness, and avenues of experiencing personal fulfillment; yet their final result is widespread deception.

Some false doctrines teach that we do not need God, and that everything we require for self-fulfillment lies within us. Other doctrines rely on physical, man-made images as their source of fulfillment; they teach the worship of idols. Again, anything that consumes your attention more than God is your object of worship. Many people have been conned by the teachings of satanic doctrine, but God is very clear concerning His view of idol worship.

For you shall worship no other god, for the LORD, whose name is Jealous, is a jealous God.   (Exodus 34:14)

We serve a God who will not allow anyone or anything to stand in the way of the worship that rightly belongs to Him. Regardless of how many doctrines we may study that promote other gods, the Lord makes it very clear that we are to worship *"no other god."* To reject this commandment is to turn your back on your Creator and Savior. Living without God brings an imbalance to people's lives that can only be corrected through repentance and an acceptance of the Lord Jesus Christ as Lord and Savior.

The dragon with the seven heads wrestles against the truth of God's Word, but God is the Victor. As ambassadors of the gospel (see 2 Corinthians 5:20), we must speak God's truth and engage in spiritual warfare by commanding the devil to release people. In order to help people come to Christ, we have to battle false teachings. These teachings never tell you about being born again; they rarely warn you of your negative behavior or reveal that if you call upon the name of the Lord, He will save you. They hide the fact that no matter what you have done, God's love will reach out to save, heal, and deliver you; that God Almighty is there to comfort, lead, and guide you. If you will just call upon Him, He will answer. He loves you and wants to deliver you from the devil.

In my vision of the seven-headed dragon and the justice scale, I noticed the angels of God fighting against Satan with swords. I saw the Word of God in action, and the angels took the scale away from the devil. When they seized it, I saw something that resembled a round ball on one end, but as I looked closer, I noticed that it was the earth. Then I saw the angels rip open a round door that was upon the earth. As they opened it, the Lord put His hand inside and yanked out deep roots that had all kinds of sins and perversions dangling from them. Everything evil you could imagine clung to these roots He was pulling from the center of the earth. God was tearing down the seven major kingdoms of false gods.

This warfare against this dragon and his defeat were extremely vital to the spiritual well-being of the people of God. I heard the Spirit of the Lord say that there are several major powers of evil that fight along with this dragon. So I began to pray and take dominion over them. I commanded them to be bound, and I also commanded that whatever they were trying to destroy would be loosed in the name of Jesus. Deep warfare was taking place against manipulation and sin in the earth—against thievery, lying, murder, stealing, adultery, fornication, hatred, bitterness, and all types of evil.

It really touched my heart because I knew that God was fighting this battle. He wanted to restore the hearts of the fathers to the children and the hearts of the children to the fathers. (See Malachi 4:6; Luke 1:17.) It was exciting to know that God was battling on our behalf. I knew that the imbalance on the scale represented the false gods that had risen up over the earth to teach us lies. I saw the justice scales begin to even out, and I knew that God was going to intervene on this earth to bring back the truth and miracles that had been stolen from us.

I am very happy to let the world know that the powers of darkness have to obey, according to the mighty name of Jesus Christ and by the blood He shed.

10

JESUS, OUR DELIVERER

SATAN'S WRATH IN THE END TIME

Just as there is a real place called hell, there is a real place called heaven. The gates of each place lead to very different consequences. The gates of hell lead to eternal torment, pain, and hideousness. In contrast, heaven's gates lead to righteousness, peace, and joy. They lead to the heavenly city, which has no need for the sun because the light of God illuminates it and reveals its glory. (See Revelation 21:23.) Each of heaven's twelve gates is made from a beautiful pearl, and they welcome the children of God to a city of gold. (See verse 21.)

While we still have time, we must respond to God's provision of salvation and forgiveness through Christ. Those who refuse God's offer and are still alive at the end of the age will experience terror both on earth and in hell. During one of my visions of hell, Jesus said, "I want to show you what is going to hit the earth once the church has been taken out."

There will come a time when God will remove the church from the earth and take His people to be with Him. With the removal of the church, the Holy Spirit's restraint of the enemy and his forces will also be removed. (See, for example, 1 Thessalonians 4:15–16; 2 Thessalonians 2:1–12.) Then Satan will pour out his full wrath on the people of the world, before Christ returns.

In this vision, the Lord gave me a glimpse of what the enemy's wrath will be like at this time. As I walked with the Lord, I heard an awful sound. We stopped, and I looked down a huge tunnel. It was round and curved, somewhat like a subway. Far back in the tunnel, I could see fire coming toward us, roaring like a train. When the fire was about fifty feet away from us, it suddenly stopped.

The flames were covering an object, and as I looked at this object more closely, I realized it was a gigantic snake, bigger than a locomotive. It opened its mouth, and a huge tongue stretched forth. It came a few feet from the Lord and me before it stopped and recoiled into the large opening of the tunnel. It continued to approach and then retreat, as flames shot from its mouth and it continued to roar.

"Oh, my Lord," I asked, "what is that?"

He answered, "This serpent shall be released on the earth when My church is called away."

Watching this, I thought, *We need to repent of our sins and turn to Jesus Christ stronger than ever before.* We need to prepare people through the good news of the gospel and warn them of this coming wrath before it is too late for them. God does not want the deception of the devil to lead people to experience eternal death. We have to be wise regarding the devices of Satan and realize that there is a price to pay for dying without repentance toward God. Though we will often go through struggles and challenges in life, we must never allow these difficulties to scare us into giving up on our loving heavenly Father.

"*For by grace you have been saved through faith, and that not of yourselves; it is the gift of God*" (Ephesians 2:8). Salvation is a gift from God. Not only does He give you this gift, but He also remains committed to your ability to hold on to it through His grace.

> *Now may the God of peace Himself sanctify you completely; and may your whole spirit, soul, and body be preserved blameless at the coming of our Lord Jesus Christ. He who calls you is faithful, who also will do it.*   (1 Thessalonians 5:23–24)

Your faith is what saves you, but you do not save yourself— Christ does. Neither does God leave you to your own devices after you receive salvation. God's Word assures you that, in every trying situation, He has already prepared a way of escape for you. (See 1 Corinthians 10:13.)

THE FINAL JUDGMENT OF GOD

In a vision, I saw millions of people before God's throne. Every tribe of every nation was there, and I saw the angels separating the people. I saw record books brought before the Lord. Angels were descending on and ascending from the earth—a sight I have seen many times in visions. This was a vision of the end of time and the judgment of God, as we read about in the Scriptures:

> *Then I saw a great white throne and Him who sat on it, from whose face the earth and the heaven fled away. And there was found no place for them. And I saw the dead, small and great, standing before God, and books were opened. And another book was opened, which is the Book of Life. And the dead were judged according to their works, by the things which were written in the books. The sea gave up the dead who were in it, and Death and Hades delivered up the dead who were in them. And they were judged, each one according to his works.*

Then Death and Hades were cast into the lake of fire. This is the second death. And anyone not found written in the Book of Life was cast into the lake of fire. (Revelation 20:11–15)

God has provided us with deliverance from eternal death through the sacrifice of Jesus Christ on our behalf. We need to respond to God's truth and get back onto the straight and narrow pathway of following Him. He wants us to know that He loves us and that He is there to forgive us.

TWO KINGDOMS—TWO CHOICES

I pray that there will be a new awakening in the body of Christ and that we all will realize that Jesus is truly real. He is coming back for a church without spot, wrinkle, or blemish, which will reign with Him forever. (See Ephesians 5:27; Revelation 5:10; 22:5.) In the meantime, He wants us to experience the miraculous power of His peace upon the earth, and to deliver others from the grip of Satan.

Though the kingdom of darkness often tries to imitate and compete with the kingdom of God, there are vast differences between these two kingdoms that continually stand out. God's kingdom is one of life, light, and love. Satan's kingdom is one of death, darkness, and hatred. God always lets us know our options and gives us the right to decide whether we will choose the enemy's way—which leads to death—or His way—which leads to life.

I call heaven and earth as witnesses today against you, that I have set before you life and death, blessing and cursing; therefore choose life, that both you and your descendants may live.
(Deuteronomy 30:19)

Which way will you choose? Have you chosen life by making a sincere commitment to following Christ and living for Him in holiness? Will you join Him in engaging in spiritual warfare and bringing deliverance to the captives?

I want to encourage all who choose to follow the Lord, especially in these end times, that you are overcomers in the name of Jesus. You will experience the attacks of the enemy, but you can be spiritually strong for the fight.

BE SPIRITUALLY STRONG FOR WARFARE

When engaging in spiritual warfare, it is essential for us to understand what it means to have a proper relationship with Jesus Christ. Many Christians suffer from frustration because they feel helpless to defeat the devil as he raises havoc in their lives through intimidation and condemnation. You can overcome the enemy's strategies by knowing your authority as a child of God and a coheir with Christ. (See Romans 8:17.) Your deliverance can be taken from you only if you *decide* to relinquish your spiritual rights.

STRONG AGAINST INTIMIDATION

One of the devil's strategies is to inflict enough strife upon you to force you to surrender before realizing the authority you have to defeat him. Demonic spirits are sent out on various assignments against us based on our faith in Christ. This is why those who truly believe God often face trials that are much more strenuous than the ones others experience. One difficulty seems to follow another, because it is the strategy of demonic forces to weigh us down with so much at once that we willingly relinquish our confession of faith and our trust in God.

Do not fall for these deceptive tactics. Regardless of how many attacks the devil may attempt to launch against you, you do not have to succumb to them. God is faithful, and He will not allow you to go through anything that you are incapable of bearing. When the weight of the struggle becomes too heavy, He will provide a way of escape. When you are in proper relationship with Jesus Christ, living in His salvation and authority, He strengthens you when you are weak and empowers you for warfare, delivering you from the gates of hell.

Through Christ Jesus, you hold the power to defeat every foe the enemy sends on assignment against you. It is your heritage as a believer in Christ Jesus to walk in liberty and power and to have victory over the devil's devices. No matter how vigilantly he attacks, remember that no weapon that he forms against you will prosper.

> *"No weapon formed against you shall prosper, and every tongue which rises against you in judgment you shall condemn. This is the heritage of the servants of the* Lord, *and their righteousness is from Me," says the* Lord.
>
> (Isaiah 54:17)

Continually submit to God's will and never allow your life to be steered by fear due to the threats of the devil. In the book of 1 Kings, we read that the wicked Queen Jezebel sought the life of Elijah the prophet because she was enraged by the news that he had killed her false prophets. She sent a messenger to relay a threat to Elijah: *"So let the gods do to me, and more also, if I do not make your life as the life of one of them by tomorrow about this time"* (1 Kings 19:2).

Despite having seen great exploits and miracles from the Lord, this threat from Jezebel consumed Elijah, and he ran for his life into the wilderness where he sat under a Juniper tree and requested to die. (See verses 3–4.) Even when you flee in fear, however, God knows how to find you and restore you to your senses. Later, Elijah was found hiding in a cave when the Spirit of the Lord came and asked him, *"What are you doing here, Elijah?"* (v. 9).

Where would God find you if you fled in fear? The worst place to flee is the dark confinements of your old habitat—your old ways of living. The safest thing to do in times of uncertainty is to run toward the voice of God so you may receive knowledge, wisdom, and strength for living life, and living it more abundantly. (See John 10:10.)

Therefore, as Satan gives orders to hell's gates to destroy your family, finances, mentality, health, or even your faith, you have the authority to counteract his evil devices by applying the Word of God. The Spirit of God will speak to you in a *"still small voice"* (1 Kings 19:12), as He did for Elijah, and give you the instructions you need in order to have victory, especially when you have yielded yourself to the Lord through fasting and prayer. God does not always speak to us with thunder; it is often much more subtle.

For instance, perhaps you are daydreaming as you are driving home from work. You accidentally take a wrong turn, so you decide to take an alternate route home. You later learn that the driver of a large tanker forgot to put his truck in park, and it rolled through the very intersection you would normally take at that time and crashed into a wall. God allowed you to daydream for a few seconds so you would respond to His prompting to take the alternate route. At the time, you thought it was a mistake. Later, however, you rejoiced as you realized God was protecting your life from tragedy.

STRONG AGAINST CONDEMNATION

Another of the devil's strategies is accusation and condemnation. When the devil sets out to judge you unjustly, he already knows that he is overstepping his bounds. (See Revelation 12:10–11.) Nevertheless, his trick is to deceive you into bowing down to his gruesome threats.

When the devil spews railing accusations against you, know that these deceitful charges are immediately dismissed because Jesus has already given Himself for our sins. *"Who gave Himself for our sins, that He might deliver us from this present evil age, according* to the will of our God and Father" (Galatians 1:4). In Romans 8:1, Paul wrote, *"There is therefore now no condemnation to those who are in Christ Jesus, who do not walk according to the flesh, but according to the Spirit."* As we confess our sins and keep our relationship with the Lord current, He validates and strengthens us so that we may be presented *"blameless in the day of our Lord Jesus Christ"* (1 Corinthians 1:8).

LIVING IN DELIVERANCE AND VICTORY

Finally, we must recognize that there is not just one method of conducting spiritual warfare and obtaining deliverance that we apply to every circumstance. At times, spiritual warfare simply means taking a strong stand against wrongdoing. At other times, it means remaining silent and trusting God when the temptation to scream in frustration is begging you to give in to it. Sometimes, it means spending a night in intercessory prayer or casting out demons. The real issue in spiritual warfare is not so much a specific form of engagement. Rather, it is the *effectiveness* of the engagement as you are guided by the Holy Spirit in doing what is appropriate for a particular situation.

Though the methods of spiritual warfare may vary, these guidelines and principles will steer you toward deliverance and victory:

+ Know your God, and make sure the devil knows that you know God as well.

+ Recognize the times we are living in and realize that the devil's assaults will increase against those who belong to God.

+ Understand that the devil always makes your situation look worse in the natural than it is in the Spirit. Don't allow mere temporal manifestations to cause you to give up. Ask God for spiritual insight and discernment. *"We do not look at the things which are seen, but at the things which are not seen. For the things which are seen are temporary, but the things which are not seen are eternal"* (2 Corinthians 4:18).

+ Realize that you have authority through Christ Jesus, and do not be afraid to exercise that authority to make way for your deliverance.

+ Understand that you need to apply God's Word to your life in all situations and to claim His promises.

+ Know that you do not have to live the rest of your life bound by a generational curse. You hold the power to rebuke whatever has cursed your life and to be set free by the power of God.

+ Recognize that it is not by your own power that you wage spiritual warfare; it is by the Spirit of God that you walk in authority with signs following. (See Zechariah 4:6; Mark 16:20 KJV.)

+ Know that though you wrestle in the spiritual realm (see Ephesians 6:12), the battle has already been won for you if you believe in Christ's provision and victory!

If you believe in the Lord Jesus Christ and ask Him to come into your heart, He will not turn a deaf ear to your cry but will rush to deliver you.

A PRAYER FOR COMPLETE DELIVERANCE

Jesus proclaimed in the Word of God,

If two of you agree on earth concerning anything that they ask, it will be done for them by My Father in heaven. For where two or three are gathered together in My name, I am there in the midst of them. (Matthew 18:19–20)

Will you allow Bishop Bloomer and me to agree with you in prayer for your complete deliverance?

Father, we pray right now, in the name of Jesus, that the person holding this book will be touched by the power of God. We come in agreement that his/her life will forever change for the better and that every generational curse that has been suffocating his/her destiny will be destroyed in the name of Jesus. We pray that every burden will be yanked from this reader's neck and that he/she will enjoy liberty and freedom of life through Jesus Christ. Father, touch this reader's heart to feel the love of Christ as never before. No longer will he/she walk in fear; may the boldness of the Lord rise up from within this person. Allow him/her to see himself/herself through Your eyes, and may the anointing that destroys every yoke become an everlasting part of his/her spiritual existence. We pray, dear God, that you would release your angels to protect, keep, and lead him/her in the way of righteousness. Deliver this person from the secret bondages that are stagnating his/her spiritual, physical, mental, and emotional well-being. Allow Your favor and Your power to be this reader's portion, today and forevermore, in Jesus' name. Amen.

Always remember—Jesus is your Deliverer!

But I am poor and needy; yet the LORD *thinks upon me. You are my help and my deliverer.*   (Psalm 40:17)

The LORD *is my rock and my fortress and my deliverer; my God, my strength, in whom I will trust; my shield and the horn of my salvation, my stronghold.*   (Psalm 18:2)

And do not lead us into temptation, but deliver us from the evil one. For Yours is the kingdom and the power and the glory forever. Amen.   (Matthew 6:13)

ABOUT THE AUTHORS

Dr. Mary K. Baxter has been in full-time ministry for more than thirty-five years, ever since she was taken by God into the dimensions and torments of hell, as well as the streets of heaven, for over forty nights in 1976. God commissioned Mary to record her experiences and tell others of the horrific depths, degrees, and torments of hell, as well as the wonderful destiny of heaven for the redeemed of Jesus Christ. There truly is a hell to shun and a heaven to gain!

Throughout her life, Mary has experienced many visions, dreams, and revelations of heaven, hell, and the spirit realm. She has been sent by God to minister in over 125 nations, and she has seen her books translated into more than twenty languages. Salvation springs forth as she walks in the miraculous power of God on her life. Signs and wonders follow her, and testimonies of God's saving grace abound in her ministry. She has a mother's heart to see all people come into the kingdom of God and become all that God has created them to be. She has birthed numerous other ministries and pours into the lives of others to see the kingdom of God expand into the emerging generations of the earth.

Mary was ordained as a minister in 1983 and received a Doctor of Ministry degree from Faith Bible College, an affiliate of Oral Roberts University. She continues to travel the world and minister in power. Mary Baxter's book *A Divine Revelation of Hell* has sold nearly 1.4 million copies. In addition to that work, her books published by Whitaker House include *A Divine Revelation of Heaven, A Divine Revelation of the Spirit Realm, A Divine Revelation of Angels, A Divine Revelation of Spiritual Warfare, A Divine Revelation of Deliverance, A Divine Revelation of Healing, A Divine Revelation of Prayer, A Divine Revelation of the Powerful Blood of Jesus,* and *A Divine Revelation of Satan's Deceptions.*

For speaking engagements, please contact:

Dr. Mary K. Baxter
Divine Revelation, Inc.
marykbaxter@yahoo.com
www.marykbaxterinc.com

Bishop George G. Bloomer is the founder and senior pastor of Bethel Family Worship Center, a multicultural congregation in Durham, North Carolina. A native of Brooklyn, New York, Bloomer overcame difficult personal challenges, as well as a destructive environment of poverty and drugs, and he uses those learning experiences as priceless tools for empowering others to excel beyond their seeming limitations. He is also the founder of G. G. Bloomer Ministries, traveling internationally and delivering life-altering messages to equip people for personal growth and spiritual fulfillment.

Bloomer has appeared as a guest on television, radio, and other media outlets nationwide, including CNN's *Faces of Faith,* the Trinity Broadcasting Network (TBN), *The Harvest Show*

(LeSEA Broadcasting), and *The 700 Club* (Christian Broadcasting Network). He is also the author of a number of books, including *Looking for Love, More of Him, Authority Abusers, Spiritual Warfare,* and the national best seller *Witchcraft in the Pews.* He has also collaborated with Mary K. Baxter on *A Divine Revelation of Deliverance* and *A Divine Revelation of Prayer.*

Bishop Bloomer was awarded an honorary doctor of divinity degree from Christian Outreach Bible Institute.

Welcome to Our House!

We Have a Special Gift for You

It is our privilege and pleasure to share in your love of Christian books. We are committed to bringing you authors and books that feed, challenge, and enrich your faith.

To show our appreciation, we invite you to sign up to receive a specially selected **Reader Appreciation Gift**, with our compliments. Just go to the Web address at the bottom of this page.

God bless you as you seek a deeper walk with Him!

WE HAVE A GIFT FOR YOU. VISIT:

whpub.me/nonfictionthx

WHITAKER
HOUSE